The Sporting Life

THE Sporting LIFE

The Duke and Jackie, Pee Wee, Razor
Phil, Ali, Mushky Jackson, and Me

IRVING RUDD AND
STAN FISCHLER

St. Martin's Press
New York

Design by Judy Dannecker

Library of Congress Cataloging-in-Publication Data

Rudd, Irving.
    The sporting life : the Duke and Jackie, Pee Wee, Razor Phil, Ali,
  Mushky Jackson, and me / Irving Rudd & Stan Fischler ; fore-
  word by Peter Golenbock.
        p.   cm.
    ISBN 0-312-04428-3 :
    1. Rudd, Irving. 2. Sports promoters—United States—Biog-
  raphy.
    I. Fischler, Stan. II. Title.
    GV742.42.R83A3 1990
    796′.092—dc20
    [B]   89-77468
                                                                    CIP

First Edition

10 9 8 7 6 5 4 3 2 1

AUTHOR'S DEDICATION

To Gertrude: not just a wife but a friend in fair weather or foul. Without her neither this book nor all the wonderful things that have transpired would have been possible.

With love to my daughters, Susan and Nanci. To my grandchildren Jodi, Allison, Davina and Tobias who make the profession of "grandfathering" a constant joy.

COAUTHOR'S DEDICATION

This book is dedicated in part to Simon and Ben, neither of whom had the good fortune to have met their grandfather, Ben Fischler, who died before their time. Irv Rudd is so much like their grandpa Ben that it was very easy to love him and not surprisingly, to love writing the book with him. For the coauthor, it was, as we say in Brooklyn, a mitzvah.

CONTENTS

Contents

Foreword

For the past fifty years Irving Rudd, diminutive and modest to the extreme, has been a paid adviser to some of the most powerful figures in the world of sports. It was never in the job description, but part of his job was to make his less-than-charitable employers seem saintly, moving the late Red Smith to joke that Irving had a way of working in harmony with anyone.

Smith once wrote, "If Irving had been around at the time, he would have been telling his friends: 'Look, the guy has changed. His real name is Attila the Hon and he's a real nice guy . . . .'"

As a publicist promoting ballplayers, horses, and fighters as gate attractions, Irving Rudd has been a legend. For the Brooklyn Dodgers he invented Camera Day, Batboy for a Day, and Music Unappreciation Night.

When he refused to flee Brooklyn with the Dodgers for Los Angeles, he was hired by the owners of Yonkers Raceway. Once he deliberately had the huge sign outside read YONKERS RACEWYA, getting front-page photos of the "mistake" nationwide. It was a coup. As Irving says, "The toughest thing to publicize is a horse. You can't interview them." After moving on to work for boxing promoter Bob Arum, to publicize an April 15 fight between Thomas Hearns and Marvin Hagler, Irving convinced the IRS to underwrite a national commercial in which the two fighters promoted their fight and encouraged the public to file on time.

Irving's job always has been to blow other people's horns. I guess that's why this book is filled with anecdotes about Jackie Robinson and his teammates on the Dodgers, the Tananbaum brothers who owned Yonkers Raceway,

Foreword

Muhammad Ali, Don King, Leon Spinks, Walter O'Malley, Sugar Ray Leonard, and Thomas Hearns but rarely about the main character, Irving Rudd. If a sentence begins with the word "I," it's usually "I remember when so-and-so . . ."

The reader has to understand that Irving doesn't see himself as special. He sees himself as a working stiff, doing his job, earning his pay. But for those of us who have known him, we know how special he is.

If you ask Irving a favor, his first thought is how he can be accommodating, not "what's in it for me?" Several years ago I asked him if I could interview him for my history of the Brooklyn Dodgers. He could have said, "I'm saving it for my own book." Instead, with great generosity he gave his valuable time and even-more-valuable memories freely.

In a world where calculating the proper move for career advancement means so much, Irving Rudd always did what he thought was right and damn the consequences. Who else would have stopped ABC-TV from making one of his fighters look like a chump when the network producers wanted heavyweight contender Jimmy Young, a Philly fighter, to punch sides of beef à la Rocky, another Philly fighter?

Rudd saw Rocky as a has-been who makes good. He didn't think the comparison to Young was flattering. Rudd risked offending the network that was paying the freight for the fight.

They backed down. The sides of beef were safe. So was Young's reputation.

Who else but Irving Rudd would have organized Pee Wee Reese Night because he felt the group of businessmen who wanted to do it were "phonies." These same businessmen had thrown a night for Dixie Walker, but they had raised only enough money to buy him a fishing rod. Rudd was embarrassed for the Dodgers, for whom he worked, and he vowed such an incident wouldn't be repeated. So Irving Rudd did it right. Thirty-five thousand fans lit candles given them when they arrived at the park and sang "Happy Birthday" to Pee Wee. Reese got a car and a small wagonload of gifts. The Dodgers looked munificent. All because of Irving Rudd.

Who else would have complained that Grantland Rice had been shunted by the New York Giants to the upper press deck for the World Series and insisted the dean of American sports writers be accorded the respect he deserved? When the Giant PR guy told Irving to bug off, Irving gave Rice his seat in the main press box.

Who else but Irving Rudd would have been aware that after Ali had lost the heavyweight title to Leon Spinks that Ali's wife was being ignored? Irving went and got her some fruit juice.

Ali noticed. "That Irvin' Rudd is thinkin' about you all the time," said the Champ. "That's my Irvin', always thinkin' 'bout others."

After Ali's fight with Earnie Shavers, Irving saw that the Champ was no longer the same fighter. Always honest, he told Ali to hang them up. "Please," Irving begged. But Ali needed the money. And he suffers terribly for staying on too long.

Irving has been special for a long time—since he was a kid, in fact. How many thirteen-year-old kids were taken out for dinner by the Brooklyn Dodgers? It happened to Irving. He didn't write it, but I know it happened, because he told me it did. Al Lopez and four of his teammates were so impressed by Irving's polite manner that they took him—a towheaded kid who asked for autographs with a please and thank you—out to a fancy restaurant for arroz con pollo, sat and chatted with him at the St. George Hotel after dinner, and then put him in a cab for the ride home.

"That night showed me that there was a big world out there," Irving said. "Who was I? A poor kid from Brownsville."

But Al Lopez and his teammates took Irving to dinner perhaps because they saw something in him they didn't see in the others: a basic goodness and a positive outlook on humanity that never seems to waver.

The "man of a few thousand well-chosen words," as Irving likes to call himself, has made his wonderful world come alive by putting some of those words on paper. With the publication of *The Sporting Life*, Irving Rudd becomes an author. And somewhere his old friends, Granny and Red and Jimmy Cannon and Damon Runyon, are happy to have him in their company.

—Peter Golenbock
October 1989

Acknowledgments

Over the decades Irving Rudd has been associated with every sport, from boxing through baseball. As he has often noted, a champion boxer or World Series winner requires high-grade cornermen and dependable coaches to produce wins. Likewise, when it comes to producing a book, extraordinary help is necessary.

In this case several people provided exceptional help above and beyond the call of duty. First and foremost, our agent Agnes Birnbaum rates our highest praise not only for having faith in Irving's project but for seeing it through to fruition.

Many others provided a meaningful boost when it was needed most. Our good friends Paul Ringe and Joe Dionisio came through in the clutch à la the Brooklyn Dodgers' 1955 pitching hero Johnny Podres.

Significant help was required in the areas of research, transcription, and typing. Enough cannot be said in praise of our research editor Miriam Greenwald, who was indefatigable, indomitable, and effervescent when the chips were down. We put Miriam in Agnes's exalted class—without her we'd be on the ropes.

Additional invaluable help was supplied by Jeff Diamant, Mitchell Polo, Ben Fischler, Jeff Resnick, Scott Decelles, Adam Reich, Keven Friedman, Josh Sipkin, Kathy Wolf, Berry Stainback and Arthur Staple, among many others too numerous to mention.

Without question, the book would not have been possible without the inspiration and insights provided by our editor George Witte at St. Martin's Press.

—Stan Fischler

Introduction

In the autumn of 1955, I was a rookie sports columnist with the *New York Journal-American*, a twenty-three-year-old with a firm conviction that I had no business being in the big leagues of journalism alongside such titans as Jimmy Cannon, Bill Corum, and Red Smith. It was then that I met a bouncy little man who persuaded me that, yes, Fischler, you do belong at the top—and don't let anyone tell you different.

Irving Rudd was that man, and in time, my professional love affair with Irving would continue through the razing of Ebbets Field, the deliberate misspelling of the Yonkers Raceway sign (see Chapter 10), and the birth of the Off-Track Betting Corporation.

At the time of our meeting in 1955, Irving was publicist for the Brooklyn Dodgers. Now, anyone in the newspaper business knows that a publicity man is paid to help the media, but only one-tenth of one-thirtieth of 1 percent actually do their job right. Lucky for me, I happened upon that precious commodity—the writer's kind of PR man.

Irving not only steered me toward stories and took me by the hand (when hand-taking was desperately needed), but he represented something I love and cherish to this day—a feeling of Brooklyn-ness. In fact, the resemblance both physically and spiritually between Irving and my own father was striking. Both made it up from the sidewalks of East New York. Both were dynamic, loveable (though occasionally cantankerous) characters. And both made it quite clear when an out-of-towner asked them where they were from—it was not New York City, brother, it was Brooklyn. With a capital *B*!

Had my dad been able to do it all over again with the

job of his choice, I suspect that he would have liked to have been in Irving Rudd's shoes. So in a sense, one of the pleasures of writing this book with Irving was enjoying an occasional fantasy, placing Ben Fischler in the role of Irving Rudd.

I would be negligent if I failed to mention that there were many, many times when I not only thrust myself into Irving's role but wished oh, so very hard that I had been in the Brooklyn Dodgers' entourage on that glorious day in 1955 when they won us our first World Series. (After that, none of the other World Series really mattered.) Being a born and bred Brooklynite (Williamsburg), I shared the heartbreak of Bobby Thomson's 1951 home run (still wishing it foul) and the unmitigated joy of watching a high-class semipro game at Dexter Park on the Brooklyn-Queens border, where the best of the black players went up against the all-white Bushwicks in the pre–Jackie Robinson days.

All of which is a rather roundabout way of saying that working with Irving Rudd on this book has been more a labor of love than love's labor lost.

After all, who wouldn't get a tremendous kick out of doing a book with his favorite Uncle Irving who knew Roy Campanella, Pee Wee Reese, Joe Louis, and Muhammad Ali!

—Stan Fischler

=Part I=

= 1 =
In Camp with
the Champ

As marriages go, the wedding of Muhammad Ali and Irving Rudd is not one that was made in heaven. When it takes place in 1976 Ali is thirty-four years old, black, Muslim, and built along the generous lines of a Clydesdale stallion.

Rudd is twenty-four years his senior, Jewish, an imposing five feet five inches tall, and tipping the scales at 135 pounds. But what does size, religion, or color really matter? Ali is the fighter and Rudd is the press agent.

Me and Ali are an unlikely combination, but I am tickled about it. For that I thank John Francis Xavier Condon, then promotional boss of Madison Square Garden and a solid, no-bullshit guy. Early in June 1976 Condon calls me up and says: "We're having a press conference at Madison Square Garden tomorrow and I'd like you to be there. We're gonna announce Ken Norton and Ali."

Condon is a tall, trim, handsome Irishman with whom press agents like me want to work because he stands behind you if you do the job right. When Condon tells me, "I want you involved in this fight," I'm happier than a pig in mud but also concerned on account of I don't know either fighter. I'd never met Norton and had only been on the perimeter of Ali's entourage. Besides, Condon is vague about what I'm supposed to do. But the paycheck beckons, so I have no choice but to show up if I want to eat next week. I rapidly screw my head on in the right direction, point myself toward the Garden, and find Condon.

"Irving," says Condon, "I'd like to send you to Norton's camp. You're gonna be Norton's camp man." I am surprised and just this side of being overjoyed. "There's only one problem," I tell Condon. "I've never met Ken Norton."

With that, Condon takes me by the arm and walks me over to a huge, very handsome, black guy built like Hercules and says, "Ken, this is Irving Rudd. He's gonna be working out of your camp and I'd like you to know each other."

Norton looks down at me (which is easy since he has a foot on me). "I want to take a good look at this dude," he says with a smile. "A real good look so I know him the next time I see him out there in California."

I look Norton up and down and frown menacingly. Then, with mock anger, I snap, "Well, you won't have any trouble with that, Ken—it's the only face I've got!"

Norton recoils as if an underdog had just surprised him with a left jab to the cheek. Quickly he shakes it off and grins. "Hey, you're a funny man. I think I'm gonna like you."

"Play your cards right," I say. "Behave yourself with me and *you're* gonna have a great training camp."

Norton's grin is now a mile wide. "Hey, that's cool, man!"

Ken swings his right hand at me and a light slap creases my face. I can tell it's Ken's way of kissing me. We are, by press agent–boxer standards, in love at first sight.

Condon breaks the spell a few minutes later. "Irving, what are you still doing here? Get the hell out to California and start working on this fight!"

It is June, and the fight is in September in Yankee Stadium, but they're willing to put me on the payroll right away. This is good because I need time to get the feel of the bout. So, off I go to Los Angeles.

Al Douglas, the smooth, sophisticated promoter who gave me my very first job in boxing, would have been proud. His Irving, the little white kid from Brownsville, Brooklyn, who the big black man had broken in at Harlem's Rockland Palace in 1935, is now working with two of the best black boxers in the world. On the flight west I say to myself, "Irving, you've come a long way from 155th Street and Eighth Avenue."

Already I'm worrying about Ali more than Norton. I'd heard and read a lot about the Champ. I puzzle over what is the reality and what is the fiction. I find I'm quietly wishing I was working Ali's camp and not Norton's, just so I could answer the puzzling Ali question. But that, I hope, will come later. Right now I'm working for Norton, and number one on the agenda is to head straight for his training base at an outlandish location called Massacre Canyon.

Massacre Canyon is about a hundred miles south of Los Angeles in the San Jacinto Valley, but it might as well be in the middle of the Sahara Desert.

Hot? You wouldn't believe such heat. In the shade it is 105 degrees Fahrenheit. Every single day, 105; and Norton doesn't want any air-conditioning. In the gym the doors are closed. Norton is a lunatic—but also a nice kid.

This is good. Norton and I are getting to know each other, and I'm wondering if he has a chance against the great Ali. I'm also hoping that Ken wins the fight, on account that in all my forty years as a fight press agent, I've never been with a winning training camp in a championship fight. Since I probably won't live more than another fifty years, and have lived well over fifty already, I figure it's about time I'm in the winner's corner. But now the important thing is to get inside Norton's head so I can send some good publicity stuff to Condon back at the Garden.

To my surprise, I really like Ken. I see he is a bright guy, not a kid out of the steaming ghetto. He says he grew up in a middle-class section of Jacksonville, Illinois. He is as polished as any college-educated white kid his age, but he's still a black in his head and, every so often, he likes to do what he calls his "nigger put-on." He makes with a shuffle and struts down the street saying, "I'm gonna be a nigger!" And then he talks "nigger talk." That's okay, but I decide I'm going to make a Jew out of him. I tell Norton about some jerk and I throw away the line, "Ah, that guy is a schmuck."

"What's a 'schmuck'?" he says.

"Ken," I tell him, "you're too young to know."

But he wants to know, so I explain that a schmuck is usually equated with a prick, anatomically and philosophically. Norton understands; the only trouble is, he can't pronounce the word. It keeps coming out as "shnook," "smuck," or "schnuck."

I give Ken a list of ten good, dirty Yiddish words to use later when he gets to the Borscht Belt Catskill Mountain hotels. I phoneticize them to make them easy for him to pronounce and tell him they should be practiced and used often when he gets to Grossinger's, and he agrees.

I know this is out of character for Ken. He is an only

child, a kind of spoiled kid in some ways and a very forceful kind of guy. In fact, the whole Norton entourage is offbeat by fight standards. His trainer, Bill Slayton, is an older guy in his fifties, yet he looks like one of Norton's sparring partners. He handles the swivel bag and works with Ken every step of the way in the gym, short of actually boxing. Slayton wears gloves that look like miniature baseball catcher's mitts. He takes Norton's blows on the gloves as he moves around the ring. Then he goes three or four rounds, directing the punches—left hooks, uppercuts, right crosses. Ken works well with Slayton, which isn't all that automatic because Ken has his dark moments.

I learn firsthand about Norton's dark side when it comes time to have photos taken of him to promote the bout. The photographer is in the ring with him and I tell Ken to arrange his arms in a certain way. He's moody and acts like he doesn't hear me. That's my cue. I tell the photographer to forget it and wait a week, until Norton is good and ready to do the kind of photo we want. When Norton turns dark, if you're smart, you back off.

The amazing thing is that Norton has a way of conveying his shit-face mood without actually being surly or nasty. And apart from these few periods on the dark side, he is a pleasant, articulate guy. I actually look forward to working with him for the next few months. To hell with Ali.

I'm feeling higher than Ben Franklin's kite as the days roll along at Norton's camp. Then one night I put on the television set and I'm hit by a bolt of lightning. The announcer says that Ali has just entered the Santa Monica hospital, complaining of bruises on his legs. They say it's on account of a cockamamy match he had with a Japanese wrestler a few weeks earlier.

"Oh shit!" I say. "The fight is off. There goes my job!"

I figure that as soon as the guys at the Garden hear about Ali's condition, the fight will be canceled and we'll all be going home in a couple of days. I phone Condon in New York. "John," I say, "what are we going to do about Ali in the hospital?"

"What!" Condon tells me he never heard the news about Ali. I can tell by his voice that he doesn't believe what he's hearing.

"Ali is *in the hospital*," I repeat for the benefit of the East Coast. Then I explain the whole story. Condon is stunned to the goddamn core. He asks me for a few minutes so he can get his head together and says he'll call back.

A few minutes later the phone rings. "Irv," says Condon, "I hate to ask you to do this, but do you mind driving to Santa Monica and finding out exactly what the hell's really goin' on with Ali?"

No info, me. I've already made calls on this and know the Champ is at St. John's Riverside Hospital. I've got all the info, and I pass it on to Condon. "Get a hook with the doctor and lemme know where we're at," he tells me. "I got to know whether he'll be able to fight or not." And then he hangs up.

Into my car I jump, and barrel the 110 miles from Massacre Canyon to Santa Monica, where I'm hoping to do the impossible and see Ali. When I get to the hospital, I realize I'd have a better chance at getting an audience with Jesus Christ himself. There's an iron wall around the Champ like you wouldn't believe. How in hell am I going to reach him?

I do the obvious; I ask for the hospital's publicity man, who, it turns out, is playing hard to get. Finally I get through to him, and the PR guy whispers the news: "I'm going to give you a jump on the bulletin that the doctor's going to give to the press later this afternoon."

This shows me the guy has class. He knows that I'm not going to break his confidence and that all I want is to have the news for my own people in New York and their

8

use. The bulletin, thank God, says Ali isn't suffering from a terrible injury that could kill the fight.

I phone London and he says to hang around because there's sure to be a press conference when the doctor releases his bulletin. Great, I figure, maybe I can get to see the Champ.

Suddenly, *bing*! There's a ring in I. Rudd's head. An idea has been born. "John," I tell Condon, "I'd like Norton to visit Ali in the hospital. This could be dynamite for us. A great thing!"

I suffer through that painful half-second pause, holding my breath while awaiting the boss's reaction. "Irv," says Condon, "that is a hell of a good idea."

Now I can exhale. I start praying that Norton will like my idea of him visiting Ali. I go to my hotel room to rest, then wake up to the ring of the phone. It's Ken Norton. "Irv," he says, "did I wake you?"

By now I can fool around with the big guy, so I come back with my standard line to the did-I-wake-you question: "Well," I say, "I had to answer the phone anyway."

Norton laughs, but I'm wondering what the hell he wants from me. Little did I dream that he was presenting me with a miracle. "Hey, Irv," Ken says, "I wanna go visit Muhammad Ali. I wanna go see the Champ in the hospital."

If I was half asleep when I got on the phone, I'm awake-and-a-half now. "Gee," I say, trying very hard to contain my glee, "that's real nice of you."

"Hey," Norton goes on, "I don't care what Ali is like in the ring. Sure, he's my opponent and I'm gonna try and beat his brains out. But as far as I'm concerned, he's a helluva man, and I respect him for that. I wanna go pay my respects to him while he's sick."

I tell Ken that I'll see what I can do. The second I hang up, I get on the other phone, call Condon, and give him the news. He's tickled and tells me to call Pat Patterson, Ali's bodyguard.

I call the Beverly Wilshire Hotel, where he's supposed to be staying, but no Patterson. I call the hospital; no Patterson. I keep trying, and finally I decide to get ballsy and take a shot at Ali's hospital room. It's five in the afternoon, and this time a half-sleepy voice says, "Hello!"

"Excuse me, is that you, Muhammad?" I say. "Yeah," the voice answers. "Who this?"

"You don't know me, but I work for John Condon. . . ."

The password "John Condon" opens the door—but wide. "*You* work for John Condon! You say you want to bring Ken Norton to see me . . . here?"

I can't figure out if he's pissed off or happy with what I'm telling him. I'm half afraid the guy is going to hang up on me in disgust. "Sure," says the Champ. "Bring that sucker up here tomorrow. But I don't want no press around when you do. No press. Ya hear?"

"Well," I reply, seeing a ray of light, "let's leave it this way. Suppose I bring the press to the reception area downstairs, where I'll give 'em a report of the meeting. I'll be like their pool reporter."

I'm beginning to sense that Ali is an ace. Right away he goes for my idea and he's giving me no grief at all. I've got my foot in the door; I've got the Champ on my side. I tell Ali that Norton and me will work it out. Now I have to get back to Norton and hope that he hasn't changed his mind.

When I meet Ken he's still enthused about meeting Ali, so we're off to Santa Monica in Ken's Lincoln Mark IV at no less than 110 miles per hour. When he sees me adjust my seat belt he looks at me like I'm a six-year-old. "What're you putting *that* on for?" he says.

"I am putting on the seat belt," I tell him, "because I want to see tomorrow and be alive when I do it."

Now he's got the Lincoln up to 120 miles per hour, roaring toward 130 miles per hour. I am not suffering a complete nervous seizure; just a partial one. I take comfort in the fact that Norton has big, strong hands and that they are gripping the wheel of the Lincoln with what appears to be enormous confidence. But the roads are getting thinner and windier as we roll through the California mountains. I try to reassure myself. "Feel confidence, Irving, he's an athlete; he's got reflexes. If he's crazy enough to be that crazy . . ." Finally we roar into Santa Monica and arrive at the hospital alive and well.

First thing I do at the hospital is find the PR guy who helped me in the first place. He tells me there's a herd of newsmen inside. Great. That's what I'm in this business for; now all I have to do is work it out right so that Ali isn't upset and that Norton gets to see him and, most important, that the news guys get their stories and we get the ink, and I. Rudd gets his paycheck.

I gather the media together and set up ground rules. "Fellas," I tell them, "don't blow it for me. No one gets in to see Ali; that's the way he wants it. I'll go in as the pool reporter and tell you what happens with him and Ken."

Knowing the press, I realize that that's not enough. Right away the photographers start bugging me. "Look," they beg, "can we get Ken in some kind of picture?"

No problem. I run into the gift shop and buy a huge Snoopy doll, they take a million pictures of Norton and Snoopy, and it's great, so far.

Now it's time for the confrontation with Ali. We tell the newsmen to be patient and we take off into some kind of secret passageway, up one wing, across a corridor, down another wing. Flanked by uniformed officers, we make a turn here, a turn there, and at last we come to a room where everyone suddenly puts on the brakes.

There, large as life, is the Champ. He's sitting on the edge of his hospital bed, completely relaxed, as if he's lounging at a country club. He's wearing pajamas and a bath robe. He looks at Norton and Norton looks at him.

They shake hands like a couple of second cousins at a family reunion.

"Hey, Ken, baby, nice to see ya!" says the Champ.

Norton pauses, seemingly in awe of Ali. Then: "Right on, Muhammad. How they treatin' ya?"

The ice is broken. Now the heavyweights are chatting like old pals, and all of a sudden I remember that I had a special request from a young black reporter from San Diego who begged me to get him an interview with Ali. I doubt that I can swing it, but I promised the kid that at least I would try. I lean over toward the Champ. "Muhammad," I tell him, "there's this kid, he wants an interview with you. I know you said no press, but maybe you can give this one kid a break."

Ali shakes his head. "No! If I give *him* a break, I gotta give *everyone* a break."

I nod. "Well, yeah. I guess I shouldn't have asked you at this time."

I'm about to turn away when I notice that Ali's brow is furrowed; he's thinking. "Where are the press?"

"Downstairs someplace. The PR guy is there and they're all waiting for your statement."

I figure he'll give me a couple of quotes for them, say good-bye to Ken, and then go back to the hospital bed where he belongs. Instead the Champ nearly leaps out of his wheelchair. "C'mon," he says to Norton. "Let's go down and see the press. How about we show these mothers we're alive."

Norton can't believe it and I can't believe it. But there is no stopping Ali now. He turns his wheelchair into the hallway and begins rolling himself toward the elevator like this is the most important move of his life. The Champ is so worked up by the time he gets himself into the elevator that you can almost see the adrenaline flowing out of his pores. He looks over at Norton, who is a little taken aback by all this, and says, "What am I gonna call *you*?"

"I know—Drum." Ali draws it out.

Drum was the name of a slave film Norton had made. Then a flash comes over Ali's face, "I know, I'm gonna call you *Mandingo*! That's what I'm gonna call you!"

The Champ has touched a raw nerve in the challenger. Norton is pissed at the allusion to Mandingo, and now he's looking at Ali and not saying a word, just chewing hard on his wad of gum. I don't think the Champ has actually psyched out Norton, but he is getting close. Norton is uptight and annoyed, but not quite afraid. Meanwhile, Ali gets out of the elevator, pushes the wheelchair around a corner, and yells, "*Stop!*"

I didn't realize where we were, but Ali did.

Like Eugene Ormandy conducting the Philadelphia Symphony Orchestra, Ali is waving his baton over the entourage, leading his big band of fight people, from press agents who figured *they* knew the business, to the writers themselves, who can't believe what they see in front of them: Ali in a wheelchair and Norton standing a few feet away.

Before any doctor or nurse can tell him to sit still, Ali gets out of his wheelchair and begins his act. He knows he has the media in his palm; the question is what tone the act will take. It doesn't take long for us to find out. The theme is, Give Norton a lot of (quasi-humorous) shit.

The TV lights are on; Ali is at center stage and shouting, "Bring him here! Bring that sucker over here!"

Norton walks over to the Champ. "C'mon kid," Ali taunts Norton. "Let's see what you got!" He throws a real punch at Ken, and now I'm shitting a brick. The Champ is actually starting a fight with the challenger right here in the goddamn hospital. Crazy. Ali already is injured, and now if Norton gets good and mad he just might kill him. I throw my five-five, 135 pounds between the two behemoths and calm them down.

Ali is hobbling (because of the contusions on his gimpy leg) but it isn't stopping him from scuffling. Ken is cool. No way is he going to hurt the Champ at this point. He pushes Ali away and leaves it at that. I step in again and push them apart once and for all. Meantime, the photographers are taking pictures like crazy and the press is eating it up. Ali is telling everyone how when they meet for real at Yankee Stadium, he's going to knock Norton on his ass. The pencils are scribbling a mile a minute, until finally, it's time for Muhammad to get the hell back to his bed and rest himself.

Good fellow that he is, Norton comes with us—after all, he *did* come here for a personal, how-are-you visit, and nothing more—and we go back to the Champ's room. Who should be sitting there but Veronica, the Champ's beautiful, brown-eyed wife-to-be. Ken says hello and sits down on the couch between Veronica and her sister, who is also a light-skinned black woman and also a beauty. Norton starts clipping back at Ali with a verbal sexual counterattack. He puts his arm, very warmlike, around Veronica's sister and croons, "You and I gonna make it good, honey."

The Champ is pissed as hell. "Hey, what you doin', Sucker?" he snaps. Ken keeps jiving. The Champ is too tired to fight anymore. Norton knows he has won the round and finally gets up, shakes Muhammad's hand, and tells him to get well soon.

I go over to Ali. "Champ," I say, "I want to thank you for being so nice today. It's gonna help publicize the fight a lot. Before I go, though, John Condon asked if I would call him, collect, from your bedside. He wants to talk to you. . . ."

"*You* work for John Condon," he says.

"That's right. I told you that once before."

"You gonna tell him how I was cooperative today? You gonna tell him that I did everything I could to push this thing?"

I get on the phone and reach Condon. "John, I'm here at the Champ's bedside." I tell Condon how well everything went and he's happy as a lark. So am I; especially since Ali and I are hitting it off real good.

Now a calm settles over Ali and his room. The Champ eyes me up and down. "You been workin' for Norton," he says with a voice so soft I hardly can hear him.

"Yeah," I say, "he ain't a bad guy, either."

"How's he treatin' ya?"

"He's treatin' me fine. You don't want me to give away any Norton secrets, do ya?"

The Champ laughs. Then his phone rings and I get another insight into what Ali is all about.

A minute ago he was talking, calmly, like a mensch (a nice young man) to me. All of a sudden he's plugged in again. It's somebody from a radio station talking to him.

Like a giant chameleon, Ali seems to change color as the interview begins. The man is turning livid red. *"I'll destroy Norton,"* he bellows into the phone. *"You hear what I say? I'll destroy that man!"*

I want to present the Champ with an Academy Award, right on the spot.

Now I understand the Champ for what he really is—a titanic performer. He is a nice, soft-spoken guy until he sees the pencils and pads and microphones and cameras before him; then he becomes a John Barrymore of the ring, the supreme actor. This is not the loud braggart I was led to believe Muhammad is but, instead, a tender gentleman who unfailingly shows a kindness to everyone around him, especially working people. They seem more important to the Champ than the big shots do. In the hospital he doesn't single out the best-looking nurse for attention. No, Ali picks out the oldest, homeliest nurse on the floor. "Come here, baby!" he says to her. Then he puts his arm around the woman and kisses her on the cheek. "Do you love the Champ?" he coos.

That little attention makes the old nurse's day. The

more I see of Ali in the hospital, the more I wish I could work for him.

But I have to go back to Norton's camp, where we have a birthday party for Ken. Later I go back to the hotel for rest and rehabilitation, which I badly need after the trip to Santa Monica, when the phone rings. It's Condon. "Irving," he says, "I'm moving you over to Ali's camp."

"How's that, John?" I say, figuring I'm hallucinating.

"Irving, you're my top man. I want my top man in the top camp. I don't want second-stringers in the champion's training camp. You're going to Berrien Springs, Michigan!"

It's a couple weeks later; Ali is out of the hospital. His base is an estate behind a huge iron gate with big letters—M.A.—stuck on the front, so nobody can make any mistake about who's training there. A guard is out in front and he asks if he can help me. "I'm here," I say, "to see the Champ."

The guard goes to a nearby phone, rings up, gives a message, and then comes back to me. "The Champ's *not here.*"

"I'll wait."

"Man, you gonna wait a long time. He's not here. Gone! Everybody gone!"

I call Condon to find out who is crazy, me or Ali. "Irving, stay where you are; hang around the phone and try to track down the Champ."

How do I track this guy down?

First I phone AP, UPI, and newsrooms in Chicago and Detroit to see if they've heard anything about his whereabouts. I try the airlines. I spend five days in Benton Harbor, Michigan, trying to find him. All I accomplish there is to learn how to do my own laundry, since I got nothing else to do but make calls and go to the local laundromat and sit with the snaggle-toothed women with their "arthu-ritis" and their grandchildren. At the age of fifty-nine I'm reduced to this. Meantime, Condon has no idea where Ali is, and between us, we don't know what the hell to do. Finally I lay an idea on Condon: "Why don't we go into town and get a consensus of what Ali means to Berrien Springs. What do the people really think of him? If I get some stuff, maybe I can push a feature on him."

Condon likes the idea. He also thinks we should keep trying to locate him and maybe plant a story with the big papers that the Champ is in fact missing.

Fine. I call Neal Milbert of the *Chicago Tribune* and tell him that there's been no sign of Ali for days.

"Yeah, okay, Irving. That's very interesting, Irving. When the Champ surfaces, give us a call, will ya?"

Wherever I go I'm getting the same patronizing shit. So is Condon on the East Coast. In other words, the newspaper guys think we *planned* Ali's disappearance. They figure this is one of those phony kidnappings, designed to get some ink. Meantime, Condon and I really don't know where the hell Ali can be.

Finally some kid out of the Grand Rapids, Michigan, UPI calls me up for background on Ali. Out of the clear blue sky he tells me that the Champ has just taken off in the general direction of Arizona. With that I get ahold of the UPI bureau in Phoenix, Arizona, and sure enough, they tell me that Ali was spotted at the Phoenix airport with a white man and a black man.

Turns out that Ali had been in Arizona a year before, doing a tour with Dick Gregory. Now, on a whim, the Champ is going back. About one hundred miles out of Phoenix he passes a town called Miami. This appeals to the Champ's whimsy. He calls up Angelo Dundee, his trainer who lives in Miami, Florida, to say, "We're opening a training camp in Miami. Yeah, man, Miami, *Arizona.*"

Once Ali surfaces in Arizona, Condon gets the details

and rings me up. I'm to go to Phoenix, where a fellow named Gene Kilroy, one of Ali's aides, will meet us.

I'm rapidly getting the idea that Ali's whole show is choreographed by Ringling Brothers, Barnum and Bailey. Anyhow, I pack my bags, and a few hours later I'm in the Phoenix airport being paged by Gene Kilroy. He's a big, good-looking Irish kid who tells me right off the bat that we have to take another plane to Show Low, Arizona.

This time my flight isn't on an American or United Airlines jet. Instead we're flying in a Cessna one-propeller job that just barely clears the tops of the mountains. I. Rudd thinks it's 1928 now and he's on a barnstorming tour with Wiley Post. Eventually we make it into a tiny air strip, "Show Low Municipal Airport," and the pilot puts the craft down. Much to my surprise, who should be right there on the strip but the Champ himself. (I later learn that he does this whenever anyone comes to see him. Always comes out to the airport; always makes sure he delivers the greeting. He's class, all the way.)

"Hiya, Champ," I say.

"Welcome to camp, Mr. Rudd," the world's greatest fighter says to me. "How's Ken doin'?"

"Lookin' good."

"Go to your room and make yourself comfortable. We'll be seeing a lot of each other."

There is no training the next day, so I figure I'll have a little time to unwind and get my act together. But before I can open my carpetbag, along comes some guy from a little Arizona hick newspaper. He walks out of the woods, finds my name, and says he wants to do a story on the Champ. Great! I. Rudd never says no to a story, so I invite the kid to the coffee shop, sit down at a booth, and pull out the menu. I feel a tap on the back. "Hey man, why doncha sit over here?"

It's none other than the Champ. He wants company. But I have this kid with me. "Champ," I say, "this young man here . . ."

"Bring him along. We talk."

I can't believe my ears. The Norton people tell me Ali has a bad camp. Yet this kid gets a full interview from the Champ and we all have a ball. The trick, though, is that it is with Ali alone. I soon discover that in a one-on-one situation, Ali is superb.

One day John Condon flies out to the camp at Show Low, looks things over, and says there is one thing he doesn't like: we are in Nowheresville. "We gotta get Ali back East," he says. "We gotta get him where there's lots of exposure, where there's press." Since Norton is moving to Grossinger's Hotel in the Jewish Borscht Belt (Liberty, New York), we figure it'd be a good idea to switch Ali to the Concord Hotel, Grossinger's rival on nearby Kiamesha Lake. This way, newspapermen could swing from one camp to the other in less than half an hour. It makes good business sense. So, within forty-eight hours we are back East in the Catskills, living it up at the Concord. The entire golf clubhouse has been turned over to Ali and his traveling circus.

Within a day at the Concord we get the verdict from the Champ: he likes it. It comes during a walk through the hotel kitchen, a monstrous place with everything from stuffed derma to shell steaks. The Champ wants some food, and they give it to him by the ton. Anything the Champ's heart desires, they produce in about two seconds.

Since Norton is nearby at Grossinger's, it means that we have a chance to coordinate promotion plans. My first day back in the Borscht Belt I go over to "the Big *G*," as Grossinger's was known to the hotel trade in the Catskills, and I have a reunion with my old buddy Ken.

It's a kick to see the guy, because as much as I like Ali, I have a soft spot for Ken for a lot of reasons, not the least of which is that I was teaching him Jewish curses and I want to see if he remembers any of them.

So now we're together again and I say, "Hey, Ken, how about those Jewish words I gave you?"

He glowers. "Hey, man, cool it! That stuff don't go around here. This is Grossinger's."

I look at him. "If Yiddish ain't going to be a hit at Grossinger's, where the hell is it ever gonna go over?"

At the Concord, Ali trains like a fiend and takes breaks only after straining himself to the very limit. On one such occasion he shows up in the Concord's enormous dining room at the very height of the dinner hour. Only the appearance of Jimmy Carter or Menachem Begin could have produced a more enraptured response. Ali walks among the tables, stopping wherever he sees a nice old Jewish lady. He kisses and hugs her. "How old are you, mama?" he says to one old woman.

"I'm eighty years old," she says.

He winks. "Y'know, you're a cute-looking chick!"

Then on to the next table, pressing the flesh, sending everyone bananas. He sees a little girl and does the same thing. One of them gets shook up when he takes her aside. "You got any boyfriends?" he asks. She begins to cry. "Hey," he says, "what're ya cryin' for? You're a pretty girl." That charm always seems to do the trick.

After touring the kosher hustings the Champ goes back to training.

One question being asked is whether or not Ali could psyche out Norton. The closest the Champ comes to pulling that off is when we're at a promotion at New York's City Hall. It happens this way.

One day we are due to be at City Hall at noon. John Condon had a great idea. He had a boxing ring set up for Norton and Ali to work out in public with Mayor Beame present.

The Champ has to walk down a corridor before stepping out into the main entrance and down the steps to the ring. As Ali walks down the hall, who is coming the other way but Norton. All the congeniality of the hospital meeting in California is gone. The Champ puts on a surly face.

"Hey, bum," he snaps. "What you doing making filthy movie pictures with your genitals hangin' out? I'm gonna straighten you out. I'm gonna whip yo ass."

Next thing I see, the Ali crowd is egging him on. "Lemme at him," yells Ali. "Yeah," one of the Champ's cronies says. "Let's get that fuck! Let's mush him!"

Meanwhile, Ken is sort of looking queer at Muhammad, staring him down. Norton reaches a point where he looks at Ali like the Champ is a lunatic. For a brief moment it seems that there is a twinkle of worry in his eyes. Ali has finally got Norton's goat, but Ken shakes it off immediately and that's the end of the fuss.

Seeing the two guys I had worked for go at it that way sets me to thinking—*do I want Ali to win the fight or do I want Norton?* I come to the conclusion that I don't care. I like them both.

The question everyone is asking is whether the Champ can handle Norton. A lot of the experts preface their answers with a reference to Ali's fight with Joe Frazier in Manila. Did he leave it in Manila? is a question that's heard almost every minute on the minute. Did Manila drain him? Some guys say no, other guys say yes. Two days before the fight I'm with a Baltimore writer, Alan Goldstein, a very bright guy.

"How do you make the fight?" he asks me.

I say, "Did he leave it in Manila?"

"No," says Goldstein, "I think he's still the same."

"Well," I say, "if he's still the same, he knocks Norton out in five."

It's like picking between good apples and good oranges; both are nice to the palate. All I really care about is that nobody gets badly hurt. (Of course, I also care that we draw a good crowd.)

The Champ is training harder than ever.

One night, though, he puts the call out to Bob Seagriff, the security chief: *"Hey, police. Police!"*

Seagriff shows up and the Champ says he wants to go to New York City. Just like that! It's three in the morning and they are off in a caravan of cars to the Plaza Hotel. Two hours later the Champ is walking along deserted Canal Street in lower Manhattan—*after* having started out from the Plaza Hotel at Fifth Avenue and Fifty-ninth Street. He walks four miles, and when he finishes touring Canal Street he turns to Seagriff and says, with a straight face, "Now I feel like walking back."

Seagriff looks at him like he's crazy. Ali breaks up in laughter. Then the gang heads back to the Plaza in the limousine.

The media gets more than enough from Muhammad. Anything a newsman wants, the Champ provides. One day I get a call from the Houston Astrodome, where a bunch of Texas writers are sitting for a telephone press conference. They want Ali right away—without any notice! I rush over to him. "Champ," I say, "I didn't know about this 'til now, but a bunch of writers in Houston want to talk to you right now."

No hesitation. No moping or bitching like so many other athletes would give you in a similar situation. "Sure," he says. And bingo! over to the telephone he goes and has another press conference.

Another time I get a call from Melbourne, Australia. These Aussies want Ali. I see an opening. "Champ, I want you to talk to Australia, where they have an all-white policy."

He grabs the phone. "Hello! This is Muhammad Ali, here. Yeah, I'm in good shape, but I want to talk to you about something else. I wanna talk to you about brotherhood." Then, he goes on for twenty minutes, lecturing the Aussies about racism. A great lecture, he points out how people can live in harmony, no matter what the man's color, no matter what the man's faith. He's got to be allowed to live his life. By the time Muhammad gets through the Australian newspaper guys are punch drunk.

At last it's fight night, and just our luck, there is a police strike. By four in the afternoon, when I get to Yankee Stadium, I hear reports of hooligans causing trouble. If the strike isn't bad enough, the weather is rotten. It's cold. Between the police strike, the hooligans, and the cold, it's a promotional horror.

The fight itself is good and close, but Norton loses by a decision—although a lot of people figure that Ken won the fight. When I get inside Ken's room, he sees me and yells out, "You were there, Irving. You saw it. What do you think?"

I'm on the spot. At first I don't say anything. Then I go over to Ken and put my hand in his. "Ken, I know that right now you probably won't believe me, and you probably don't want to hear it, but what happened tonight is all for the best. You're gonna be a bigger hero, a bigger fighter. You're gonna make a lot more money. You didn't get hurt. You didn't get knocked out. You didn't get disgraced. You feel, I know, you got robbed. It's too bad. But wait and see; it'll all turn out for the best."

I'm satisfied that Ken, my first client, is okay. As for my second client, Ali, I see the Champ briefly at a press conference the next day and then we part company.

Months go by and the camp with the Champ becomes a distant memory. Then I get a letter from a Soviet comrade of mine, Dimitry Urnov, who lives in Moscow. The last letter I sent him, I casually mentioned that I had been in training camp with the heavyweight champion of the world. Much to my surprise, never thinking that Ali was that well known in Russia, Dimitry's ten-year-old son, Fedya, writes to me and asks if I can get an autographed photo of Ali for him. He also requests that I pass along a note to the Champ.

A couple of months later I'm working in Miami Beach, where Ali is putting on a boxing exhibition. I go over to see the Champ and give him Fedya's letter, which says: "Dear Muhammad Ali: My father is a friend of a friend of yours. I see you on television. I love boxing. Could you write me a note?"

A day later I go to the Champ's room and he gives me his photo with the inscription: "To Fedya. Love, Muhammad Ali." Then he turns the picture over and writes a letter to the kid.

"Be a good little man," he writes. "May God bless you. I hope we can meet someday. I'll come to your country and you come to mine."

I thank him and begin to take Fedya's letter back. "Hey," says Ali, "you can't have *that*. Y'know, I don't get letters from Russians every day."

It's a precious moment, and for my personal treasury there are the words he utters to his wife, Veronica, as I leave: "That's Irvin' Rudd. Always looking out for you."

For my momma, who fifty-five years earlier wanted her Irving to be a doctor, those words would have been *noches*.

= 2 =
"He Should Only Be a Doctor!"

Mr. and Mrs. Nathan Rudd are not particular when it comes to the subject of vocational guidance for their son. Nathan and Sarah decide that their slightly brittle Irving, if he can somehow survive a ruptured appendix, a rheumatic heart, and a "bed" comprised of three well-taped wooden kitchen chairs, will be a credit to the tribes of Abraham, Isaac, and Jacob. Thus, Nathan and Sarah Rudd agree that their designated genius should become, in order of importance: (a) the chief surgeon of Mount Sinai Hospital; (b) secretary of labor; (c) a specialist in eye, ear, and nose infections (two of which he actually suffers from, so already Irving is an expert); or,

at the very least, if he flunks medical school, (d) a rabbi—
Orthodox, of course!

The thought that young I. Rudd will grow up to be a
press agent for athletes would be as palatable to them as
the notion of his aspiring to the papacy. So Mama and
Papa Rudd do their best to steer "Oiving" in the right
direction—to elementary school and, most important,
Hebrew school. Then they cross their fingers and go back
to the business of scraping out a living.

Mama is busy running what we in Brooklyn call an "appetizing store" in the East New York section of the borough. In the late twenties East New York still has cows
roaming on farms and is regarded by sophisticated Manhattan Jews as *yenevelt* (a distant world). An appetizing
store is well named. It sells specialty foods that are—at
least to Jews—appetizing. Her big items are lox (smoked
salmon), herring, and pistachio nuts, not to mention I.
Rudd's personal favorite, dill pickles, which for my nasal
passages creates a more delectable odor than Chanel No.
5. Then there are bottles of bubbling seltzer, which Alfred
Kazin rightly describes as "the poor Jew's dinner wine."
To a Brooklyn Jew, Good Health Seltzer is more important than pasteurized milk.

Papa is in a related business—smoked fish. Unlike
Mama, he never actually touches the stuff during working
hours, because Papa is a truck driver for the Max Finkelstein Smoked Fish Company, an outfit that I deduce is a
holding company of some Egyptian pharaoh. Finkelstein
Smoked Fish is located on Havemeyer Street in the shad-
ows of the Williamsburg Bridge. While Mama is wrapping
fish, Papa is delivering kippers. It is a hell of a double-
play combination, and it helps keep their Irving in U.S.
Keds while he, they hope, is at school.

There are many schools, because the Rudds move
around like pawns on a chessboard. Talk about the wandering Jews, the Rudds touch almost every poor neighborhood in Brooklyn.

*   *   *

Tough as it is, I like school. Good teachers, good kids; like Bernie Friedkin, who launched my boxing career at age twelve by tapping me on the back and asking a simple question: "Rudd, can you fight?"

Not quite sure what this Friedkin fellow has in mind, I hedge my bets. "Yes, I can fight, but no, I don't care to indulge at the moment."

Friedkin is a chubby kid who will not take my half-assed no for an answer. "Oiv," he says, "I want ya to come over to my house. I got a gym, gloves. We're gonna box like they do at da Garden."

Before I can come up with an alibi, Friedkin takes me home with him and I realize that here is a kid who *really* lives on the other side of the tracks—not just the Long Island Railroad tracks but also the BMT elevated tracks. The kid is living in luxury. Why, they have not only running water but also steam heat and, wonder of wonders, a shower in the bathroom. To I. Rudd, the Friedkin home at 651 Alabama Avenue is the Taj Mahal of Brooklyn.

While I'm still suffering a case of awed lockjaw, Friedkin takes me down to his basement. Sure enough, there is a "boxing ring"—four ropes tied loosely around the steam pipes—as well as a couple of dozen *Ring* magazines stacked halfway to the ceiling. All over the walls Bernie has pictures of fighters: Jack Dempsey, Gene Tunney, Benny Leonard. Even a few bums, to boot.

What I'm seeing at Chateau Friedkin is completely at odds with the teachings I had absorbed in the Rudd household. Jewish boys are raised to be doctors or rabbis or lawyers. At worst, teachers. But Bernie Friedkin wants to be a professional fighter! Worse yet, he wants me to be his professional punching bag.

Against my better judgment, we put on the gloves and, all of a sudden, my head feels like a springpost in a pinball machine!—bop! bop! bop! Bernie pops me with more jabs and hooks than I've seen in my entire life. He beats the hell out of me and is very courteous about it. "Oiv," he says as I pick myself up off the floor, "yer a terrific guy. Let's do it again tomorrow."

Too punchy to understand him, I agree to return the next day. Day two is just like day one, another drubbing, except this time my survival instincts are working better and I begin to look for Bernie's weaknesses. He is cute, for sure, and in his heart Friedkin is a fighter, but I can tell that he has a China chin, although I would never get to break it. In fact, I am in grave danger of becoming the first punch-drunk grammar school kid in New York.

"All right, already," I tell Bernie, "you can beat me up; but where's it gonna get ya? Jewish kids don't become fighters; don't ya know that?"

"Bullshit," says Bernie. "I'll show ya a dozen of dem."

Before I can say I believe ya! Friedkin has me by the hand, giving me a grand tour of his neighborhood. In the windows of the kosher butcher, the candy store, the hardware store, there are big cardboard posters advertising professional boxing bouts at the local clubs, Broadway Arena and Ridgewood Grove. I see names that are neither Irish, Polish, or German: Pal Silvers, Lou Feldman, Georgie Goldberg, and Marty Fox. Friedkin tells me about Ruby Goldstein, one of the world's great lightweights. "Dey call him," says Bernie, "da jewel of da ghetto." Bernie says that if Ruby ever loses a fight, the whole Jewish community sits *shivah* (goes into mourning). Listening to Friedkin, I get the urge to become the world flyweight champion, but Bernie beats me up too often to pursue that idea, so I turn to dreams of glory as a big-league baseball star.

That presents problems. I stand only five feet tall and am growing slowly. Worse than that, I am a lefty, but my pop bought me a righty glove. Playing shortstop I have to wear my right glove backward. But who will tell that to the Brooklyn Dodgers' scout watching me from the stands?

For two years I persist in my baseball ambition, but when I reach age fourteen I realize there is no place for me—and never will be—in the National League. While other kids on the block are getting bigger and stronger, I. Rudd remains five feet and 110 pounds wearing a $2.95 pair of actual spiked shoes.

Since baseball and boxing are out of the question, there is some speculation about I. Rudd's future vocation. Medicine and the rabbinate have been given up as lost, so that means that I can either get a "regular job" or be a bum. On Powell Street in Brownsville, "makin' a livin'" can mean pushing a hand truck in the garment district of Manhattan or working behind a store counter or peddling shoes.

Instinctively, I know that the seven A.M. rush-hour crush and the drudgery of a nine-to-five job doing what I figure is meaningless work, is not for I. Rudd. I sense that somewhere out there is a working world of fun and adventure and I want a whack at that. I know it won't be easy since I have no uncles or brothers named John D. Rockefeller, but first I have to figure out my geography—like where *am* I going?

The answer comes from the corner newsstand. Day after day I find that I gravitate to the sports pages. I read every sportswriter I can lay my eyes on—Dan Daniel in the *World-Telegram*, Dan Parker in the *Mirror*, Bill Corum in the *Journal-American*, and Tommy Holmes in our own *Brooklyn Daily Eagle*.

I devour every word these guys write and rhapsodize and fantasize about the world of sportswriting. I dream of seeing the glorious words *by Irving Rudd* on a page of newsprint. Lo and behold, I discover that it's not so hard to accomplish after all. The thing to do is go to high school, which I have to do anyway.

In my freshman year at Thomas Jefferson High School on Pennsylvania Avenue in Brooklyn, I find out that there is a full-fledged newspaper, written and published by the students. It's called the *Liberty Bell*, and you don't have to be six feet tall to write for it; even a kid who is five feet nothing can get on the staff.

So I become an actual, factual writer for the *Liberty Bell*, which for me is like signing my first pro contract with the Dodgers and then being assigned to the minors. Who cares, I am writing. While Lepke Buchalter and Abe Reles are doing their thing for Murder Incorporated on the streets of Brooklyn, I'm learning how to write.

Jefferson High is a terrific academic setting, mostly because the principal, Dr. Elias Lieberman, is a gifted poet who treasures high-class academia. Our instructors include such teachers as Gordon Kahn (author Roger Kahn's father), who is the blood and guts and brains of the "Information Please!" radio show. All of a sudden, bright new worlds are opening for the kid from the wrong side of the tracks. "Rudd," says the newspaper editor, Saul Goldstein, "I want you to interview Helen Hull Jacobs (the tennis star) at Forest Hill Stadium."

Irving Rudd interviewing Helen Hull Jacobs? To me, the odds would seem better for me to reach the moon than to get inside Forest Hills Stadium. But there I am amid the English-style clubhouse with its striped awnings and freshly trimmed grass courts. I meet the great Helen Hull Jacobs at the tennis club's restaurant, which is a million light-years away from Grabstein's delicatessen on Sutter Avenue. I keep asking myself, Irving, what *are* you doing here?

Yow! I'm thrilled to the teeth and can't wait to get home and put the interview down on paper. I enjoy my first literary orgasm. (I still didn't know about the other kind.) I can't wait to see the actual story in print. A week, two weeks go by. Finally the *Liberty Bell* comes out with another edition.

Ah! There it is, in black and white. I read it over and over again, concerned that maybe the first time I was just dreaming. Fortunately, the story never disappears, and I know in my heart that this writing business is for me. Further proof comes a week later in the form of a fan letter. Bertha Orchowsky of Class 7B writes to the editor: "In the first issue of the *Liberty Bell* there was an interesting interview with Miss Helen Jacobs. This was the first interview with a woman and it proved to be a success. Why can't we have more famous women interviewed?"

I do my full share to fulfill Bertha Orchowsky's request. Next I interview Eleanor Roosevelt, wife of the President of the United States. I'm now fifteen years old, five feet one inch tall, and I'm interviewing *the* First Lady! After that I take a crack at some famous men, too, including Jimmy Durante (who told me, "When I was a youngster like you I had dreams of becoming a great concert pianist") and George Gershwin (who said, "The music of today is the classical music of tomorrow").

After a year of interviewing I come to the conclusion that my favorite subjects are sports people, like Ford Frick, a sportswriter (who would become president of the National League and commissioner of baseball), and Nat Fleischer, publisher of *Ring* magazine.

In the summer of 1927 I start going to baseball games at Ebbets Field—where I can get in free—and, finally, to Yankee Stadium. To get to Yankee Stadium from Brownsville is like going on a safari. It starts with the packing of supplies, the most important of which is a monstrous bakery roll the size of a flattened bowling ball (and less digestible). The rolls, known as *"bumbahs,"* are slit in half and filled with anything that happens to be in Mama's icebox. (That is not to be confused with a refrigerator. An icebox is what it says it is, a big wooden box where you put a large hunk of ice delivered by a wagon, pulled by a horse, driven by—who else?—the iceman. Only rich people own refrigerators in Brooklyn.) With the bumbahs well stocked, the Bronx-bound expeditionary force takes the overland route to the IRT subway. Although they call it a subway, the IRT is an ominous, dark-steel elevated line along Livonia Avenue, where the colored people (nobody calls them blacks) live. The overland route takes us past pushcarts loaded down with vegetables, junk shops where the owners plaintively wail, "I cash clothes," and the tailor with the sign: WILL ALTER TO SUIT. We march past the candy store with the big picture of an Optimo Cigar in the window, then the poolroom, and up the wooden stairs to the el station.

The excitement heightens as we get to the platform. I can't get over it; we're at eye level with the third floor of the Livonia Avenue tenements. I look across the tracks and see a man in his bathroom, shaving, as if nobody in the world is around him. I would keep on looking but I hear the telltale click-click of the steel plates under the rails. Any kid who has ever ridden the Brooklyn el knows that this means the train can't be far away. The official tip-off is when the TRAIN COMING sign lights up and rings in the station. I look up the track and there is the IRT express, with its two outside front windows looking like a pair of eyes to me and the middle window like a nose. It's only the IRT, but to young Irving it is as good as the 20th Century Limited on its way from Grand Central Station to Los Angeles. The train screeches to a stop, the huge sliding door with the fat rubber cushion at the end slowly slides open, and we rush in, grabbing a seat for the splendid excursion to 161st Street and River Avenue in the Bronx.

I'm in heaven, pressing my nose against the front window of the IRT, making a whiny sound of my own, pretending to be the motorman, moving the lumbering steel giant all by myself. When the express finally rolls out of the tunnel portal in the Bronx, my heart does a paradiddle and all thoughts drift from piloting the subway train to the heroic figures I would soon see at Yankee Stadium.

In a way, my first game at Yankee Stadium is a

buildup to a letdown. I climb the stairs, released from the IRT, and am awed by the mountain of concrete that is "the house that Ruth built." We push through the turnstiles, climb the concrete ramp, and at last are deposited in the grandstands, from where we can see the most important men in the world working out on the field. The first thing that hits my senses is the magnificent grass: it is so well kept and the smell is sharp and beautiful. The great names that I had only heard around the neighborhood candy store are all there—Lou Gehrig, "Jumpin" Joe Dugan, Tony Lazzeri, Waite Hoyt, Benny Bengough, Cedric Durst, Bob Meusel, and Johnny Grabowski. But most of all there is Babe Ruth, in the flesh. More than anything, I want to see this Goliath of a slugger put one into the so-close right-field bleachers. But on this day Babe lets me down; not one lousy home run (though he does get a couple of hits). The expeditionary force returns to its Brownsville base defeated.

Well, if I can't have Babe Ruth, I'll settle for Clise Dudley. Unlike Ruth, Dudley makes his living a lot closer to where the Rudds live—in Brooklyn. In fact, Dudley is a pitcher for the Brooklyn Dodgers. That in itself is not something to go crazy about, except that the Dodgers play at Ebbets Field in Brooklyn and that's only fifteen minutes from my house. Even though Dudley is relatively unknown, his name has a ring to it that tickles my ears, and I become a Clise Dudley fan for that and other good reasons. Dudley is a big, handsome, strapping right-hander playing for the Dodgers, managed by Uncle Wilbert Robinson. Uncle Robby likes his pitchers big, and if they can beat the Giants or at least hold their own, they'll win. Dudley has all the qualifications. Now all I have to do is meet him. That means getting into Ebbets Field, and since my annual allotment of baseball ticket money already is spent on the visit to Yankee Stadium, I have to figure a way of getting past the turnstile without money.

After a little investigation I learn that that's not so hard to do; the trick, I'm told by some older guys at the candy store, is to hang around the outside of Ebbets Field and find an opening.

The "big" guys tell me that the best thing is to show up at Bedford Avenue and Sullivan Place (near the center field entrance to the bleachers) at about ten in the morning and get a turnstile ("stile boy") job. A stile boy stands behind a manually operated turnstile that lets one person at a time enter the ballpark when a foot pedal is depressed by the boy and the stile makes one revolution. The ticket taker stands to the right of the stile boy, chopping the tickets and handing back the rain check.

So I show up at 10:00 A.M. and, sure enough, there's an opening, and I. Rudd, erstwhile Yankees–Babe Ruth fan becomes Brooklyn Dodgers employee and, naturally, fan. I get a quarter for three innings' work and then I'm admitted inside—no cost, no obligation. There are hundreds of empty seats around and I'm in like Flynn. I can't believe how easy it is; and all for turning a turnstile. It doesn't take me long to figure out that the better jobs are those on the gates leading to the grandstand or box and reserved seats. After a couple of days I decide to bring my autograph book. Already I know all the players by sight, and even if I don't, it's easy to spot a ballplayer.

Naturally, my eyes are always on Dudley, the big pitcher who whips our rivals, the Giants. I still haven't the nerve to approach him, but one day while I'm working the turnstiles I see this big, nice guy and I holler, "Hello, Dud!" He answers, "Hi-ya, son." The words are like the most beautiful tonic in the world. Soon I get to know him, and one day, while I'm trying to line up another stile job (the pickings are tough this day), Clise comes along, takes me by the hand, and passes me right through the employees' entrance with him. After the game I wait for him and we take the subway together, and there's a doll on the train, the most beautiful lady I've ever seen. She knows her baseball and soon she's talking to me and Dud. Her name is Jean Kern. I don't know who she is, but she has this great big hat and long gloves, and I figure she's the most beautiful lady in the world. Next day she takes me to the game. We sit in a box seat and I have peanuts, popcorn, a scorecard, soda pop, the works. I still don't know who she is—and I never did find out—but she seems to know everybody. But best of all she knows Dudley and he knows me and I figure our love affair will go on forever.

Then one day the roof falls in on me. I'm with Dudley outside the park and along comes Mickey Finn, the infielder. Clise puts his hand on Mickey's shoulder and says, "Well, Mickey, this is it. I'm on my way." Dudley had just learned that he has been traded to the Phillies.

By this time other favorites have crept into I. Rudd's life. One of them is Evar Swanson, an outfielder with the Cincinnati Reds. To me, Swanson is one of the great human beings, on or off the ball field, and he cements our relationship by warmly shaking my hand, which no other ballplayer has done up until now. It may not seem like much, but the handshake is worth all the money in the world, especially since it comes just seconds after Swanson caught a fly ball for the final out of the game against Brooklyn.

Much as I like Swanson and Dudley, I remain unalterably a Dodgers fan through and through. To me, being a Giants fan is worse than heresy; it's like being a goy (a gentile). In my neighborhood I could be killed for being a Giants fan. Only a special few can get away with that. One of them is a storekeeper on our block.

This shopkeeper has a lot of balls. He is a Giants fan, which is bad enough, but on top of that he's a big supporter of Bill Terry, who is considered the worst of the worst by Dodgers people. Terry is the guy who seems to beat us more than the other Giants. (Besides, he once insulted the honor of every Brooklyn fan, man, woman, and child, when he cracked, "Brooklyn? Is Brooklyn still in the league?") So we hate the bastard, Terry, so much that when we find out that the shopkeeper is a Giants fan, we call *him* "Terry." That is the ultimate gesture of contempt we can deliver against anyone living in Brooklyn who is so low as to root for the Giants.

The only big conflicts I have are when the Phillies—and my man Clise Dudley—come to town. Then I make a brief exception and root only for Clise when he pitches or comes up to bat. My friends in the bleachers seem to understand, and give me no grief. Meanwhile, me and Clise become closer and closer. Whenever the Phillies come to town I go to visit him at the Governor Clinton Hotel in Manhattan, where the club stays. One day Clise tells me that the Phils are going to play a twilight exhibition game in Bayonne, New Jersey, which is not all that far from New York.

"Can you guys use a batboy?" I ask Clise.

Dudley says he doesn't know, but he'll ask Burt Shotton, the Phils' manager. "Better yet," says Clise, "why don't *you* ask Shotton?" I nearly shit a brick. But Dudley points across the hotel lobby. "You see that man; that's Burt Shotton. Go on, ask him!"

So I walk over, barely touching the floor with my shoes, I'm so scared, and confront this kindly man. "Why, sure, we'll need a batboy," he says. "Report here tomorrow at four o'clock."

I hustle back to Brooklyn, borrow a uniform from my coach at Thomas Jefferson High School, pack my bag, and go to bed. It rains all night and all the next day. The game is called off and I am crushed to the core. After all, I had never been farther from Brooklyn than the Bronx. My big chance to get to Bayonne is rained out the window.

To me, being a batboy is about the best thing that could happen to a kid, which is why I'm always a little jealous of Babe Hamberger, the Dodgers' batboy, who took a liking to me after a while. Next thing I know, Hamberger is giving me broken bats after the Dodgers' games.

These are the most expensive Hillerich and Bradsby Louisville Sluggers, the kind that any kid from Brownsville would give his right arm to own. Here I am getting, free of charge, an autographed Babe Herman model and another from Johnny Frederick and from Rube Bressler. I tape up the cracked parts, bring them home and—poof!— I am now a very big man on Powell Street. Who can afford to buy a Louisville Slugger in 1930?

Eventually I become a batboy, although not with the Dodgers. Thomas Jefferson High School needs a batboy, so I take the job. Okay, so it's not the majors, but it's a start.

= 3 =
Winning
the Fight Game

The writing experience on Thomas Jefferson High School's *Liberty Bell* has given I. Rudd enormous confidence. That as well as several kayos at the hands of my pal Bernie Friedkin leads me to think that (a) I can become a professional writer and (b) I can write about boxing, on account of Friedkin teaching me so much about the pastime. So that's how I come to meet such marvelous people as Jetty Royal, Havana Kid, Yoshio Nakamura, Yusin Sirutis, Willie Cheatum, and, of course, the ever-popular Kid Bon Bon. These and other upstanding citizens make their home away from home at a place called Stillman's Gym. It is soon to be home for I. Rudd as well.

Stillman's Gym is housed in a narrow, dirty, airless three-story structure within shouting distance of Madison Square Garden on Eighth Avenue between Fifty-fourth and Fifty-fifth streets. The gym is ruled by a tough-talking, harsh-faced martinet named Lou Stillman. It is Lou's practice to tout whoever happens to be working out at his place, thus, the huge banner on Eighth Avenue proclaims: HENRY ARMSTRONG NOW TRAINING. Or Sixto Escobar or Lou Ambers or any of dozens of other great fighters.

From one until four in the afternoon, Sundays and holidays, a parade of pugs climbs in and out of two rings, including my friend "Schoolboy" Bernie Friedkin. From upstairs, the walls echo the drumfire of punching bags and the snorts and grunts of fighters shadowboxing or doing calisthenics. To the left, on a high stool under an automatic ring timer, sits Lou Stillman, regulating the flow of fistic traffic.

I am impressed with Stillman, who reigns supreme. He's the undisputed king who takes no bull from anyone, even if the temperature happens to be ninety degrees outside and a fight manager asks Stillman to open the windows. "Look," bellows Stillman with dictatorial finality, "don't tell me the place needs air. Take your fighter and get the hell outta here!" Like I say, Stillman is undisputed.

Away from the king's throne and near ring number one is a lunch counter at the rear. On the opposite side is a row of telephone booths. A placard warns that the use of slugs in the telephones will result in banishment from Stillman's for life. The stand-up lunch counter and the phones are the rialto of the gym. Top matchmakers, from Madison Square Garden down to Ridgewood Grove, Broadway Arena, Bronx Coliseum, and Laurel Gardens, close their deals over salami on ryes at Stillman's lunch counter. This is the place where Friedkin takes me one day, and I am instantly hooked on the aroma, the thump-thump sounds, and the general ambience. When I walk down the steps onto Eighth Avenue that day, I know that

I must come back to Stillman's like my Jewish brethren are lured back to Jerusalem. Never mind the "next year in Jerusalem." For I. Rudd it is "next week at Stillman's."

So I keep coming back, and the fight guys there get to know the little squirt from Thomas Jefferson High School who likes to write. Then the break comes, quite unexpectedly, while I'm watching some fighters work out. A big, handsome black guy approaches me and asks me if I want a job.

I'm amazed. The black guy is Al Douglas; and everybody at Stillman's knows that Douglas not only owns 10 percent of Joe Louis but also is the fellow who runs a boxing emporium in Harlem called Rockland Palace. Douglas wants me to be his press agent.

Press agent? What kind of creature is that? I ask Douglas what a press agent does, and he tells me that I have to "write releases." To which I respond, "What's a release?" Unperturbed by my abject ignorance, Douglas pulls out a mimeographed sheet with a letterhead on top and shows it to me. "By Jesus!" I shout. "I can write that kind of crap. Why, I write better stuff for the *Liberty Bell!*"

Douglas smiles paternally. "You're on, kid. I'll start ya at eighteen dollars a week."

I don't tell this to Douglas, but I would have taken the job for nothing. It is an honor to be press agent for Rockland Palace on a lot of counts, not the least of which is that I'm the only white guy on the payroll. And why not? Rockland Palace is located at 155th Street and Eighth Avenue, just catty-corner from the Polo Grounds baseball park in the very heart of Black Harlem.

I'm not sure why Douglas has hired me, but I don't really care. All I know is that from the very start he raises me like a son; he teaches me all I have to know about the fight game. Lesson one is plain and simple: since I'm working for a black fight club, I'm going to be shafted by the white press. In 1936 the black boxer, unless he happens to be Joe Louis or Henry Armstrong, is disdained by the newspapers as well as the fight managers. I soon get the word when I hear about a fight, matchmaker who needs to fill an empty spot on his card. I tell him about a good black boxer. "Sorry," he tells me, "but I can't use coal!" Right away I know that my job is not going to be easy. I have to crash the daily papers with news of fighters like "Tiger" Jack Fox, "Jersey" Joe Walcott, Elmer "Violent" Ray, "Snooks" Lacey, and "King Kong" Mathews. To these black fighters, Rockland Palace is the big time.

The Palace isn't closed to whites, but there are two sets of unwritten rules, I learn. One is for the fights between blacks and blacks and the other for fights between blacks and whites. It's not hard to figure; when a black guy goes up against "one of his own kind" the fight is a regular one, no deviations. But if a white guy is going against a black, the black fighter has to wear "handcuffs" (take it easy) or do a tank job.

Like Stillman's Gym, Rockland Palace has a flavor all its own. It is Harlem's answer to Madison Square Garden. While the Garden's ringside is graced by the likes of Toots Shor, Leo Durocher, and Mayor Fiorello LaGuardia, the Palace's ringside features Duke Ellington, Bill "Bojangles" Robinson, and Cab Calloway, the elite of the black show biz community. Seats go from $.55 to $1.65 for reserved ringside. Handsome men dressed to the gills escort equally handsome women down the aisles. Always on hand are such regulars as Satisfaction, Plenty Money, the Deacon, and Vivian. Better characters you won't find in Damon Runyon's *Guys and Dolls*. Vivian is a perfect example. A bartender by profession, Vivian (these guys only have one name) sits out in the aisle at every fight and shadowboxes, excitedly rooting his favorite boxers on.

Characters such as Vivian are not limited to the audience. Our ring announcer, Harry Balogh, is in a class by himself; he's the first ever in boxing to wear a tuxedo while working. Balogh treats every fight like a Shakespearean epic. Where one word will suffice, Harry uses a dozen. As the crowd watches, Harry closes his eyelids, as though troubled with a great secret sorrow, and introduces the fighters. Over and over again Balogh slays the crowd with lines like: "May the arm of the worthier participant be elevated in token of victory," or "A giant heavyweight, he weighs, tew, tew, tew and a half" (222.5), or "Introducing Tony so-and-so, that up-and-coming youthful youngster."

It is nothing for Balogh to switch to a sermon on jay-walking. One night, after the last bout ends, Harry grabs the mike and intones: "Please don't pass any red lights or wooden nickels—I thank you."

Balogh usually wins his bouts with the King's English, although one defeat was recorded during a war benefit. A group of pretty gals from the American Women's Volunteer Services stood primly poised at the back of the house, waiting to take up a collection. Balogh, with his serious stentorian delivery, intoned: "These girls will soon pass among you with their little cans. Give 'til it hurts."

At Rockland Palace, Balogh never steals the thunder from the worthy men on the card, be they newcomers, regulars, or fighters on the way over the hill. Our biggest draw is "Tiger" Jack Fox, a fearless, long-armed, light heavyweight with a knife-scarred face ornamented by tin ears. He is somewhere between good and very good, depending on how you analyze fighters. One night I watch him go up against a terrific puncher named Jack Trammell, a tall, skinny man with a chicken wing for a right arm. When Trammell straightens that wing, something generally drops—and not Trammell. Fox looks like he's in big trouble, spotting Trammell about twenty pounds and six inches in height. The Tiger walks out and invites Trammell to park his right on his thrust-out, unprotected chin.

Trammell connects and rocks the Tiger back on his heels. But Fox pulls himself together in no time at all and chases Trammell right out of ring. Next they throw "Jersey" Joe Walcott in with Fox. In the first round Walcott nails Fox on the chin and knocks him through the ropes onto the apron of the ring, where he lies absolutely still for seven seconds. The crowd goes wild; after all, nobody had done that to Tiger Fox before. But Fox manages to roll back into the ring and get up, and by the eighth round he knocks Walcott out cold. The Tiger is the king of the Palace.

Even though Walcott takes the count, he still shows enough for Douglas to want him back at Rockland; and it's a good move, too. Anyway, Walcott returns to Rockland in September 1937 as part of a card Douglas stages for the benefit of the five "Scottsboro boys," who are black kids in an Alabama jail. My press release reads: "Each dynamite-laden fist will swing a solid, crushing blow against the forces of Southern lynch justice."

Walcott's final bout at Rockland is against George Brothers, a 170-pounder who was an International Golden Gloves light heavyweight champion. Jersey Joe drops Brothers right after the bell in the first round. Brothers gets up, Walcott moves in, and—whamo!—knocks him down again.

Brothers is a skinny kid, and he seems no match for the brawnier Walcott, especially since he's been on the floor twice already. But he gets up, and for the third time, Walcott deposits him horizontally. The rule that three knockdowns in a round automatically ends a fight is not yet in effect, but the crowd has seen enough. All around ringside they are getting out of their seats and heading for the exits. As one guy leaves he waves at Brothers and says, "Good-bye, boy. Don't get up or he gonna knock you down again!" Brothers sits there looking at the fan, spits out a mouthful of blood and teeth, shakes his head, and just glares. Then he pulls himself up and carries the fight to Jersey Joe. Brothers lasts eight rounds and comes off with a decision. Jersey Joe is a fine boxer, just a shade below greatness and, as far as I know, the only fighter who has ever knocked out a father-and-son combination. In 1936 Joe stiffens Phil Johnson and fifteen years later he knocks out Harold Johnson.

Meanwhile, I. Rudd is having a ball. I'm learning the

fight game and I'm learning the press agent hustle. Even though the odds are stacked against us, being a black club from Harlem, Al Douglas always seems to come up with a promotable character for me—like the ever-popular King Kong Mathews.

But let's start at the beginning. Before King Kong steps into the ring as King Kong, he is Oscar Mathews out of Tallulah, Louisiana, who can write his name but that's all. He is five feet ten inches tall, weighs two hundred pounds, and is surrounded by unbelievably massive arms and a huge corded neck. They put Oscar in with Heinz Kohlhaas and Oscar walks out and throws a right hand. Off to the hospital goes Heinz with a concussion. Then they put Oscar in with one Jack Tebo and Oscar throws a right hand. There goes Tebo, also with a concussion. Then they bring in a fellow named José Muniz, who I bill as "the Portugese heavyweight champion," although he probably is a flamenco dancer out of some East Side bistro. Muniz dances away the night and Oscar comes walking after him. Then, whiff! When Oscar hits, mountains move, let alone Portugese champions. Oscar throws a right and all over the house there is a single sound—"*oough!*" Then the crowd goes home.

After these impressive wins, Oscar shows up at the Palace wearing a new bathrobe. Across the back it says "King Kong." When Oscar starts down the aisle, from way back in the house the chant sweeps through the hall: "King Kong, King Kong, *King Kong!*"

Douglas and I figure we've got a winner here, so we send out promotions with King Kong's picture. He's got a crown on his head with big letters asking: "Is King Kong Mathews greater than Joe Louis?" In Harlem they are naming babies for Oscar. Mathews is not only very likeable, he suddenly becomes very challengeable. As it happens, Tiger Fox wants a payday and asks for King Kong.

Ever shrewd, Douglas wants no part of Fox beating up on his new hero—Al really respects Tiger as a fighter—so Douglas picks Jack Trammell instead. By now even folks outside of Harlem are talking about King Kong Mathews, and the Palace is sold out before 6:00 P.M. of the first preliminary bout. Finally King Kong makes his entrance and the crowd goes bananas. There's only one problem: Trammell is no lemon. In the first round, Trammell sticks and moves, sticks and moves. Right away we all know how it will go unless the King gets lucky. Halfway through the round, Trammell lets fly with a right and steps back.

King Kong doesn't fall backward. He doesn't fall on his face. He rockets about six feet forward into Trammell's arms. It is as if Trammell has grabbed him by the lapels and snatched him close. The King hangs on and Trammell tries desperately to shake him off. Then the King gets in one little chop. It lands on the head—high. (Trammell tells me later that he had a headache for four days after that love tap.) Now the referee separates them. Trammell keeps backing away and jabbing with his left hand as the King walks in . . . but too far. Trammell winds up his right, way out in center field so everybody in the Palace can see it; that is, everybody but King Kong. The poor King is on his back faster than you can say Kong, and they are throwing water in his face. For a half hour they are working over him before he finally wakes up. When that happens, one of the last customers in the place, an old man with his head down talking to himself, picks himself up and leaves.

"The King," he is saying. "The King is dead!"

Well, he isn't physically dead, but he isn't the man he was a few hours earlier. Nor is Rockland Palace the same place it was when I. Rudd was conscripted out of Stillman's Gym by Al Douglas. It is time for Rudd to move on. Douglas and I have an amicable parting of the ways, although I am committed to boxing for life, the proof being that I immediately return to Stillman's to meet friends and find new work.

Being around Stillman's, like being around Rockland Palace, is basic training in the boxing business. You learn things like "Gainford's Law" and you meet characters such as Beezy Thomas.

Like Al Douglas, George Gainford is a pillar of the black boxing community. He is a huge, handsome man, nicknamed "the Emperor" by some. He handles Golden Gloves champions and one day will gain fame and fortune as the man who guides "Sugar Ray" Robinson to the middleweight championship.

Gainford's Law, I learn, is based on an incident that takes place while George is in a tank town discussing some potential bouts with the promoter and the town's mayor. "Mr. Gainford," the mayor says, "I want you to know that we have a spanking new auditorium in this city; and we've got twelve thousand seats for boxing." To which Gainford replies: "Mister Mayor, it ain't the seats you got for boxin' that's important. It's the *asses* you all put in them seats that counts." Hence, Gainford's Law.

By Stillman's standards, Gainford is a rather upright, stable character, but Beezy Thomas is somewhat to the left of normalcy. For some unfathomable reason, Beezy is called "the Champ of the Congo." A fragile man of flyweight dimensions, Beezy is a mass of facial scar tissue surrounded by a pair of muffin ears. Short and bullet-domed with a fuzzy pate, he shuffles around the gym. Like so many former boxers, he is now down but not out, a bootblack who does odd jobs but mostly is mascot to the superb boxer Tony Canzoneri.

Beezy is a master of the whammy. In top hat, white tie, and tails, Thomas goes to all of Canzoneri's fights. He leads the way down the aisle to ringside. Then he invokes the spirits and curses against Tony's opponent. He goes into a trance, rolls his eyes, foams at the lips and wallops his head against the nearest wall with frightening force— five, ten, as many as twenty times without apparent injury. Judging by Canzoneri's winning record, Beezy must be doing something right.

Likewise, I. Rudd must be doing something right at

Stillman's, because one day I'm introduced to a fellow named Benny who I only know as a sweet guy who hangs around the gym.

With a big cigar plugged in the middle of his kisser and a little bald spot on top of the head, Benny is one of those fat guys who wheezes every few words without fail, like an old locomotive letting off steam. *"Whoosh"* almost sounds like a part of Benny's monologue, because whenever he talks there's a *"whoosh"* stuck somewhere in between. "Oiv," Benny says, "I'm openin' a (*whoosh*) little fight club (*whoosh*), and I need a (*whoosh*) publicity man. Oiv, you're my man. Fifteen a week to start."

Who could say no to Benny with the *whoosh*? So I'm back in action, only now I. Rudd is based at Fort Totten Arena in Bayside, Queens. This is a very special fight club because it's located on an army base, which means you don't need a license to promote or referee a fight, since it's government property. Benny tells me we're going to have our cards on Friday nights with five four-round bouts among the soldiers. The topper on our card will be a professional match.

Somehow we can't get the promotion off the ground. For starters, our big problem is that we're an outdoor arena and every Friday, it seems, we get rain. Meantime, I'm working like a beaver trying to come up with a gimmick that will bring the people to Fort Totten. My plan is to build up two neighborhood rivals—Peanuts Barbetta and Jimmy Falco.

The way I do this is to match each of them with a stiff for several weeks so both Barbetta and Falco develop winning records. Then we put them together and sell out the joint. So finally the big night comes, and what happens? Barbetta gets sick and we have to find a substitute to go in against Falco.

It's not a complete disaster, though, and when the card is over, Benny counts up the money and pays off the fighters— for the soldier bouts it's nine bucks to the winner and six

47

bucks to the loser. Now I noticed that Benny has run out of bills; there is nothing left for his publicity man. "Benny," I say, "this is the third straight week you ain't paid me."

First Benny comes back with a *whoosh*, then: "Kid, stick with me (*whoosh*); next week I'll have something for ya."

Next week comes and the beloved ex-champ Benny Leonard is supposed to be our referee and also tell stories from the ring. Just before the fights are to begin, we get word that Leonard's plane is grounded somewhere and he can't make it. Meanwhile, I'm taking tickets at the gate and doubling as usher when Benny, the promoter, comes running up the aisle, grabs me by the arm and says: "Oiv (*whoosh*), *you* gotta be my (*whoosh*) referee tonight."

Before I can tell Benny I've never been through the ropes in my life, he's pushing me into the ring. I get through the soldier bouts all right and now comes the wind-up, main event, between Johnny Lasinski and Joe Baynes, blown-up light heavyweights. Lasinski is a blond with a cowlick, a tatooed Joe Palooka with "Mother" drawn on one arm and "God Bless America" on the other; Baynes is also a tough-looking guy.

How do I handle two *bullvahns* (bruisers) like that? I scramble around; there aren't many clinches, thank God, and then Baynes does the job. He chops one to Lasinski's belly and there's an "oooff" moan of pain. Baynes does it again, and this time Johnny goes down and I count him out. Am I ever glad to get out of that one!

I can still see the headline the next day in the old New York *Sun*: "Baynes Kayos Lasinski in Ring at Fort Totten." And the comment: "Impressed into service as a referee, Irv Rudd did himself proud, especially by the masterful manner in which he handled the behemoths, Lasinski and Baynes. Tossing those big boys around isn't exactly easy work." With a review like that I figure I might even get a bonus from Benny. He puts a ten dollar bill on the table. "That's it (*whoosh*), Oiv. That's all (*whoosh*) that's left." I grab the tenner, seeing as it was going to be four weeks without pay if I don't.

The next day, I'm back at Stillman's looking for action when there's a phone call for me. It's Benny. I'm figuring maybe he's got more dough for me. "Oiv," Benny says, "you still got the ten bucks I gave ya?" (Yeah, I still have it.) Benny sounds desperate. "Oiv, can you get over to the (*whoosh*) Long Island City Magistrate's Court (*whoosh*) right away?" Now Benny is pleading. "I got caught in a (*whoosh*) crap game and the fine is (*whoosh*) ten bucks, or I sit here three days."

Who could say no? I rush over to the court and fork over my ten-spot. I figure it's worth the price of buying my freedom from Benny the Whoosh. Then it's back to Stillman's to make more contacts. One of my favorites, who always seems to be around the gym at the time, is Barney Nagler, who covers the fights for a paper called the *Bronx Home News*.

In his calm moments Barney is a sweet guy and a great writer. But all his moments are not calm; like the time he got into a row with the fight manager George Sheppard. That's not exactly a good match—Barney weighs in at five-one, maybe 140 pounds, while Sheppard is six-three, 250 pounds, and once was a damn good professional fighter. The trouble starts when Nagler writes something about one of Sheppard's fighters, suggesting that the fighter, Sonny Horne, find a new manager. Naturally, that bugs Sheppard, and when he meets Nagler he quietly invites him aside.

"What the fuck do you want?" Nagler supposedly says to Sheppard.

"Gee, Barney," Sheppard says, "you really hurt me with that story yesterday. It wasn't quite right."

Nagler, all five feet of him, stares up at Sheppard through his funny little glasses. "You big prick. I'll bust you right in the mouth. . . ." And then he starts swinging at the startled Sheppard.

George has to protect himself. He puts his hand out, like

a football player's stiff-arm, and knocks Nagler's glasses off. Barney is an awful mess. Before any more damage is done, cooler heads intervene, but Nagler isn't finished with Sheppard. At the next Boxing Writers' Association meeting a resolution is brought up that Sheppard, because of the way he manhandled Nagler, should be barred from getting any publicity for himself or his fighters.

That would be some miscarriage of justice. And one honest writer, Bill Heinz, realizes it and jumps up yelling, "Wait a minute! You guys are gonna wipe out a man's livelihood, Sheppard's existence." The others listen to Heinz and finally agree that all Sheppard has to do is send Nagler some letter of apology; otherwise, drastic measures would be taken.

Everybody is wondering what Sheppard is going to do, and at the next meeting of the Boxing Writers' Association we get the answer. A telegram has arrived from Montreal. It reads, "To Barney Nagler: Right or wrong, I apologize."

Right or wrong, I soon learn that one young man who never apologizes is Al "Bummy" Davis, a fighter who will soon become the most hated man in the ring and—right or wrong—one of I. Rudd's best clients. "Bummy" Davis is a very much disliked fighter except to those who really know him at close range. Why is he hated? To begin with, he comes from a family of toughs. At the age of eight he was "lookout" for his dad's speakeasy. He's the kind of kid people are always trying to shove away from their places. He has a nasty streak and he'll fight with older men. His entire milieu is tough. His brother, known as "Big Gangy," is equally rough. With Bummy it's a survival thing, and he has survived through toughness. When he turned pro as a fighter the mean streak came through, especially when he pulverized Tony Canzoneri. Bummy beat him up so badly that he developed a bully persona from that point on.

= 4 =
Mushky Jackson, Razor Phil, Beau Jack, Joe Bostic, and Other Great Characters, Black and White

I never regret working with Bummy Davis, but as characters go, he is still a piker compared with some of the beauts I get to know around Stillman's Gym. Right at the top of the list is Mushky Jackson, whose real name is Morris Ladisky. Mushky speaks in malaprops. When it is raining he looks out the window and says, "Y'know, it's grizzling out there." Or after rushing to make an appointment at the gym, Mush runs up the stairs, huffing and puffing, and announces with a grin, "I got here in the knack of time."

One day Mushky is sitting in the office when somebody opens the paper and sees a big story about crime. John

Condon, the boxing publicist, is telling about a gangster who has managed to elude the cops for a number of years. Mushky is sitting there all ears as the conversation goes back and forth. He looks like he is watching a tennis match, his head is going from one speaker to another, and then Mushky blurts out, "Dis case, da one yer talkin' about. How long ago did he pull this heist?" Somebody tells Mushky it was many years ago. "Too late," snaps Mushky, "da Statue of Liberty has run out on him."

Another grand Stillman's character is Razor Phil. When he isn't hanging around the gym, Phil handles a bunch of low-grade fighters, a sharp contrast to Phil's high-class look. The Razor's eccentricities can fill an ocean liner. For instance, in the middle of the summer Phil walks around wearing a white shirt, a necktie, and a coat. He has earned the nickname Razor Phil because he feels a need to carry a straight razor on his person at all times. Although Phil's clothes give him an outward appearance of savoir faire, Phil will never be mistaken for Albert Einstein. Or, as Mushky Jackson so aptly puts it: "Phil is illiterate; and what's more, he can't read or write!"

One of Phil's more literate cronies is fight announcer Harry Balogh. When the guys gather on Friday afternoon, Harry likes to drop this precious malaprop: "Okay, boys, let's reminisce about tonight's fight." At least Balogh knows how to write, which is more than we can say for Razor Phil.

When Phil has to write a letter, he asks a pal to handle it for him. Once he asked matchmaker Teddy Brenner to author a terribly nasty letter to another matchmaker. Phil really was pissed as hell at this other guy, and he dictated the most insulting letter imaginable to Brenner. When he got to the end he said to Brenner, "Sign it 'Your Friend, Phil Lewis.'"

Razor Phil isn't giving me any grief, but one night I learn a real lesson about the bad side of boxing. There's a fight manager, Lou Shiro, at ringside who handles Joe

Governale, a good Brooklyn middleweight who is on the card. Shiro, who lives in suburban Long Beach, Long Island, comes over to me and says, "Irving, do me a favor and tell Judge Charley Shortell that I'm driving home with him tonight. I left my car at home."

Like a naive jerk, I go over to the judge, who is an honorable man, and tell him that Shiro wants a lift. Shortell grabs my arm: "Irving, what's the matter with you? Listen, I'll forget what you just said—if you'll forget it. Don't go back to Shiro and don't tell him a thing. Ya hear?"

Now I get the message. Shiro is trying to make sure that his fighter, Governale, gets a break from the judge. But Shortell won't have any of that shit. After the fight he takes me aside. "I'm going to keep this between you and me, kid, rather than go to the commissioner." He realizes that I'm only a dupe.

That is the secret word: *dupe*. In the boxing business, I learn that dupes are as commonplace as mouth swabs. Dupes are all over the place, and sometimes in the least likely places. One of the hardest things to take is the discovery that occasionally, sportswriters are in on the duping. One of them, to my everlasting astonishment, is the legendary and revered Damon Runyon. He not only covers fights for the Hearst newspaper chain but also owns a piece of the promotions. You never find Runyon the reporter putting the knock on a fight he has arranged.

At the New York *Daily Mirror* the boxing writer has a good piece of Sugar Ray Robinson. This reporter is in so deep with Robinson that his editor refers to the reporter in print as "Sugar." In no time at all I. Rudd is being "denaived." I get a part-time job at *Ring* magazine, the so-called bible of boxing, and learn that the *Ring* ratings aren't worth the paper they're printed on. The reason is simple. Nat Fleischer (alias "Mister Boxing"), the boss of *Ring*, can be reached. He plays favorites, and some of his trophies are as phony as a three-dollar bill. Fortunately, there are enough good fellows and enough colorful characters for me to be able to put up with the clowns. How can boxing be all bad when you have people like Tin Can Romanelli, Hard Rock Harden, Hobo Williams, Millionaire Murphy, Bearcat Wright, Dynamite Jackson, Long Sing Que, Foulproof Taylor, and Hype Igoe?

The characters are matched only by the number of laughs. Sometimes the laughs come in strange places, like a hotel room, when a pimping attempt for an elderly reporter fails before a big fight. (The idea, of course, is to fix the guy up with a beauty and thereby guarantee a good press. But sometimes even pimping has its drawbacks.) One night there is a knock at the door of this grizzled old reporter. He opens the hotel room lock and pulls open the door. There, facing him, is a most gorgeous belle. She smiles and says, "Mister so-and-so has sent me for your private pleasure." The boxing writer thanks the lady but says, "Thanks, but no thanks."

A moment after the woman of the evening departs from the scene, the writer picks up the phone and calls one of the big guns connected with the fight promotion. "Did you," he asks, "just send up a gorgeous broad to my room?"

"Yes, yes," the fight guy replies magnanimously. "Enjoy! *Enjoy!*"

The sixtyish writer is not impressed. "You forgot to send something else," he snorts.

"What's that?" asks the amazed benevolent despot.

"A good, stiff hard-on!"

Another gem is Charlie Kaminetsky. As people in Brownsville go, Charlie is physically a giant—or, as they say on Pitkin Avenue, a *shtarker*. To put it mildly, Charlie is not a man to trifle with, even if you have a truckload of longshoremen to back you up. He is a big man and he has earned the name "Charlie Duke."

When Charlie Duke isn't busting heads, he gets himself into the fight racket and winds up managing a few pretty good local fighters, including Harold Green and Georgie Small.

I see Charlie Duke because I'm always around fight managers and the men's rooms of fight clubs. This may sound strange, except that men's rooms are places fight managers always seem to do business in. Like the time I do work for a guy named Joe Vella, who manages Gus Lesnevich, and he owes me $150. So I see him one night at Madison Square Garden in a cluster of people near a hot dog stand. Joe waves me over and then starts walking down a flight of stairs to the men's room. There, against the wall by the urinals, he says, "Here you are, kid—you did a great job!" And he peels off $150 worth of bills.

Who can say no to Charlie Duke and expect to lead a long and healthy life? Of course I plant a few items about Georgie Small. Lo and behold, the notes get into columns all over the place, including a very big one written by Jimmy Powers of the *Daily News*.

I don't take any deep bows for that; after all, I am feeding notes to newsmen all over the place. As far as I'm concerned, the Georgie Small note is gone and forgotten the day after it appears. I forget about it and go on to my next chores until one afternoon, weeks later, I am walking up the steps of Stillman's when who do I see coming down the stairs but Charlie Duke himself.

"Charlie," I say, "it's nice to see you."

Kaminetsky smiles and says, "Oiving, it's nice to see you, too."

I figure that's the end of our dialogue, since I have business upstairs and, I assume, Charlie Duke has business in Brownsville. "Wait a minute!" Kaminetsky says as I continue up the staircase. "I wanna take care of ya."

I stop in my tracks and watch in amazement as Charlie Duke hauls out a bulging bunch of bills and fans them out in front of me like a card shark opening a new deck. He has nothing but fifties and hundreds. Shiny C-notes.

"Oiv," he says, "help yerself. Take what you think is fair."

I almost fall down the steps, looking at all that cash. I know for sure that if I pluck a few hundred out of his wad Charlie Duke will be thrilled to pieces. But I don't take a thing from Kaminetsky, and it's not because I know the guy is a hood. I simply don't feel that what I did—place a few notes about Georgie Small—warrants the kind of money he is offering me. I can tell from the look on his mug that Charlie Duke understands me. I am glad; in spite of his tough guy background, I rate him a good fellow and a great character on the Stillman's beat.

Why is it that I'm always winding up on the side of some crusade or other? Having worked with black men all my life, maybe it shouldn't be surprising that I'm involved in a breakthrough—although nobody knows about it—involving Negroes in the fight game. This case involves a fellow named Joe Bostic, who writes a column for New York's leading black newspaper, the *Amsterdam News*.

All his life Bostic wants to be an announcer at a local fight club, but he can't get a break on account of nobody hires blacks for that kind of stuff. I'm in touch with Bostic and remember him as a hell of a guy when our paths cross in 1947. I am doing publicity for the Queensboro Arena when one night, the regular announcer fails to show up, so they stick me in at the last moment. I do good—so good that the promoters, the deputy commissioner, and everybody's twin brother want me to take out a license as an announcer. I nix the idea and the Queensboro crowd tries to sign someone else up. That's when I think of Joe Bostic and his dream of being a fight announcer. Why shouldn't he be? If ability has anything to do with it, I know he stood head and shoulders over half the guys around. Mickey Kelly, the fellow who had been our announcer at Queensboro, was a stiff; a "Dees, dems, and does" guy who wasn't even Irish. (Imagine being a Kelly and being

Italian!) No matter, ability is what counts. Kelly was so bad that once, when he was handling a main event, he forgot one of the fighters' names and had to lean over and ask, "Hey, by the way, what's your name?" You won't find that happening with Joe Bostic.

I'm not pushing Joe because of the money he can earn; it's a matter of principle. I want to see my friend Bostic get a break in boxing. So I go to see Pat Kiefer, the Queensboro promoter, and he agrees to hire Bostic. No fuss, no trouble at all.

Except now I'm damned worried that Bostic might fall on his face—in front of a largely white audience—and he'll look like a horse's ass and Kiefer will figure me for some kind of schmuck. I begin counting the minutes before his opening bout. Come the night of Bostic's debut and I'm a nervous wreck. There's no Bostic around. We're less than an hour away from the opening bout and there's no sign of Joe.

"Jesus H. Christ!" I grumble to myself. "What the hell did I get myself into this time?" I'm about to jump out of the nearest window when Bostic comes running down the aisle, all out of breath. Turns out his car broke down enroute to Queensboro; he winds up taking a cab and arrives on the fly. That at least enables me to exhale.

Up until this point, nobody but I. Rudd, Joe Bostic, and Pat Kiefer know what is about to happen: a monumental racial breakthrough at a New York City fight club. Finally Bostic climbs into the ring. A gradual murmuring can be heard from the audience, growing by the second like an advance of a swarm of bees. Angry bees. The crowd realizes that a black man is about to do the announcing. "Look, a nigger!" one of them shouts. "Who in hell is he?"

Up to now Bostic is cool, but then, as if fate is conspiring against us, the microphone breaks down as Joe is about to make his first announcement. Bostic is talking into dead air and it looks like we're in for a real disaster when, just as quickly, the mike comes on again and Joe thanks the crowd for its patience, fair mindedness, and all-around good sportsmanship.

What a move! One second the crowd is hostile and ready to lynch the guy and the next minute they're going wild with joy. That is not to suggest that *everyone* in the joint is a 100 percent behind Bostic. Rank-and-file fans who see he knows the ropes are fine, but there is a bloc of bigots in the boxing commission, not to mention a few local politicians and fight managers who bombard me from all sides. They try with veiled threats, ridicule, and assorted—and sordid—sneaky tricks to make me turn against Bostic. But I don't go for their shit, and besides, Joe is getting better by the week. He makes my faith in him look good. In fact, he gets so good, so fast that soon he is working Ridgewood Grove and even the most hardened bigots begin to accept him. It is no accident that once Bostic proves himself as an announcer, the boxing commission appoints Jimmy Freeman, a black man, as the first Negro referee.

The Bostic episode leads I. Rudd to believe he is becoming an expert in race relations. But not an expert-expert. There are more lessons to learn, and I get a beaut in Cuban-American-Jewish relations when I have the pleasure of being press agent for the great Cuban fighter, Kid Gavilan, who is to fight Sugar Ray Robinson. This is July 1949, and after watching me work with Gavilan, Red Smith, writing in the New York *Herald-Tribune*, calls me, "Chairman of literature in the Kid Gavilan camp and a student of psychological warfare."

My momentary marriage with Gavilan is directed toward his bid for the world welterweight championship in Philadelphia. Our honeymoon begins with the start of training camp. As is so often the case, we choose an arboreal spot that is within striking distance of New York City so that we can convoy the writers back and forth without too much hassle. That means we want the Jewish

Catskills again, and this time our choice is the Lash Hotel in Parksville, New York. Why the Lash is picked, of all places, I'll never know. Unlike Grossingor's, the Concord, Laurels Country Club, and other jumping joints in the Catskills, the Lash has a crowd of *alta cockahs* (senior citizens)—so much so that a male chauvinist line is coined: "There is no gash at the Hotel Lash!"

Since sex is on nobody's agenda, we can turn our attention to the interaction between my Cuban fighter and the elderly Jewish guests, most of whom are intrigued by this young man who is training at *their* hotel for a boxing championship. The *alta cockahs* only naturally figure that anyone involved in so serious a pursuit should be, well, serious. So they can't figure what Gavilan is all about. If anything they see him as very *un*serious. The Kid comes off like some kind of dodo, a first-class crackaloo with all kinds of eccentricities. One of them is the Kid's propeller fetish. Gavilan is crazy about beanies with propellers on the top. Whenever he goes out for a long run, he wears a beanie. The Kid gallops up and down the main (and only) stem in Parksville while the propeller on his beanie spins like a crazy helicopter. The sight of this pretender to a boxing throne making like a noodnick brings out all the latent antiblack, anti-Latin (Gavilan is both black and Cuban) prejudices of my serious brethren at the Lash. Sitting on the hotel porch, I see them watch the Kid and his twirling beanie and I hear them utter in obvious Yiddish-American contempt, "This is a prize fighter?" Convincing the patrons that Gavilan is a tough fighter and not a crackaloo is not going to be easy.

The one factor in Gavilan's favor is that he basically is a nice boy—except that he keeps getting himself into dopey situations, and right in front of the guests. One such near-disaster occurs right in front of the front porch of the Lash, where there is a big shuffleboard court. Gavilan and one of his stablemates, a heavyweight named

Agramonte, like to play shuffleboard, and the guests like to watch them.

The problem is that whenever the Kid or his partner miss an easy shot or have a close call on the lines, they swear up and down (in Spanish, of course), using the most obscene words. Having a passing knowledge of Spanish, I know what they are talking about, and I know that if any of the Lash patrons ever find out what they are saying, they will have collective shit fits. Luckily, none of the grandmothers or grandfathers understand a word. They just sit around watching the Kid and say, "What a sweet language that Spanish is. How musical it sounds when these two fine chaps talk it."

When it comes to English, Gavilan says little. Which is very good for I. Rudd because it gives me a lot of verbal room with which to operate on the Kid's behalf. As press agent it is my job to stir up news for Gavilan and stimulate interest in the big fight with Robinson.

That's where I bring my knowledge of psychological warfare into play. I know that Gavilan is a natural welterweight who has no trouble making the division limit of 147 pounds. On the other hand, I have been around boxing long enough to realize that Robinson always has a weight problem when it comes to the welterweight division. In fact, up until now, Robinson, during his reign as champion, has consented to train down to 147 pounds just a couple of times.

The summer of 1949 is hot and especially tough on Sugar Ray, who is forced to fast on a diet of tea and toast to get down to his proper weight for the fight. By contrast, Gavilan, who stays skinny no matter what, is eating like a dinosaur. That gets me thinking: Here is this kid feeding as he pleases, and down near Greenwood Lake, New York, Robinson is working at that camp he calls the "cabin in the sky." He is sweating in the ring and galloping over the mountains and working up an appetite and dreaming of fried chicken. How he must be suffering, poor lad!

I run for my typewriter, licking my chops in high glee, and sit down to write a letter to Sugar Ray: "Dear Mr. Robinson—Kid Gavilan's menu for today is as follows: . . . ." Everything is included, from bagels to blintzes. Meal after meal, day after day, the torture is increased. Blini and latkes. Pirogi and kashe-varniskes. I ordain a war of the calories, an ordeal by bill of fare for Robinson. Then I teach the Kid an assortment of *klulas*, or curses, for him to call down upon the head of Robinson.

Cries of "Arriba" are heard up and down the porch of the Lash Hotel as the day of the big fight draws closer and closer. When the Kid struts across the lawn, his beanie twirling on his head, the Yiddish mamas yell, "Belt him in the kishkes, yet!"

For Gavilan this is a problem. He fought the great Sugar Ray the previous September and now a lot of people figure that Robinson is toying with the Kid. Unfortunately, Gavilan is only a fairly good puncher, and all the eating in the world can't develop a knockout punch. As Red Smith points out, "A Gavilan victory would be a joint triumph for vegetables, *smetana* and *crangrejos morro rellenos*."

The day of the fight, at Municipal Stadium in Philadelphia, the feeling is very strong within me that Gavilan will be the new welterweight champion of the world. However, my Machiavellian plot to psychologically undermine Sugar Ray at the dinner table does not carry over into the championship ring. True, Gavilan extends Robinson for fifteen rounds, but Robinson handily takes the decision, the blintzes and pirogi notwithstanding.

Not all fighters have an image problem as easy to overcome as the Kid's. Rocky Graziano is a case in point.

Graziano, alias Rocco Barbella, is a tough kid from the

Lower East Side with a penchant for getting into hot water, from which I have to extract him. When the Rock fights at Fort Hamilton Parkway Arena, a couple of times he is AWOL from his army base. Irving Cohen, his manager, doesn't know what's going on. The MP's come to get him and Rocky is court-martialed and dishonorably discharged. (He also flattens a couple of lieutenants on the way.)

One time Rocky fails to report a bribe offer and they come down hard on him. The DA's men pick Rocky up at his house and take him down for questioning. He gets a suspension, and so his manager asks me for help. What do I do? I realize that some of my friends are putting on a boxing show for the American Legion somewhere in New Jersey. It looks like a good way to change Graziano's image—wrap him in a Legion flag.

I ask if it's all right for Rocky to come out with me to be greeted by the head of the Legionnaires. The answer is yes, but when we get there the reception is less than cordial. The guys refuse to pose for pictures with Rocky. I feel it's time to speak up; so I remind them that *they* invited us. I tell them they can turn their backs to the camera when the picture is taken. That they go for, and I must say that the Rock is well received by most of the people there.

Well, some anti-Rocky guys never quit, and someone gets hold of Dan Parker's ear. He tells Dan about the American Legion trip and Parker writes a really tough column on how we try to run Rocky past the American Legion to get their sanction, and all that crap. It's the start of tough times for Graziano, but Rocky eventually pulls out of the pits and, after retirement, makes a name for himself on television. Every once in a while I bump into him, and Rocky never forgets. He always says, "Irv, you tried to help me that time in New Jersey."

Guys like Rocky you want to help as much as possible. In some cases it is possible, in others you just lay back and hope that they don't get screwed too badly. Among the fighters I know, no one's story is more depressing than Sidney Walker's

Sidney Walker, known in the fight game as Beau Jack, is a muscular little guy from the backwoods of Georgia. He can neither read nor write. In the late thirties Beau gets himself a job as a bootblack for millionaire golfers at the Augusta National course, home of the Masters. A few of the golfers happen to see Beau use his fists, so fifty of them chip in fifty dollars apiece and launch him on a pro boxing career. By 1942 Beau is lightweight champion of the world. He beats Terry Young, knocks out Allie Stolz and Tippy Larkin, and whips Fritzie Zivic twice, among other good men he handles. Pretty soon Beau is worth more than a million and it looks like the sky is the limit for him.

Then the sky falls down on Beau Jack's head. Sharpies take advantage of his illiteracy and trusting nature and fleece the poor guy. Beau accepts checks that *he* thinks are made out for $2,000 but are actually worth only $20.

Once it's clear that Beau is on his way down, his pals desert him like rats leaving a sinking ship. One of the few that sticks by Jack is my pal Chick Wergeles, who winds up working for me years later at Yonkers Raceway. One day a reporter meets Wergeles while Chick still is trying to arrange matches for the aging Beau. "If you let him fight again," the reporter says, "you should be arrested."

Wergeles shrugs. "What am I gonna do? Look at these." Chick pulls two letters from his pocket. "Every time he gets one, he brings it to me and tells me I got to get him a fight."

Poor Beau is being chased by the men from Internal Revenue. They are hounding him for payment of back taxes, plus interest and penalties. The reporter pleads with Wergeles to keep him from fighting again. "Let the government take any tangible assets he has."

Wergeles looks at him like the reporter is nuts. "Tangible assets? What are they?"

"Property and stuff and things like that," says the reporter.

"Uh-uh," says Wergeles, shaking his head. "Beau Jack ain't got nuthin'."

Pretty soon Beau disappears completely from the fight scene. He fought a total of 128 bouts and earned $2,500,000 and even was voted into boxing's Hall of Fame. And that is the last I heard from Beau until one day when I'm in Florida in the mid-fifties working for the Brooklyn Dodgers. I'm at the Fountainbleu Hotel in Miami Beach and I go down to the barber shop. As I walk in I notice a bootblack standing just inside the door. His back is to me but there is no mistaking him.

I instantly recognize the broad shoulders and his muscles practically bulging through his white jacket. "Hello, Sid," I say, and he turns around. It is Beau Jack, of course. Or Sidney Walker, as I prefer to remember him.

"Why Mister Rudd," he says. "What brings you here?" I tell him and we talk about the Dodgers for a few minutes—it seems he is a Dodgers fan and Roy Campanella is his hero. Then, he says to me, smiling, "Can I shine your shoes—for nothing?"

Beau doesn't know it, but a large gulp comes to my throat and I can hardly get the words out of my mouth. I don't know whether it is comprehensible, but seeing Beau like that brings tears to my eyes. Finally I say to him, "No, Sid, you *can't* shine my shoes."

"Why not?" he asks.

"Because," I say, "*you* were the lightweight champion!"

=Part II=

= 5 =
From Boxing to Baseball—or Getting to First Base

The fight game and I. Rudd get along just fine until a new invention comes along that puts both of us out of work for a while. Video, they call it, and all of a sudden the fans who once were coming to Ridgewood Grove, Broadway Arena, and St. Nick's are now staying home to watch a guy named Uncle Miltie. Slowly but surely I see the crowds dropping off at all the local fight clubs, and I also see the handwriting on the wall. No clubs, no money. By the start of the fifties my worst fears are realized. Coney Island Velodrome is closed; Ridgewood Grove is closed; Fort Hamilton Arena is closed; Queensboro Arena is closed; Rockland Palace is closed. It is time for I. Rudd to find another job.

By this time I am pretty well known in New York sporting circles; after all, it's more than ten years since I started out as a fight press agent. But boxing is my middle name and I'm nothing but a cipher in baseball circles, which are the circles I would like to enter. Also I'm married, and I need to earn a living for Gert.

I met Gert in October 1939 on a blind date arranged by my friend Bill Dezortt and his girlfriend Norma. I had no fights coming up, so I said yeah, I'll try it. Bill tells me her name is Gertrude Bean and she lives at 406 Dumont Avenue in Brooklyn. Right away I figure she can't be all bad on account of there's a famous grammar school around the block from her. So the time comes for the date. I go to the house and meet her mother and her five kid sisters. I feel a crisis. But Bill and Norma help me out after I'm introduced to Gert. (I later find out that Gert, who is an Orthodox Jew, thought I was a goy. She wanted to know how Norma could do such a thing as bring a *shegats* into their house. Not to worry, Norma assured Gert, he's a Jew and we can all go out and eat.)

The blind date couldn't have been a disaster since Gert agrees to see me again—alone. This time I'm playing the big shot and take her to the Loew's Premier Theater, one of Brownsville's best, on Sutter Avenue. This is big-time stuff. I like this eighteen-year-old girl; I want to impress her. But I couldn't have rigged it better than what is about to happen. We get to the theater and I walk up to the window to buy the tickets, when suddenly I see a man in a blue uniform standing right next to the cashier. He is not only a New York City policeman but happens to be Officer Quigley, who knows me since I am knee-high to a grasshopper. He gives me a big "Hi, Irv, how've ya been?" And I introduce him to Gertrude Bean. Next thing

I know, Quigley turns to the doorman and tells him to let us through—without even paying!

It is J. Budd's first freebie, and Gert is suitably amazed by all this. She is from a poor family. Pretty soon me and Gert are "an item." The sisters are convinced that I *am* Jewish and her mother doesn't mind me either. (Years later she tells me, "I thought you were a funny little kid who knew from theater and roller skating—and you're still a funny kid.")

So now I'm looking for work and I don't feel funny anymore. But a break comes when I learn that the Brooklyn Dodgers are backing a sandlot baseball foundation and they need a guy to organize and publicize the whole shebang. Walter O'Malley is boss of the Dodgers at the time, and I get the word that if I do the job right for O'Malley I will be in Brooklyn with the Dodgers for a good, long time.

The sandlot job is a cinch. I'm working with kids, which I love; in Brooklyn, which I love; with the Dodgers' organization, which I am getting to love. O'Malley realizes this, and in February 1952 I get my first big assignment from the bossman, one that will make or break my career with the Dodgers. It all centers around O'Malley's anger at the way the Dodgers have been failing to make money during their spring training exhibitions in and around Miami. "The O," as we call the great man, figures that a team as popular as the Dodgers should pull in a pile of dough for their exhibitions.

The trick is to send an advance man to stir up the gate a few weeks before the exhibition schedule actually begins. O'Malley realizes this because, among other things, he can read. And one of the items he reads is in Hy Goldberg's column running in the old *Newark Evening News*. Goldberg points out that in the spring of 1951 the Dodgers played nineteen games in Miami Stadium, one of the most beautiful ballparks in the country, and the gate was sub-awful.

"O'Malley," writes Goldberg, "is not a promoter. He's a lawyer, but there seemed to be something illegal to him about poor turnstile counts at Dodger games."

Just after Christmas 1951 The O calls me into his office in the old building at Montague Street overlooking Brooklyn Borough Hall and gives I. Rudd the word. He says it is no good for only 750 people to be sitting in Miami Stadium, which holds 14,000, watching the Dodgers. "Go to Florida in February," he tells me, "and *do* something about this, Irving."

God has spoken. I know what he wants, he wants me to be Brooklyn's answer to Dexter Fellows.

In the publicity business, Dexter Fellows is lionized as the archetypical advance man. For years he worked for Ringling Brothers, Barnum and Bailey Circus. Before the circus arrived in a particular town, Fellows would precede the clowns and elephants by a few weeks, drumming up business for the show to come. In those days the headlines in local papers used to read: "Here Comes Spring; Here Comes Dexter Fellows!"

O'Malley and I agree that the advance man-techniques of Dexter Fellows will be the same we will use for the Dodgers to bring people to Miami Stadium. The O shakes my hand and tells me that his private plane is at my disposal for the flight south. This I can't believe, since I have never been south of Hoboken, New Jersey, in my life. (Once, as a batboy for the Polish Falcons baseball team in Williamsburg, Brooklyn, I went to Ansonia, Connecticut, and considered *that* an overseas expedition.) My ultimate destination is Vero Beach, the Dodgers' official base, but the real hustling is going to be in Miami, where we want to fill the big stadium. Already I am getting goose pimples. How could I. Rudd ever have dreamed that one day he would show up at LaGuardia Airport and board the official Dodgers' plane with the beautiful blue-and-white team logo on the fuselage?

I arrive at the airport and discover that O'Malley, his wife (a charming person who lost her voice to cancer), and a few writers also are on the plane. While the high command enjoys itself, I. Rudd is busily trying to lay out a blueprint for filling the seats. The deal is for me to spend a few days at Vero Beach, meet the players, then scoot over to Miami and hustle my ass off.

The days go fast at Vero; I talk to as many Dodgers as possible, and now it's time for the real business. "Take the plane," says O'Malley, "and do your stuff." Leaving from Vero Beach Airport is I. Rudd, the pilot, and nobody else—my first chauffeured flight. When we land in Miami I feel a lot better, even though I am inwardly concerned about doing the job. Here I am in Miami, brand new, and I am going to sell the Dodgers to thousands of people who don't know me, don't know I am here, and couldn't care less. I remember Hy Goldberg's warning to me that I am going up against the horse and dog tracks, nightclubs, sunshine, jai alai, and broads. That's a hell of a parlay.

I get the message on my first day prowling the sandy shore of Miami Beach in search of baseball customers. While I am hustling one of the beachcombers, he looks at me strangely. "Baseball? If you're not planning to flash pari-mutuel prices on the scoreboard, you better forget it!"

What to do? I need a friend and I need advice. Finally I realize that Paul Grossinger, the son of Jennie Grossinger, grande dame of Grossinger's Hotel, is in Miami running a hotel of his own called the Grossinger-Pancoast. I know Paul from my days working the Borscht Belt, so I call him up and he invites me over. Already, I am feeling better. Paul makes me feel at home and gives me some free advice. "Irving," he says, "you're going to have to knock on more doors and talk to more people than you ever have in your young life."

For a split second I'm scared; then a vision of an O'Malley paycheck looms in my head. I thank Paul Grossinger and get on my way. I knock on doors, all kinds of doors, telling Miami that the Dodgers are coming. I arrange cabana parties at the big hotels, where the fans can meet the players, and soon people start buying tickets—and more tickets.

One of my main objectives is to get a good crowd for a game we have lined up with the Philadelphia Athletics, a lousy draw. O'Malley has told me that in 1951 the Dodgers-A's game drew only five hundred people to Miami Stadium. I am aiming for five thousand at the very least. To get that I have to do a lot more hustling and I need a few breaks.

The first break develops when I walk into a local radio station one night while a disc jockey named Alan Courtney is on the air. It's 11:30 P.M. and Courtney is spinning records. While he's on the air, I. Rudd slips him a business card. He looks down at it and his eyes light up. Next thing I know he is telling his listening audience: "Guess who we have here with us, folks? None other than Irving Rudd of the Brooklyn Dodgers. What brings you to our fair city, Mister Rudd?"

Courtney puts me on the air and I promptly tell Miami listeners that the Dodgers are coming to town. But I'm not getting away with a free plug that easily. Courtney shoots back: "Mister Rudd, why should people pay three-fifty for a box seat to a meaningless exhibition game?"

I'm not only on the spot, I am up shit's creek without a paddle if I don't produce the perfect squelch. "Well, Mister Courtney, you're wrong," I tell him. "The fans are not going to see a meaningless exhibition game; they're going to see a young man named Johnny Podres who will soon become the best left-hander since Watson Clark pitched for the Dodgers in 1931."

72

Courtney smiles. He likes that, and now we go back and forth for nearly an hour; meanwhile, the Dodgers are getting a Miami hype like they've never had before. I make that discovery the next day when I'm working hotel row. Guests, bellhops, everyone tells me how they loved hearing me give Courtney hell on the air. Some even say they'll come out and see the Dodgers.

But I. Rudd has just begun to fight. I hustle some more radio shows and get myself a column in the *Miami Herald*. Then I borrow a leaf from Dexter Fellows's book and hire a few circus hucksters to plant Dodgers' signs in every store they can find. I buy a bunch of old-time cardboard boxing show cards that say THE DODGERS ARE COMING! Pretty soon you couldn't walk anywhere in Miami without seeing those signs.

After a week of hustling Miami I am hoarse and minus $500 in expenses. This is a lot of money for a kid from the slums, and suddenly I begin to wonder what the hell is accomplished. I can't see any results because we haven't had a game yet. When I get back to the hotel that night I get very depressed. I am pooped, can't imagine the fans will come out, and tell myself it's time to quit and go back to Brooklyn and become an accountant.

When I open the door to my hotel room I see a telegram. It is from the man himself—O'Malley. He has wired me from Vero Beach: "KEEP UP THE GOOD WORK. I KNOW WE'RE GOING TO DO BETTER IN MIAMI."

Reading the wire is like hearing the inspirational voice of Notre Dame's Knute Rockne. All of a sudden I. Rudd is feeling fifteen years old and ready to fight. Not long after the sun lifts over the palm trees I go back to the oceanfront, booking more autograph parties, selling more tickets. My goal is to top the Dodgers' previous average attendance—4,000 a game, or a total of 76,164 paying customers. Time will tell.

At last the Dodgers have checked out of Vero Beach and are heading for Miami. They arrive at the McAllister

Hotel and I'm sitting in the lobby awaiting them. Who walks in first but my favorite right fielder, Carl Furillo. He looks me up and down and says, "Irv, where the hell have you been—in the closet? You've been in Florida for weeks and you're still pale as a ghost. How come?"

Already I'm feeling good. "I'm pale," I yell back, "because while you guys are playing ball in the sun, I'm marching in and out of hotels tryin' to sell tickets for you. And when I'm on the beach I'm still wearin' a suit, but with the pants rolled up so they don't get wet when I'm hustlin' people in the water. *Ka-pish?*"

Furillo understands. I know that my lack of a suntan means I was hustling my ass off. More than that I know that it paid off, because within a day, the sun worshipers begin following the Dodgers from the cabanas to the ballpark. In thirteen games we draw 91,077, compared with 76,164 the previous year. The big test, of course, was getting a crowd for a stiff team like the Philadelphia A's. Again I get lucky. I run into the Philly press agent a few days before the game and he says to me, "Irving, how would you like to meet Connie Mack?"

Mack, it seems, has been around baseball a million years. He is really old but still considered a god of the game, and everyone calls him "Mister Baseball." When the guy asks me if I want to meet Mack it is like asking a Jew if he'd like to shake the hand of Moses. Who could refuse such an offer?

The thought is pressing hard on my brain that we will be playing Mack's awful Athletics on the following Monday, and the vision of empty seats gives me cramps. As I am introduced to this living legend I think fast. "Mister Mack," I say, "do you know that we're having a night in your honor next week at the A's-Dodgers game?"

Of course old Connie Mack didn't know it, since I had just made it all up. "Mister Mack," I go on, "the youth of Florida would like very much to honor you for your many contributions to baseball."

At first he seems ready to shake his head no, but the line about kids honoring him appeals to the old guy, and Connie slowly nods that it wouldn't be such a bad idea after all. "Holy Christ," I think to myself, "I actually talked Mack into it!"

With Connie Mack as my starring attraction, I tout the otherwise nothing game all over the place and we get a fantastic crowd; like the kind we were getting for the great Dodgers-Yankees games. As Hy Goldberg writes in his column, "People poured into the Miami Stadium in huge gobs. It wasn't ever thus."

All the advance hustling is paying off; the crowds are coming, and for that I should be tickled. But I have another problem in Miami, one that I never bargained for when I left dear old Brooklyn. Discrimination. I forgot that Miami is in the South. And in the South they use a different rule book than we use in Brooklyn. One of the rules says that a black man can't go on the beach after sundown unless he has a special pass. The rule book says that our Negro stars—Jackie Robinson, Roy Campanella, Joe Black, Jim Gilliam, Don Newcombe—can't even stay at the same hotel as our white ballplayers. There even is a color line at Miami Stadium, but I. Rudd is proud to say that he is figuring out a way to break it. One day I realize that the black fans are segregated in a corner of the bleachers at Miami Stadium. Even if you are Dr. Ralph Bunche of the United Nations you sit on the wood bleacher seats if you are black.

Not only is it morally wrong, it also happens to be bad business, and I, for one, figure something should be done about it. But what? I head for the Negro quarter of Miami and look up a black guy named Rudy Fitzgerald, who manages the Lord Calvert Hotel. "If you can get us into the grandstands," says Rudy, "you'll sell a lotta tickets. Do that and our people will come."

Now my only problem is my own kind, the white folks. I head for city hall and the mayor of Miami, a nice little

Jewish man named Abe Aronovitz. "Mister Mayor," I say, "isn't there some way we can lick this Jim Crow business? Can't we find a loophole in the law?"

Mayor Aronovitz tells me that he couldn't care less whether the blacks sit on home plate, the grandstands, or the box seats. "The guy I'm worried about," the mayor tells me, "is my police chief."

I get my ass over to police headquarters, warned in advance that the chief is a redneck cracker with a deep-grits accent. Face-to-face with the man, I feel a surge of Yankee pride in a cause well taken. I tell the chief straight out that I have to get the blacks out of the bleachers and into the grandstands.

"Man," he shouts, "you *cain't* have those niggers all over Miami Stadium!"

Undaunted by the cracker, I. Rudd plows ahead, this time searching for a logical route. "Chief," I say, "what if we have *separate* sections for the Negroes within the box and reserved seats sections. Put them there and you wouldn't be putting them with the whites; they'd be in their own area."

He looks at me, strangelike. "How you'all gonna do that?"

I see a flicker of light at the end of the tunnel. "Simple, Chief. We'll get some nice velvet ropes and we'll run them along the railings. On one side of the red ropes will be whites and on the other side of the ropes will be blacks."

Granted, it isn't complete desegregation, but what I am doing is bringing the blacks out of the distant wooden bleachers and into a respectable section of the ballpark behind the dugout, behind home plate, and behind first base. In that sense I will be breaking the color line. The chief—somewhat stupified by the ease of it all—agrees, and a first step toward breaking the color line is taken.

Another time a golf pro comes to me and asks if he can get Don Newcombe, Jackie Robinson, and some of the other black players to play in a baseball players' golf tournament. I say sure, they will welcome the invitation, but that we won't tolerate any Jim Crow. The Negroes have to be able to use the same locker rooms in the dressing area and have total equality and privileges with the white ballplayers. This isn't going to be easy, because the color line has never been broken on a Florida golf course. But the promoters know that if they are going to get guys like Junior Gilliam, Newcombe, and Robbie that they will have to break the color line. And they do.

Still, the victory is not total. Once I get out of a cab with Joe Black at the McAllister Hotel and the doorman, seeing me with a Negro, wants to know where I am going. Like, there is no way a black man is going into that white hotel.

Newcombe comes up to me very plaintively one day and says: "Irv, why can't we go on the beach [at Miami] for dinner?" He means at one of the better hotels. I tell him that even a Sammy Davis, Jr., in 1954 has to carry a card (identifying himself as a Negro) allowing him to be out after dark. So we go to five hotels and get turned away because we have black guys with us.

Finally I fall back on my friend, Paul Grossinger, again at his hotel, the Grossinger-Pancoast. I tell Paul about my problems getting the black players into the hotels. Paul Grossinger has been around. He knows the hotel scene inside out and he knows the pulse of Miami. I don't want a favor so much as I want advice.

"Bring them [the black Dodgers] over to my place," Grossinger tells me.

"Paul," I say a bit sheepishly, "you realize that some of your guests [all white] might not like that. I dare say, some might even get up and leave."

"Irving," Grossinger replies, "I *don't care* if the guests leave."

So, very timidly, I might add, I take my boys (and, by this time, I feel that I can call Robinson, Newcombe, Gilliam, and Campanella "my boys") over to the

Grossinger-Pancoast and hope for the best. Well, we all walk into the hotel's restaurant, we sit down, the waiter comes over, we order, and not a guest gets up and leaves. Quite the contrary; they are tickled pink over the idea that the great Brooklyn Dodgers are in the same restaurant as themselves. We have a ball. The black ballplayers love it, the white guests love it, and we all strike another blow against Jim Crow.

The fans really don't give a shit who is sitting where as long as they can get a good look at the Dodgers. They get it in droves, and finally the Florida exhibition season is over and I am back at Vero Beach getting ready for our trip north and the start of the regular season. Just before leaving, I am at breakfast with Bobby Bragan, a former major leaguer now coaching the Dodgers' farm team in Fort Worth. I'm slurping my oatmeal when I feel two arms pulling my shoulders down to the floor. I can't even get my head up. Then there is a stentorian voice in my ears; the inimitable deep, gravely voice of Walter O'Malley: "Marvelous job you did in Miami, Irving. I shall never forget the initiative, the devotion, the hours. It all paid off; you were superb."

What a great feeling, to be recognized by this great man. It has to be the first time an exhibition home stand has made money for a team. Columns are written about me—how I. Rudd developed a new concept for promoting exhibition games. Big guns like Dick Young of the *New York Daily News* are on my bandwagon. "The only reason," says Young, "that the Brooks did as well as they did in Miami was because of the innate color of the team and the energetic promotion of Irving Rudd, the one-man dynamo."

Now I am wondering what to do for an encore. Miami is already ancient history, and Ebbets Field is the place that has to be filled. Fortunately, I am blessed with a team that is easy to promote. Jackie Robinson, for example, is a press agent's dream come true. All I have to do is ask Jackie and he agrees to appear—radio shows, TV shows, clinics, Lions Clubs, He never says no.

The manager, Charley Dressen, is a sweetheart of a character, even though he's a bit of an egomaniac. Our running gag is that if someone took the letter *I* out of Dressen's typewriter he wouldn't be able to write a letter. Charley is intensely proud of his baseball knowledge and thinks nothing of giving one of his players a lesson, even if it means showing him how to throw a curve—as he does with pitcher Joe Black—in a hotel lobby. Dressen likes to say, "There isn't a thing about baseball that I don't know." And the fact of the matter is that Charley is right about that. But Dressen is merely the front man for one of the most colorful flock of characters I'd ever want to meet. And I use the word *flock* deliberately, because that's the nickname the *Daily News* pins on the Dodgers when the editors want a shorter name to fit on a back page.

I get to love some of the characters in this flock so much that I get carried away talking about them. One night I am making a speech at a Brooklyn synagogue when the talk gets around to our large first baseman, Gil Hodges. To me, Hodges is the all-American boy—trustworthy, loyal, helpful, courteous, kind, obedient, cheerful, thrifty, brave, clean, and reverent.

"Gil is the sort of fellow," I tell the audience of Jews, "that you'd be happy and proud to have your daughter marry."

Just then, a guy stands up at the rear of the shul and cries out, "No! No! No!"

I'm thrown off guard. Floundering around the dais, I mutter, "What—why—what's the matter?"

"Hodges," shouts the voice from the rear, "he is a *goy!*"

Goy, shmoy; black, white—they are all the same to me. Our catcher Roy Campanella is a black man but like a brother to me. Roy loves baseball so much he sometimes cries when he talks about the game. "Baseball don't owe ol' Campy nothin'," he says. "Ol' Campy owes every little thing he is to baseball." And his eyes fill when he says it.

We have a lot of stars but no prima donnas on this Brooklyn team. One day I bring a group of GI's who had been prisoners of war in Korea to Ebbets Field. For an added kick I decide to take them into the clubhouse to meet the players. After clearing it with Dressen, instead of simply having the soldiers come in and shake hands with the players, I ask the Dodgers to serve lunch to the GI's. Preacher Roe, one of our best pitchers, brings rolls, lox, and chopped eggs. Jackie Robinson dishes out coffee, and every single Dodger sits down with a GI, man-to-man, to talk baseball.

Our ballplayers have a thing about falling head over heels over anyone who traipses into the dressing room. Once the syndicated columnist Walter Winchell shows up in the stands and I notice him. Winchell is like a little kid when it comes to idolizing the Dodgers, so I ask him if he wants to go into the dressing room and say hello to some of the players. "Gee, gee, yeah," he shouts. "I'd love that." So we go down to the room and it's hard to tell who is idolizing whom, Winchell or the players. Walter is terribly impressed by their reaction to him and writes a whole column about the event. O'Malley is very impressed by that.

One of the classiest guys on the club is our captain, Harold "Pee Wee" Reese, a walking definition of the term *star*. Reese is a gentleman and a leader. He doesn't have to say it for you to know that his philosophy is anything for baseball, anything for the team.

There is the time when Pee Wee is posing for photos with a kid in a wheelchair for a poster to be used in a muscular dystrophy fund-raising campaign. The photographer finishes, packs his gear, and departs, leaving Reese still down on one knee with an arm around the boy's shoulders, chatting. They talk for a long time. Later on I walk over to Reese and ask him what he was gabbing about for twenty minutes with a ten-year-old. "He told me he used to be a Dodgers fan," says Reese, "but switched over after we lost the World Series to the Yankees. I was trying to persuade him to come back."

Jackie Robinson is that way too. For all his fire, he has a heart of gold. One time a guy asks Robbie to do a radio interview and says there's a $50 merchandise order in it for him. Jackie says all right, he'll do the show, but the order must be drawn not to him but to a charity he is aiding at the time. Robbie is always trying to help the needy, the underdogs of life.

Joe Black, the rookie right-hander who will relief-pitch us to the 1952 pennant, is one of the most modest people you could meet anywhere. Like Reese, he has an innate sense of public relations that has absolutely nothing to do with phoniness. Toward the end of his rookie season Joe sends a bottle of whiskey to every guy in the Ebbets Field press box. With each bottle there is a little note thanking the newspaper guys for the way they treated him. Stanley Woodward, an old-time newsman, says of Black, "The only other ballplayer I can remember who ever distributed such largesse was Stan Musial."

Black never loses his sense of humor, not even in the World Series. During the 1952 Yankees-Dodgers classic, Joe comes up to hit against New York's superb pitcher Allie Reynolds. Black stands there, knowing he's the third out. Yogi Berra is the catcher for the Yankees.

"What kind of a hitting stance is that, Joe?" says Berra as Black moves into the batter's box.

"Why, Lawrence," says Black, "that's my home run stance."

"You'd like a nice, straight one, right down the middle, I bet. . . . Hey Allie, throw it right here."

So—bang—he does, for a strike.

"You weren't ready, Joe," says Yogi. "We'll give you another."

Bang. Strike two.

"One more time, right down the pipe," Berra tells Black.

Joe tenses up and waits. Poor Black; he never even sees the straight fastball as it goes by for strike three.

I don't know whether it is because I am from a poor little Brownsville family or what, but I have a special feel for the underdog and I find myself gravitating toward the black ballplayers on the Dodgers, who are the real underdogs of baseball.

Most of the Negro ballplayers have toughened up to all the shit hurled at them, but one who remains frightened is Dan Bankhead, who I figure could be one of the greatest pitchers in baseball history if he were white. But Dan is a frightened black man from Tennessee who has been emotionally scarred by racism. Once, Bankhead and I are driving to a speaking engagement in Stamford, Connecticut, when he pulls over to a gas station to fill up the tank. As we pull up to a gas tank we see a police car right behind us. The cop pulls up to the driver's side and asks Dan if he owns the car. At first I figure that there is something wrong with the taillights. But once the cop starts talking tough to Dan I realize he's simply pissed off that a white man is riding with a Negro.

"Hold it!" I say, while taking out my pencil to write down the cop's badge number.

"What are you, a wise guy?" he shouts at me.

I tell the cop that my name isn't Wise Guy, it is Irving Rudd, and that I am promotion director for the Brooklyn Dodgers. "Now, sir," I request in my most discreet Brooklynese, "can I have *your* name?"

The cop gets the message and gets the hell out of there, fast. The Brooklyn Dodgers name is gold, even in Connecticut. We take off from the gas station without any more trouble.

Mostly, though, being with the Dodgers is fun, especially at our home, Ebbets Field. "Everything happens at Ebbets Field" is a bromide but a good one. The bizarre,

the zany, the dramatic, the tearful, the humorous, the unexpected—if it is going to happen, you can bet a armful of
Harry M. Stevens's peanuts it will take place at the fabu-
lous Flatbush ball orchard that houses our beloved Bums
of Brooklyn. Sometimes it happens by design; sometimes
we help something happen. One day I see a king visiting
us, then a great general, governors, movie stars, and even
a contingent parading from the Israeli navy. Getting stories into the paper is easy because the Dodgers are good
copy and, better still, they cooperate.

One of my jobs with the Dodgers is fulfilling requests
for autographed baseballs. All the time I hear from
groups—church groups, civic groups, you name them—
who want the players to put their signatures on baseballs.
Fulfilling this demand is tough but we have a special way
of handling it. The "magician" in question is Charley Di-
Giovanni, the Dodgers' batboy. Charley is a friendly kid in
his late twenties who has developed a knack for autographing a baseball in thirty seconds flat, not with his own
signature but with a perfect copy of any Dodger's autograph, from Robinson to Dressen. Charley goes through a
complete act when he does his autograph routine. First he
takes out the boxes of baseballs. Then he yells across the
dressing room, "C'mon fellas, it's time to sign the balls!"
When the players feign anger, Charley tells them that
Mickey Mantle and Willie Mays sign baseballs. "You're
not such a big shot," says Charley, "why don't you sign
some?" Then, with the speed of light, DiGiovanni sits
down, pen in hand, and duplicates the signatures of Duke
Snider, Gil Hodges, and all the rest of the Dodgers.

Charley is famous for another reason: he was involved
in baseball's most top-heavy fight—DiGiovanni vs. Earl
Torgeson of the Boston Braves. We are playing the
Braves when, as we say in Brownsville, "somebody starts
something up." Next thing we know, guys are running at
each other from all directions, brandishing their fists. At
the very edge of the milling mob are Torgeson and Di-

Giovanni. Earl is six foot two and Charley five feet nothing. Earl glares down at Charley and growls: "Do I have to challenge you?" To which Charley replies: "Gee, I hope not!"

They shake hands and wish each other well, and by the time they do that, the big fight is over.

Charley isn't the only batboy to come into my life. Quite by accident I become very much involved with batboys as a result of a promotion worked up by a fellow at the National Broadcasting Company. His name is Max Buck and he figures that baseball should do a takeoff on the successful radio and TV show called "Queen for a Day." Buck's idea is called "Batboy for a Day." The deal is that a kid will write the Dodgers, telling why he wants to be Brooklyn's batboy. I'd pick the best letter and the kid would come down to the ballpark and handle the job (with DiGiovanni overseeing, of course).

We get tons of letters and the contest works like a charm, especially the time we do it in Miami. A tiny kid named Craig wins the contest in Miami. The kid writes a really unique letter telling about how his dog would be tickled to be the batboy. The promotion catches the attention of the *Miami News*, which sends a reporter over to meet Craig and cover the kid's day with the Dodgers. His mom and dad sit in box seats while he does his batboy chores, running around with the bats and carrying towels to the players. I can tell the little guy is enjoying every second of his experience, and I. Rudd is getting a vicarious thrill because the kid reminds him of himself thirty-five years earlier.

The reporter from the *Miami News* follows Craig right up to the point where he kneels down in the batter's box next to Gil Hodges, and he writes a terrifically sensitive piece. I find out that the reporter is Damon Runyon, Jr., the son of one of America's most legendary writers. (For some reason I keep thinking of a harrowing book called *In Father's Footsteps* and I am reminded of my brief meeting with young Runyon. A few years later I nearly fall over in my chair when I read that Runyon kills himself by throwing himself over a bridge in Chicago.)

Such maudlin moments are few and far between at Ebbets Field. Even when the club is losing we know we are going to have laughs because of the characters who inhabit section 8, row 1, seats 1 through 7. This is where the Brooklyn Dodgers Sym-Phony Band holds court. They are baseball's zaniest musical combination and they perform every day and night when our beloved Bums are at home. The Sym-Phony has a dual purpose—to amuse the crowd and to harass the opposing players. The musicians include JoJo Delio on the snare drum, Brother Lou Soriano belting the bass drum and conducting, Patty George, Jerry Martin, Joe Zollo, and Zollo's son Frank. (The group was founded by the late Shorty Laurice.)

At any Ebbets Field game, the first to get the musical razz from the Sym-Phony are the umpires, who are greeted with a chorus of "Three Blind Mice." (This presented a problem when a fourth umpire was added to every game. "We can't help it," complained Brother Lou. "We cannot come up with the fourth mouse.")

When an enemy batter comes to the plate they toot and drum him back to the dugout if he strikes out. The Sym-Phony provides a very rhythmic cadence that gradually slows down until the player sits down on his dugout bench, at which time they blare forth with a big chord that can be heard all the way out in deep center field. If it takes a long time for the player to sit down, the Sym-Phony waits a long time, but the blare always comes as soon as the flannel trousers touch the bench.

The Sym-Phony nearly gets its comeuppance in July 1951 when Local 802 of the American Federation of Musicians questions the amateur standing of the band and threatens to throw a picket line around Ebbets Field. The union, however, doesn't bargain for their opposition. The Dodgers schedule a Musical Unappreciation Night. Admittance is free as long as you bring a musical instrument. And so they come, more than thirty thousand strong, with harmonicas, drums, kazoos, and every conceivable type of portable instrument, including—yes!—even two pianos, which are brought into the rotunda at the main entrance. What a night for music! The weird noises unleashed by the capacity crowd of roof raisers traumatize music lovers for miles around.

If Beethoven were alive he would turn over in his grave. "It is magnificent," says Brother Lou Soriano. "It is our *second* finest hour." (The *first* finest hour came when the Sym-Phony was invited to stroll the aisles during the 1948 Republican Convention in Philadelphia. A Brooklyn politician named Johnny Crews introduced them to Governor Thomas E. Dewey, who was the party nominee against the great underdog Harry Truman.

"Governor Tom says we were great," Brother Lou recalls. "Then Dewey says that when he wins the election we're going to give a concert in the White House. Now that's beautiful, because it's a sure thing that Harry Truman can't win. But, sure enough, our bum loses and we lose our concert in the White House.")

Today baseball belongs to marketing consultants and special properties people who have hearts like cash registers. They don't understand the Sym-Phony and they never will—which really tells you all you need to know about what they once really meant to me and Brooklyn.

= 6 =
Butch's Day,
Pee Wee's Night

With characters like the Brooklyn Dodgers Sym-Phony around, it is not difficult to keep people entertained at Ebbets Field. But Walter O'Malley wants more than that; he wants the seats filled as often as possible and this means that I. Rudd has to wind up his think machine and promote.

There are many theories on promotion. P. T. Barnum says a promoter never should overestimate the public's intelligence. I. Rudd doesn't buy that theory. I figure that the average Joe and Jane have good heads on their shoulders and should be treated that way. To me, the key word is *entertain*. Proving my promotional point are two different kinds of shindigs at Ebbets Field involving totally different kinds of people. One is a special day for a Scotsman named Butch Forbes and the other is a night for an ace named Pee Wee Reese.

The Forbes episode is one of the most unlikely I'll ever encounter. It starts with a letter our public relations director, Frank Graham, Jr., receives. It comes from a guy who signs his name Alistair "Butch" Forbes. He is from Aberdeen, Scotland (Bridge of Don, pronounced "Brigadoon") and he likes the Brooklyn Dodgers. A lot. In fact, a whole lot.

Like so many other out-of-town fans, Forbes requests a Dodgers yearbook. His letter explains that he is a grain warehouse worker and that he listens to Armed Forces Radio and that he loves the Dodgers' players and fans. So Graham very nicely sends him the yearbook.

Back comes a letter from Forbes, and God, is he a shrewd one. "Thank you for the yearbook," he writes. "I am twenty years old, six feet tall, and I love the Dodgers. Will you please send me an autographed picture of my favorite Dodger, Gil Hodges. Friends tell me that my hands are as big as Gil's."

This time we get a return letter from Forbes with a photo of him wearing a set of kilts. He asks if we would please pass the picture on to some "Dodger dames" who can give him "all the news."

When Graham shows me the photo of Butch, a bell in my cranium goes *bing*! I sense that we might be on to something big. I ask Frank for the picture and tell him that I'm going to run with it and maybe we'll get a little ink out of Butch Forbes. For the moment Graham can't understand how this will happen.

First I think of newspaper guys who like to write funny features. Turns out that there's a guy at the New York *World-Telegram* named Murray Robinson. Murray is a dour, introverted guy until he sits down in front of his Smith Corona; then the funny words pour out.

I get on the phone. "Murray," I say, "I've got a helluva story for you." I spin the Butch Forbes yarn, tell Robinson I've got the letter and a photo of this mad Dodgers fan. I point out to Murray that this Forbes is so wild about our club that he stays up until four in the morning listening to our games on Armed Forces Radio. Murray flips over the idea and writes a very funny piece about the great Brooklyn fan living in Scotland. An hour after the *World-Telegram* hits the stands, the phone starts ringing like a Las Vegas slot machine that just hit the jackpot. Already I'm getting great results.

One of the first calls comes from a guy named Jim Forbes—no relation to Butch—a PR guy for Pan American Airlines. He says he read Robinson's article and Pan American wants to fly Butch all the way to the United States and back—for free! All I have to do to clinch the deal is make sure that Forbes gets fed and bed.

"You got it!" I tell the guy at Pan American, and the Butch Forbes caper is underway. Next I get hold of the Hotel St. George, which we consider the Waldorf-Astoria of Brooklyn, and tell them that they are about to play host to a great Scotsman. Better still, the St. George is going to get good ink out of it. The hotel's manager gets the message. Good ink means free suite. So we have the plane fare on the cuff, the hotel on the cuff, and who knows what else. O'Malley has to love me for this. Meantime, I am building the visit up on radio and in the papers. By the time Butch lands at Idlewild Airport he is surrounded by the Brooklyn Dodgers Sym-Phony and dozens of media types. In a sense this worries Graham and me. We wonder how Forbes will handle all the tumult. It doesn't take long for us to realize that Butch not only is a nice kid but is a terrific promoter himself.

Finally we have "Butch Forbes Day" at Ebbets Field, and it is dynamite. Butch is dressed up in his kilts and is driven around the ballpark in a jeep. Then he meets the Dodgers themselves and even takes some swings in the batting cage. Forbes hits one pitch so hard he nearly takes the pitcher's head off.

The next concern we have is Butch and sex. Graham says he's worried that Forbes might be like the sailor in *Don't Go Near the Water*. The character in the novel and the movie is a foul-mouthed lecher who is taken to a Hollywood party and wants nothing more than to screw all the starlets he meets.

But not our Butchie. The only gal he has eyes for is Walter O'Malley's good-looking daughter Terry. Fortunately for all concerned—especially me—nothing comes of that brief infatuation.

From the moment Butch sets foot in New York he thinks he is living a dream. One night Graham and I take him to dinner at Toots Shor's restaurant, which is *the* sports hangout. When the waiter brings the menus over and we order a steak for Forbes, the kid bursts into tears. He says he just can't contain himself anymore. Back in Scotland, where he comes from, there still is austerity and here he is getting what amounts to a week's rations at one sitting. I am amazed at Butch's reactions to various items. He is fascinated by paper goods—paper towels, paper napkins—more than he is by the sight of the Empire State Building. He buys box after box of them to bring back to Scotland.

We also arrange for Butch to spend some time with The O in his private box and I'm worrying that, God forbid, Forbes will tell O'Malley that he is madly in love with the boss's daughter. That's all we need.

Fortunately, Butch keeps his mouth shut this once and Forbes Day runs perfectly. We make the front page of the *World-Telegram* with Butch wearing his kilts. (Nobody really wears kilts anymore, but this kid is smart.) Finally we send Forbes home with a ton of gifts, including some new threads from Wallach's.

In fact, Butch Forbes leaves Ebbets Field with everything he's ever wanted in life—except, of course, Terry O'Malley!

Unlike Butch Forbes, who was a total unknown before he was given a day at Ebbets Field, Harold "Pee Wee" Reese comes very close to sainthood as far as Brooklyn fans are concerned. Pee Wee has been the Dodgers' shortstop since pre–World War II days and is as classy on the field as he is off—something that Jackie Robinson knows as much as anyone. When some of the redneck Dodgers threaten to boycott the club in Jackie's rookie year, the pro-Robinson group need a respected name in their corner. Pee Wee is the guy who has the nerve to stand, publicly, for Robinson. That ends the revolt!

If anyone rates the title "Mister Dodger" it is Pee Wee, and sooner or later you know that he will be given a night to honor his years of service to the ball club. Early in 1955 I begin to hear rumblings on the hustings that certain important people—perhaps *self*-important is a more apt description—are going to put together a Pee Wee Reese Night. The people involved are a collection of merchants, politicians, and manufacturers, all of whom alarm me.

The reason I'm worried is because I remember how these same clowns had put together a "Dixie Walker Night" for "the People's Cherce" a few years earlier, and it turned into a debacle. They wound up giving Dixie a fishing rod, which was such an embarrassment that when he heard about it, Branch Rickey, who was pretty tight with a buck himself, went out and bought a TV set for Walker out of his own pocket so there would be something decent for Dixie at home plate.

I don't want that to happen to Reese, so when I find out who is behind Pee Wee's night I go to O'Malley and tell him why *we*—not those pompous asses who ruined Walker's night—should run the Reese night. "But let's not run a night where the fans are asked to kick in money," I tell the boss. "It's not right for the dock worker, construction guy, or clerk to pay for gifts when the ballplayer is making forty thousand."

What I propose to O'Malley is that since the game will be shown on television that night, there is a terrific opportunity for merchants to get free plugs. I tell the boss that I will go around to these storekeepers and hustle them for gifts in return for the mention.

O'Malley is more than sympathetic, especially since it isn't going to cost him anything, so I then go to Dick Young, the *Daily News* baseball writer, and tell him about the idea. Young bites and we become the "Committee for Pee Wee Reese Night." Our broadcasters, Red Barber and Vin Scully, love the idea and huckster it on the air. Now we have to see if we can hustle the gifts.

The response is amazing. Chock Full O'Nuts bakes him a 250-pound cake and gives Reese a lifetime supply of coffee. Paul Grossinger of Grossinger's Hotel in the Catskills gives Pee Wee a lifetime pass to the hotel for himself and his family and tosses in a set of golf clubs. We get trips to Europe and clothes from Wallach's and Botany clothes and hairdressing for Mrs. Reese and dresses for their daughter Barbara. And, of course, the pièce de résistance, as they never say on Flatbush Avenue, is to be the car Pee Wee will win. After all, what's a night for a ballplayer without a car?

My next move is to set up a meeting with the Flatbush Automobile Dealers Association. I go to them with Frank Graham, who comes up with one of the greatest single strokes of promotional genius for Reese Night. Frank proposes that the Chevy dealer, the Olds guy, the Chrysler rep, and so on each put up a car along with the keys. They'll bring the keys to the pitcher's mound, put 'em in a big bowl, and then have one of the Reeses pick the key out of the bowl. Whichever car the key fits will be the car Pee Wee gets.

All of this is tied in with Pee Wee's thirty-sixth birthday, which is going to be the day after Reese Night. I wonder how to get the fans to honor the birthday itself, and then I hit upon the idea: why not have everyone in the building light a match, with the lights turned off, and then we can all sing "Happy Birthday, Pee Wee!"

Well, by the time the night comes we have more than $10,000 worth of goods. You name it, we have it, from washing machines to vacuum cleaners to tape recorders to gift certificates.

Naturally, the big question is not how many gifts we can get for Pee Wee but also how many people we can put in the ballpark for his night. There are a few skeptics, to be sure.

The day before the game Buzzy Bavasi, our general manager, asks me, "Kid, what do you think you'll draw for Pee Wee's night?"

I tell him, "Maybe twenty thousand, if we're lucky."

"Tell ya what," Bavasi comes back. "I'll give ya a buck a person for everyone over eighteen thousand who shows up."

It isn't until 7:00 P.M. the night of the big event that I begin breathing a little easier. Word begins filtering in from the cops stationed along the subway route to Ebbets Field that big crowds are gathering. I begin hearing about mob scenes at the Franklin Avenue station of the IRT line and at Eastern Parkway and Prospect Park stations on the BMT line. Pretty soon the word gets out that we will have to *turn people away.*

When Pee Wee's night actually begins there are between thirty-three thousand and thirty-four thousand people in the ballpark, and not many of them give a damn that the Brooks are playing the Milwaukee Braves. They have come to toast Captain Pee Wee. We finally get the party started by opening the center field gates—the ones that face onto Bedford Avenue near Sullivan Place—and roll in truckload after truckload of gifts. As each truck makes its way to the infield, the public address announcer intones the name of the donors. It sounds like an early version of "Beat the Clock."

I have my eyes on Pee Wee from time to time to see how he is handling the affair. "If I had to go through this every day," he says, "I'd quit baseball."

"With what you're getting," kids Bill Roeder of the *World-Telegram*, "you could afford to retire!"

In between presents we read off congratulatory messages from President Eisenhower, Vice President Nixon, and General Douglas MacArthur. All of which leads up to the grand finale—the parade of automobiles.

The crowd is already tipped off about the car that Pee Wee will receive, but of course nobody knows which one of the seven cars will be the Reese car. Neither do I; and that may be the biggest mistake of my promotional career. Obviously, the 34,000 fans and Irving Rudd want Pee Wee to win the big, fat, expensive Chrysler, not the cheap little Chevrolet or one of the in-between cars. But I work out the procedure to go this way: each car will be driven to the infield grass, where Pee Wee's daughter Barbara will draw the key to the winning car.

As each car is introduced and driven from Bedford Avenue—where, believe it or not, a cop threatened to give them a parking ticket—the crowd lets out a roar. Now all seven cars are there and the fans are yelling like mad for Reese to get the Chrysler.

I'm not yelling, but I'm hoping very hard as Barbara Reese starts working her key on the cars. Damned if the key doesn't work on the Chrysler or the Buick or the Dodge but winds up fitting the cheap Chevy. The crowd is pissed and, as one reporter says in the next day's paper, "they breathed the biggest collective sigh of disappointment."

Luckily I have a gimmick to quickly erase the ill feeling. Quickly the PA guy comes on and says, "Now, ladies and gentlemen, we also want you to know that it's Pee

Wee's birthday. We're going to turn off the lights and we would like everyone to light a match."

All of a sudden the ballpark is black as pitch and, a second later, the matches start lighting and everyone begins singing "Happy Birthday." It is a sight to behold. Then, for a topper to the topper, we stun Pee Wee by having his mom, Mrs. C. M. Reese of Louisville, Kentucky, on hand.

Pee Wee's mother steps out of one of the cars and gives him a great big kiss. I could see the tears well in the captain's eyes. It is a magnificent evening except that Pee Wee now is worried that he'll stink out the joint once the game starts. I am worried too, until Pee Wee comes out to bat and beats the kishkes out of the ball. He raps two doubles off Gene Conley, leading to a couple of runs that help Brooklyn to an 8-4 victory.

I. Rudd couldn't be happier. It is a great night and, furthermore, it didn't cost O'Malley a quarter. For that alone he should love me. On top of that, we draw thirty-four thousand fans when The O expects eighteen thousand.

The ink we get is unreal. Typical is the coverage in the *World-Telegram*. The main headline reads: "Happy Boitday, Pee Wee!" The subhead is: "Ebbets Field Reese Park for a Night."

The only downer I get out of the whole thing is an exchange with Roy Campanella. The next morning Campy grabs me at the ballpark. "How come," he says, "you let li'l Barbara get the key to the Chevy and not the Imperial?"

Naive Irving explains that it is because Barbara *picked* the key to the Chevy and not the Imperial. Campy looks at me like I am the dumbest guy between here and Timbuktu. "Shit, man," he says, "you could have *arranged* for her to pick the Imperial."

"But that wouldn't be honest," I. Rudd replies.

"Honest?" shouts Campanella, disbelieving the words he hears. "Now there's a Chrysler Imperial available to Pee Wee for nothin', and the Chevy is there for nothin', and you're giving me this honesty shit. Man, if the Chrysler is there and there is six feet of shit between me and it, *I* go to the Chrysler!"

Campy is not being nasty but rather pragmatic about the whole thing. Truthfully, if I could do it all over again, I'd do it the Campanella way.

Class guy that he is, Pee Wee couldn't care less whether he has a Chevy or a Jeep. Besides, he already has a Chrysler. A couple of days after the event I finally get a clue as to how Reese actually feels about his night. He asks to see me in the locker room. He is sitting alone on his stool.

When I walk in Pee Wee looks me up and down like he is studying my suit. He is acting more like a tailor than a shortstop. Finally he says sharply, "Irving, where in hell do you get your clothes? It's awful, the bullshit you're wearing. Awful!"

Next thing I know, Pee Wee hits me in the head with a piece of paper. "What the hell is the matter with you, Pee Wee?" I demand.

Again he asks who is my clothier. "Irving," he goes on, "who lets you outa the house every morning?" Then he hits me with another piece of paper. And another! "I can't stand the sight of you," he yells. "Take these things and get yourself some clothes!"

I look at the pieces of paper he's hitting me with and see that each is a $100 gift certificate—one from Wallach's, one from Macy's, and another from Broadstreets.

This is Pee Wee Reese's way of saying thanks.

What can I say? I love the guy like I love every one of the guys on the team. All I am trying to do is promote the Dodgers any legitimate way I know how. Sometimes the thoughts are my own. Sometimes they come from left field.

I am called a son of a bitch more times than I can remember, but especially at World Series time. That's when, as promotion director, I don't want to see tickets "sold." For the World Series we have a guaranteed full house. People start calling me a son of a bitch a few days before the series actually begins. My telephone begins to ring, and ring, and ring. At the office all day. At home all night. All of a sudden I become the most popular guy in the world.

And why? Because the world around me figures that I. Rudd can produce World Series tickets, just like that! You wouldn't believe the calls that come in. "This is your cousin from Ellenville. . . . I know you won't mind, because I didn't want to bother Walter [O'Malley], but I would like to get a couple of sets for the series."

So in order to keep my sanity—and inject a bit of humor into the situation—I borrow a few quotations I first saw thirty-seven years ago on Al Douglas's office wall at Rockland Palace. These are biblical quotations, which I distribute vocally and visually to those who figure they can shake me down for passes, including my "cousin" from Ellenville.

Thou shalt not pass. (Num. 20:18)
Though they roar, yet they cannot pass. (Jer. 1:22)
Suffer not a man to pass. (Judg. 3:28)
The wicked shall no more pass. (Nah. 1:15)
None shall pass. (Isa. 34:10)
This generation shall not pass. (Mark 13:30)
Beware that thou pass not. (2 Kings 6:19)
There shall no stranger pass. (Amos 3:17)
Neither any son of man pass. (Jer. 2:43)
No man may pass through because of the beasts. (Ezek. 14:15)
So he paid the fare of and went. (Jon. 1:3)

= 7 =

Bobby Thomson, General MacArthur, and Other Disasters

It would be nice to say that every promotion attempted by I. Rudd at Ebbets Field was as socko as the Pee Wee Reese and Butch Forbes capers. But alas, I win a battle and lose a war with none other than General Douglas MacArthur.

When you think of General MacArthur you are reminded of grand triumphs on the battlefield. When I think of MacArthur I suffer daytime nightmares about a great disaster in Dodgers history. The disaster is the Giants-Dodgers pennant race of 1951. Hard as it is to believe, those of us in the Brooklyn employ blame the general as much as Bobby Thomson for the Dodgers' demise in September 1951.

Yours truly also shoulders some of the blame in *l'affaire* MacArthur, because I am the one who originally made contact with the general. It happened this way: One afternoon I read in *The New York Times* that MacArthur has been fired by President Harry Truman and is coming home. When the general returns to New York he is greeted like a conquering hero, confetti and all. Once he settles into his suite at the Waldorf Towers, MacArthur starts frequenting baseball games—at the Polo Grounds and Yankee Stadium. I say to myself, how come General MacArthur never comes to Ebbets Field? Does he have an allergy to Brooklyn?

MacArthur is a red-hot item, and his appearance at our ballpark would mean lots of good ink and prestige for the Dodgers. The name of the game is get the turnstile spinning, and I know that MacArthur's presence will sell tickets for us. I phone Eldorado 5-3000 and ask for MacArthur's suite. I get Colonel Anthony F. Story, the general's aide-de-camp. He wants to know what business I have with MacArthur. I tell him straight out that the Dodgers (meaning me) are pissed off with the general. He demands an explanation.

"What gives?" I demand. "The general goes to Yankee Stadium and the Polo Grounds but he's boycotting Brooklyn. How come he's discriminating against the Dodgers?" That shakes up the colonel. Before he can even produce an answer I pipe up: "And furthermore, you better tell the general that nobody has really lived until he has been to Ebbets Field!"

Before I get all the words out, I start to shudder. Who the hell am I to be talking this way to General MacArthur's right-hand man? I'm figuring he's going to tell me to bugger off and hang up on me.

Whew! The colonel laughs and I. Rudd stops quaking

in his oxfords. "When can we meet?" Colonel Story asks. I know then and there that I have him on my side, so I decide to come up with a complete battle plan, just like the general would do. "Before we try anything," I suggest, "let's sit down at a restaurant and map things out—real militarylike."

This appeals to the colonel. We have our lunch and then head out to Ebbets Field, where I introduce him to *our* five-star general, Walter O'Malley. The O is in fine stentorian form and impresses Story. He okays the expedition to Brooklyn.

MacArthur decides that he'll come see us play on a Saturday afternoon, which means that the time has come for the final battle plan. Frank Graham and I. Rudd huddle like we are planning MacArthur's return to the Philippines. We arrange for the general to arrive at the Sullivan Place entrance after driving down Bedford Avenue. At exactly 12:30 P.M. the corrugated metal wall at the right field wall will roll up and MacArthur will ride in his limousine down the first base side to his box seat behind our dugout.

Now it's D day, H hour. I'm standing there with Louis Goldberg, the chief inspector of the New York City Police Department, a rare achievement for a Jew. We're wondering how late the general's entourage will be, when all of a sudden we hear a siren and see the swirling lights of police cars. The gates open and Louis and I both check our watches—it is 12:30 on the very button, not a second on either side!

The general rolls down the first base line and climbs out of the car, wearing his scrambled eggs and braids and ribbons. He is an imposing figure, seeming to say to the mass of Brooklynites, "I am here!"

Now comes the real military part—security for the general, how many seats he'll need, protocol, all that shit, until the whole visit is covered, including the most important question of all: what happens when the general has to go to the toilet? How does he get to the Ebbets Field crapper?

This seemingly insignificant matter suddenly becomes a cause célèbre with Colonel Story. I suggest that the best thing is for the general to go down the stairs by the Dodgers' dugout. Unfortunately, the stairs date back to when Ebbets Field was built fifty years ago. They are rickety and steep. "It's terrible," screams Colonel Story, "the general can't climb those stairs!"

My counterproposal is that we discreetly unlatch the gate near his box seat. When the general wants to go to the john he just slides out of his seat and walks down the players' clubhouse stairs, where he can use the same toilet as Duke Snider and Skoonj Furillo.

We move the general and his entourage all the way to home plate, where a microphone awaits him. When the audience stops cheering he takes the mike and says: "I have been told that one hasn't really lived until he has been to Ebbets Field. I am delighted to be here!"

With that the crowd goes bananas. Then we add a few more touches when the general takes his seat in what amounts to a reviewing stand. We bring in the nisei "Go-for-Broke" battalion, which had fought on the Italian front in World War II and suffered many casualties. They parade past MacArthur and deliver the big salute. And so it goes, one great bit after another until it's time for the ball game. When it's over and MacArthur leaves the ballpark, I assume that it is the last we have seen of the general.

As luck would have it, I am wrong.

A few days later we are having a night game and I'm loose as a goose, walking around the infield before batting practice wearing a Harry Truman Hawaiian shirt, when all of a sudden one of the ushers tells me that I'm wanted at the press gate.

Now, that isn't unusual; I mean, there always are a handful of freeloading friends of mine who are apt to have me come over to get them into the ballpark. So I amble over to the turnstile, and there, big as life, stands General MacArthur.

Again I nearly lose my pants when I see the guy; after all, I'm wearing my *shmatah* Hawaiian shirt and here's Mister Five-Star General standing in front of me. With a little stutter here and a little stutter there, I blurt out a "Hello, how are ya; what brings ya to Ebbets Field tonight?"

The general very calmly tells me that he just decided to come out for the evening, and that's why he showed up unannounced. It teaches me a lesson: always wear a tie on the job, don't go dressed like a bum.

When I first invited the general—and tried to lure him away from the Giants and the Yankees—I figured one appearance was all I needed to get ink for the Dodgers. Little did I imagine that MacArthur would become an instant Dodgers' fan. This second, surprise visit is not his last. MacArthur comes to Ebbets Field thirteen times that year, and that's why I blame the general for costing us the National League pennant in 1951. We don't win a single ball game when he comes to see us in Brooklyn! Without MacArthur we could be world champions! Remember, this is the season when we have a thirteen-and-a-half game lead going into the homestretch and blow it all on one pitch at the Polo Grounds on October 3, 1951.

As far as I can tell, there will never be a more memorable day in sports history than the final game of the Dodgers-Giants playoff, which decides the National League pennant winner. For me the day begins in downtown Brooklyn early in the morning. First I check into our office on Montague Street. At 10:00 A.M. my sidekick, Frank Graham, Jr., and I walk down Montague Street and across to Clark Street to the huge St. George Hotel. That's where the Dodgers team bus is waiting for the players, and at ten o'clock the guys begin climbing aboard. I sit next to Clem Labine, who pitched the 10-0 shutout over the Giants the day before to tie the best-of-three series at one apiece. Soon the engine starts groaning and we are off for the Polo Grounds across the river up in Harlem.

The bus zigzags its way through Manhattan until it reaches 155th Street and finally comes to a stop in front of the ancient green-painted clubhouse underneath the el just beyond center field. We all pile out, each group splitting off to its work area. For the players it is the dressing room, for the coaches and managers it is Charlie Dressen's office away from home, and for me it is the press box.

Because this playoff is getting such international attention, the Giants are overwhelmed with press requests. As a result they create a second press box to accommodate all the extra writers in the first rows of the upper grandstands behind home plate. My job is to see that everything is okay for our guys up there, but without stepping on the toes of the Giants' press agents, who actually are in charge.

The Giants have two main press guys. One is Garry Schumacher, a warm, lovable man who runs the show. His assistant is a cantankerous guy who is working the upper, makeshift press area. I like the assistant and get along well with him, but I also know he can be a big pain in the ass, so I handle (or avoid) him accordingly. Well, it just so happens, on this biggest of big days, that I notice Grantland Rice, the dean of American sportswriters, in the upper press area. Granny is the guy who coined the expression "the Four Horsemen" to describe the famous Notre Dame backfield of 1924. He's also the fellow who wrote, "It's not whether you win or lose but how you play the game." Granny has to be one of the nicest guys you'd ever want to meet and a guy you have to hold in reverence for what he did for his profession. Anyhow, Granny is wandering around the press box like a duck out of water. I go over to him to find out what the hell the trouble is all about.

For one thing, I can't understand why the dean of writers is stuck here upstairs. "Irving," Granny says, "can you figure out where I'm supposed to be?" The poor old guy is getting on in years and it is obvious that he is all screwed up. Considering his importance, Rice belongs downstairs in the regular press box with the Red Smiths, Jimmy Cannons, and other superstars of the writing world, but here he is up in heaven with the whatevers.

I figure I'll try to help the old guy out, so I call over to the Giants' PR assistant, since it's *his* press box and not mine. "Hey," I say, "Granny Rice is here and—" Before I can finish my sentence, the cipher snaps, "I don't have time for that bullshit!" and walks away.

It is a sin of human relations and a sin of public relations, but it's a sin that has been committed over and over again by numerous untalented flacks who work for the Mets, the Yankees, the Knicks, the racetracks, and other corporate sports outfits. With them, the I-don't-give-a-shit philosophy prevails. These poor saps posing as PR men just don't understand what their function in life is supposed to be, what their job is all about. Then you have a guy like Granny Rice, a thorough gentleman, a great poet who understands life, and he's treated like shit by a flunky.

I give Granny my seat and wind up sitting in another part of the press box with Allan Roth, the Dodgers' statistician. My luck, on the other side of me is some clown covering the playoff for a Spanish-language newspaper. This guy is a legitimate newspaperman only in the sense that he knows which direction to drop his fingers on a typewriter keyboard. Anyway, this guy is bugging me from the first pitch thrown, and I'm putting up with his gibberish because it's my job to put up with schmucks like him.

The game is moving along, and by the sixth inning it's shaping up pretty good for us Dodgers. We're leading big and Don Newcombe still looks good on the mound for us. But I'm not happy. For one thing, I know the game is far from over, and for another, this Spanish guy is pestering me beyond belief

We're right in the middle of the most exciting game in history and this guy is more concerned about what we're going to serve at the press (victory) party at the Bossert Hotel in Brooklyn after the game. "Not now!" I shout. But it makes absolutely no impression on the bum, and over and over again he comes back with "About that party . . ." And I holler, *"Not now!"*

One reason I'm hollering so much is because I'm scared—scared that we're going to blow this goddamn game. Over and over, whenever our guys come to the plate, I'm yelling "more runs, *more runs!"* This bothers Arch Murray of the *New York Post*, a well-known Giants' fan as well as a regular writer on the beat. When I yell for more runs, Arch moans, "Have a heart, Irv, will you please! Look at all the runs your guys got already."

I'm not impressed. In my heart I am the eternal pessimist. What's a four-run lead? Nothing. "Not enough," I say to Arch. Then I look out on the field and bellow: *"More, more!* Stick it to 'em!"

So now we're in the bottom of the ninth, and even though we're still nursing a lead, I'm not feeling that terrifically confident about the score. On one side of me our statistician, Roth, is worrying as much as I am, and on the other side my Cuban "friend" is saying, "About that party . . . How do you get to the Bossert for the party?"

Finally it comes down to Bobby Thomson. He steps up to the plate. We're still leading 4-2. There is one out, and runners on second and third. I turn to Roth: "Allan, Allan, what are the statistics on Ralph Branca pitching to Thomson?" Roth shakes his head, kind of sad.

I want to leap out of the upper press box and parachute to Charlie Dressen imploring him not to use Branca. Allan Roth told me so!

I can't jump, but I feel so lousy. I'm thinking to myself, "Oh Christ, it's all over." I want Clem Labine right back, or even Preacher Roe. Anybody but Branca. Someone in the press box tells me that Roe is supposed to pitch tomorrow, but what sense does that make? I think of Leo Durocher. He always says, "Go now, because tomorrow it could rain!"

What the hell good is a starter like Roe now that the game is almost over? How sore-armed can Labine be? He only has to throw a couple of pitches, and he beat the Giants 10-0 the day before.

So we're going at it in the press box: why Branca? Why not Branca? It is reported that Branca has the best stuff in the bullpen, and you have to respect the word of the bullpen coach.

There is not much we can do up in the press box but pray and hope that Branca does the right thing. But on the first pitch, he does the wrong thing. It's an easy one, right down the pipe, the kind I figure that Thomson will flog for a home run.

Instead Thomson looks at it for a called strike. Jesus, if he blows that one, maybe we'll get out of this madness alive. But it isn't to be; the pitch that should have been a ball, Thomson swings at. I. Rudd holds his breath.

Once the bat hits the ball there is no guarantee, like you sometimes know when you hear that sound, that it is going to be a home run. I mean, it is hit pretty well, but pretty-well-hit balls ain't always home runs; except, of course, in a two-bit ballpark like the Polo Grounds, where the left field wall is right behind third base.

Our guy in left field is Andy Pafko. He's the guy all the Brooklyn fans are watching, because if Pafko looks like he can get it, we win the ball game. But Andy takes a good look, and the ball that is an easy fly out in a lot of other ballparks sails over Pafko's head into the stands. It has to be a bad dream. Right? All kinds of things are flashing through my head, but mostly that whenever General MacArthur was at Ebbets Field, we lost.

Well, by the time I get down to the field, I'm trying very hard to be philosophical about a very traumatic event. It's a long walk from home plate to the clubhouse in center field, the longest walk in my life, and everybody on the Dodgers' team is walking around in a state of shock.

I come into the clubhouse and the first thing I see is this big hulk of a guy sitting in front of his locker sobbing. Ralph Branca. It is a hell of a contrast, because in the ancient Polo Grounds clubhouse, the walls are paper thin. Our room is so quiet you can hear a feather fall; right next door is the Giants' dressing room, and we can hear all the yelling and screaming for joy, and that just makes our misery all the more tough to take. All there is for us is silence and shock. No recriminations among the guys, just players wondering what might have been.

An hour later, my pal Carl Erskine, always a classy, nice man, says to me, "Irv, I guess I deserve all the blame."

Erskine telling me that *he* deserves all the blame. I don't understand it. "Why, Carl?" I ask.

"Let's not forget that *I* lost *on opening day!*"

And that's how General Douglas MacArthur lost Brooklyn the pennant in 1951.

═ 8 ═
Inside
Jackie Robinson,
Roy Campanella,
Don Newcombe,
and Other Black
Stars

There isn't a black athlete, past or present, from Bill Russell to Kareem Abdul-Jabbar to Willie Mays, who shouldn't bless the name of Jack Roosevelt Robinson every night before he goes to bed—or counts his millions. If Jackie Robinson hadn't blazed the trail for black ballplayers it would have taken another ten years before we saw a black in the bigs. You have to be at least 60 years old today to really appreciate how difficult it was to break the color line in 1947. Actually, "color line" is an understatement. A Great Wall separated the white from the black athletes. You can get a good idea about it from the

movie *Bingo Long*, which shows what a primitive existence the Negro ballplayer suffered.

I see it firsthand, working occasionally at Dexter Park
in Brooklyn, where the Negro National Leaguers frequently play. And I see it again in Miami when I first
start promoting the Dodgers for O'Malley. Robbie is
taunted beyond endurance. He is a short-fused guy, yet
he can't retaliate, because his "rabbi," Branch Rickey,
tells him right up front that he can't hit back. "I know
you're a good ballplayer," says Rickey. "What I don't
know is whether you have the guts *not* to fight back."

Jackie proves that he has the guts, first in the International League with Montreal and then in 1947, when the
Dodgers bring him to Ebbets Field to stay. At first the
treatment he receives is brutal—even from his own teammates. "Some of the Dodgers refuse to accept me because
I'm black," says Robbie. But he perseveres and his natural talent cannot be denied. He takes all the crap the nee-
dlers can give him while remembering Rickey's order. In
retrospect, I am certain that Jackie's forced cool during
those first seasons in Brooklyn cost him a couple of decades of his life.

On the other hand, there is no way that Jackie makes
it as a big leaguer if he doesn't get support from some key
white guys on the club. Pee Wee Reese, Rex Barney,
Ralph Branca, and Carl Erskine make Robbie's Dodgers
career possible, because there were some real rednecks
out to ruin that black man's career before it ever started.
I'm not with the club when Jackie comes up in 1947 but
Pee Wee is, and later he tells me about it, as does Rex
Barney. The redneck in the act was Fred "Dixie" Walker.

"One thing I remember," says Pee Wee, "is the petition some guys passed around. But I wouldn't sign it. I
wasn't trying to think of myself as being the Great White
Father, really. I just wanted to play the game, especially
after being in the navy for three years and needing the

money, and it didn't matter to me whether he was black or green, he had a right to be there too.

"Then you'd hear a lot of insults from the opposing benches during games, guys calling him things like 'nigger' and 'watermelon eater,' trying to rile him. But that was when Jackie started to turn the tables: you saw how he stood there at the plate and dared them to hit him with the ball, and you began to put yourself in his shoes.

"You'd think of yourself trying to break into the black leagues, maybe, and what it would be like—and I know that I couldn't have done it. In a word, Jackie was winning respect."

From some Dodgers, Jackie wins respect instantly. Rex Barney, the fastball pitcher, is the first player to shake Robinson's hand when he comes to Brooklyn. "I was born and raised in Omaha," Barney explains. "I'm Irish Catholic, and I grew up with blacks. I never thought about it one way or another. Ralph Branca and Carl Erskine were the same way. But the guy who did more for Jackie than anybody else was Pee Wee Reese."

Although you won't find it in any baseball record book, the most pivotal day for Robinson, in terms of his acceptance as a black man with the white Dodgers, comes on a day in Philadelphia when the Brooks are playing the Phillies, then managed by a first-class redneck named Ben Chapman. Rex Barney, who was there, tells me about it one day. "Chapman is needling Jackie something good from the third base line," Barney recalls, "then the inning ends. Pee Wee walks over to Jackie and just puts his arm around Jack's shoulders as if to say, 'He's my friend and my teammate and I'm with him all the way.'"

After Robinson comes Campanella and Newcombe, but neither owns the chutzpah that is part of Jackie's character. In the late forties, for example, black players are not permitted to room with white players at St. Louis hotels. One day the Dodgers arrive in St. Louis for a series with the Cardinals, and Robbie announces that he is going to the white hotel with Reese. This bugs Campy who urges Robbie not to rock the boat.

Pee Wee remembers the incident. "Jackie paid them no mind," Reese tells me. "He joined us on the team bus, went right into the hotel, and registered, and Campy and the others followed. That was Jack—he got the job done."

One of the beautiful interpersonal sights in the Dodgers' locker room and on the field is the relationship between Reese, the shortstop and captain, and Robinson, the second baseman and other half of the double-play combination. One day when I'm with the team, I hear Reese talking serious with Robbie. "Y'know," says Pee Wee, "I didn't particularly go out of my way just to be nice to you."

To which Jackie replies, "Pee Wee, maybe that's what I appreciate most—that you didn't."

The essence of Robinson's success as a Dodger is in his unquenchable competitive fire. Nobody puts it better than Duke Snider, our center fielder, who tells a story about the vintage Jackie. Says the Duke: "We're playing a real good game against the Chicago Cubs that winds up tied, 2-2, in the top of the ninth. Their pitcher is 'Sad' Sam Jones, a long black guy who is one of the best fireballers in the bigs. I'm at bat and Jackie is in the on-deck circle, and he's yelling at Jones in that high voice that you could hear everywhere. 'Sam, you're no good! Sam, I'm gonna beat you. You got no guts.'

"After I fly out, it's Jackie's turn at the plate. He moves into the batter's box, yelling at Sam until we can tell that Jones is madder'n hell. Finally Sam hits Jackie with a pitch, and now Jackie is on first.

"Now Jones is in real trouble, because Robbie is dancing off the bag and yelling and Sam keeps throwing over there, trying to keep him on the bag. It gets to Jones, and this time he tosses the ball at Robinson instead of the first baseman. Jackie ducks and the ball sails down to our bullpen in the right field corner, and Jackie legs it all the way to third.

"Sam is beside himself, and Jackie's still yelling and laughing and dancing up the line on every pitch and screaming, 'Sam, I'm gonna beat you. You got no guts.'

"By now Sam is looking at Jackie and cursing and paying him more attention than the batter, and he throws the next pitch into the dirt. It's a short passed ball, and here comes Jackie with the winning run. It's 3-2 Brooklyn and we win another. That Robinson was something else!"

As a ballplayer, he is nonpareil. As a person, he is terribly complex. He has a sense of humor but he is not a king of one-liners. He is not a congenial backslapper but he is more sensitive than most people believe. More than anything, he is a competitor; and this I learn firsthand during a vacation with Jackie and his family at Grossinger's Hotel in the Catskills. It is January 1952, when any normal visitor to The G (what we call Grossinger's) should be swimming in the indoor pool. Not Jackie; he decides he wants to learn to ice-skate.

Now, ice-skating is a fine sport for you and me to take up, but for the best second baseman in the world in the prime of his career, it isn't so wise. (Luckily, Walter O'Malley isn't aware of Robbie's new interest.) What happens if Robinson breaks his leg getting a skate caught in a rut on the ice? That would put him, and the Dodgers, in a fine fix for the 1952 season.

But Robbie, God bless him, can never resist a challenge. He insists that we take up ice-skating, so the two of us get ahold of Irving Jaffee, the former Olympic speed-skating champion, who happens to be winter sports director at The G. We take lessons from Jaffee that afternoon, and thank God, Robbie doesn't break a leg.

Now it's almost dinnertime and I'm anxious to get back to my room and change. I leave Jackie at the rink and figure he is having his one and only skating lesson. The next morning, for some inexplicable reason, I return to

112

Cub reporter Irving Rudd is held in place by two *Liberty Bell* editors at a Thomas Jefferson High School football game.

The Kid and the Champ—with Jack Dempsey, 1946.

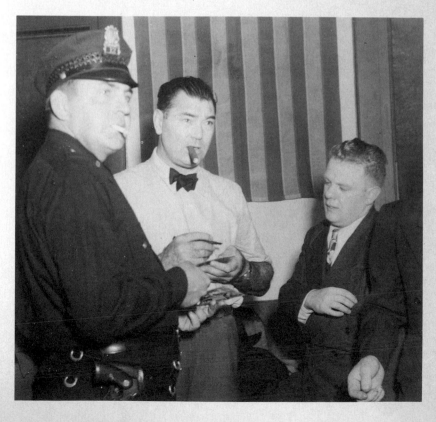

Surrounded by heavyweights Joe Louis and Dave Soden, a Brooklyn philanthropist, at Joe's camp in 1948.

Enjoying a laugh with Duke Snider at a Father and Son night, Brooklyn 1948. (Ed. Lowy Photograph)

With Brooklyn Dodgers Gil Hodges, Jackie Robinson, and Roy Campanella.

We got all kinds at Ebbets Field, from playwright and novelist William Saroyan (above) to King Faisal of Iraq, here shown talking with Jackie Robinson on Jackie's radio show. (photo by Barney Stein)

With Rachel and Jackie Robinson at a Catskills resort in 1953. (photo by Barney Stein)

Pee Wee Reese night in 1955. The lights go out at Ebbets Field as 35,000 fans, holding candles, matches and lighters, sing "Happy Birthday" to the Dodgers' captain. (photo by Barney Stein)

Enjoying cake with Pee Wee and George Shuba after the game that evening.

I even met Joe Palooka in Ham Fisher's famous comic strip, on September 2, 1954 in the *New York Daily Mirror*.

How to (mis)spell *raceway* and get a lot of ink, to help publicize the re-opening of Yonkers Raceway in 1958. (Yonkers Raceway Photo by Michael Cipriani)

With the great horse False Step at the farm of harness driver Cecile Devine in Christchurch, New Zealand, in 1961.

I traveled all over the world to find horses to race at Yonkers. Here I'm on a farm in Sydney, Australia, with the champion mare Sibelia.

To Russia—with lox! At the Moscow Hippodrome, 1967.

Meeting with Ed Sullivan and harness drivers Carmine Abbatiello and Stanley Dancer.

Reunion with Gil Hodges, one of my favorite people, at Shea Stadium
in 1967. (Yonkers Raceway News Photo by Michael Cipriani)

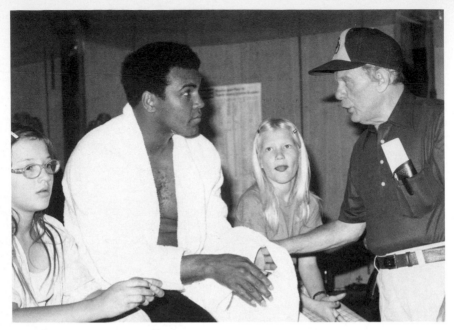

In camp with the Champ: Muhammad Ali in Show Low, Arizona, getting ready for a 1976 title bout with Ken Norton.

With Ken Norton and his trainer Bill Slaxton, preparing for the same fight.

Up in arms with the world's strongest man, Vasili Alexeyev of the Soviet Union, in Las Vegas.

Visiting with heavyweight champ Larry Holmes in 1979.

With Red Smith in Johannesburg, South Africa, before the 1979 WBA heavyweight title fight between John Tate and Gerrie Coetzee.

Legendary trainer Ray Arcel gives me some tips at Grossinger's in 1983.

Two great fighters with heart: Roberto Duran (above) and my friend Ray Mancini, pictured here with trainer Murphy Griffith.

the rink, and who shows up with a pair of skates under his arm but Jackie. He has a broad grin on his face and I'm worried. "Good morning, Jackie," I say, hoping against hope that he is returning the skates he had rented the day before.

He is still grinning. "Irving," he says, "why don't you and me have a race?"

A skating race, Rudd vs. Robinson, I say to myself. *Oy vay!* By the look in Jackie's eyes—two searchlights beaming at me—I. Rudd knows there is no way to get off the hook. "Okay, Jackie," I say, "you're on."

Our first race is from scratch—without practice—and frankly, I am scared shitless. Robbie didn't look good taking his lessons the previous day from Irv Jaffee. He looked more like a clown from the Ice Follies than a graceful athlete. Every time he takes a step the skates seem to fly right out from under him. Son of a gun! He gets up, and after four flops he is skating and the Rudd-Robinson race now is taking on epic proportions. Not only does Robbie skate better than me but he wins the race by a lot of yards and without suffering any permanent injury.

I am satisfied that the ice classic is over until Robinson shouts across the rink: "This time, Irv, I'll give you a five-yard handicap."

I need this like I need an ice-water concession in Greenland. But Robbie will not have no for an answer, so we race again, and despite the handicap, Jackie wins with ease.

Enough already! I am whispering to myself. No, Robbie is not satisfied. "This time, Irv, I'll give you half a rink's lead."

It's a gigantic handicap and I huff and puff my way to the finish line, only to be nosed out by Jackie once more. I am a little pissed off that I can't even win with that gigantic handicap. Before I can work myself into a depression, Jackie comes over and shakes my hand. What he says next tells me more about the man than a volume of psychological studies. "Thanks a lot, Irv. *I just had to beat somebody before I went home!"*

Robinson's will to win is matched only by his intense pride. Nothing for nothing is his philosophy. Once Lena Horne, the great singer, and a few other prominent blacks get together and buy Jackie a new Cadillac as a token of their appreciation for what he is doing for their people.

The first day Jackie brings the car to Ebbets Field he overhears a black guy nearby say, "Hey, man, I helped buy that Cadillac." Robbie is so pissed off, the next day he sells the car and gives the money to charity. Then he goes out and buys another, smaller car. "Nobody," Jackie tells me, "is going to say he bought *me* a car!"

My fondness for Robinson is rooted in several incidents, each of which helps bail me out of a tight spot, the way a stand-up guy always will when you're in trouble. For me, Robbie never stands taller than the time when television journalist Ed Murrow is doing a show called "Person to Person" on CBS. It is right in the middle of the repressive McCarthy era, when every conservative worth his weight in Republican buttons is finding Communists all over the place. The very liberal Murrow is one of many media people fingered as a "pinko."

It happens that Murrow has done a "Person to Person" show with our great black catcher Roy Campanella, and Ed takes a liking to our organization. He begins visiting the Brooklyn clubhouse and gets friendly with some of the Dodgers, a fact that thoroughly enrages one of our ultra-conservative baseball reporters, Mike Gaven of the New York *Journal-American.*

Gaven knows that Senator McCarthy is after Murrow's ass, and Gaven hates Murrow's guts as much as the senator from Wisconsin does. When Gaven sees Campanella on "Person to Person" he probably pukes on his TV set. And when Murrow comes to the Dodgers' clubhouse Gaven is peeved even more. Finally Gaven comes over to me one day and says, "Hey, Irving, I don't want you bringing any more Commies [meaning Murrow] into the dressing room."

"What are you talking about?" I ask him.

"That Ed Murrow. He's got no business in this clubhouse."

I am on the spot. Gaven, the man on the beat for the largest evening paper in New York, is important to us. I know that I shouldn't cross the son of a bitch, much as I loathe him.

"Mike," I snap back, "Murrow *does* have business in our clubhouse. He's a regular correspondent for CBS. Besides, *you* have no right to tell *me* that he doesn't belong here."

We go back and forth, the decibels getting higher, until Gaven says, "Murrow is a Commie and we got no room in the clubhouse for Commies."

Now I don't know what to do; I realize I've carried on way too much with a jerk, and I need help, badly.

Suddenly a voice from behind me pipes up: "Irv, anytime Ed Murrow wants to come to the clubhouse, he's *my* guest. Bring him in and make sure I see him." The words belong to Jack Roosevelt Robinson, helping out in a jam.

Likewise, I always feel a special urge to help out Jackie whenever possible. I get my chance one night after a game at the Polo Grounds.

It is at a time when Robinson has been having a running feud with several umpires as well as National League President Warren Giles. In the dressing room after the game, Robbie calls me over, takes out a handwritten letter, and asks me to read it and tell him what I think.

The letter is to Giles, and it is tough. Real tough. He blasts the National League president for being prejudiced against black players, calls the umpires a bunch of no-good racists, and rants on and on about the injustices of big league baseball. "I want to stick it to this bastard," Robbie tells me. "I'm sending it off to Giles right now, but I wanted you to see it first."

A warning signal flashes in my cranium. The letter is so far to the left of reason that I get goose pimples just thinking about it. "Jackie," I plead, "you can't send this out."

"The hell I can't," he argues, as if I'm his enemy instead of his pal.

"Let me ask you one thing, Jackie. Why in hell did you bother showing me the letter if you didn't want my advice?"

That hangs him up like a high, hard one across the wrists. "What are you doing right now?" he asks, his tone mellowing by two decibels.

I tell him I'm planning to go home; it's getting late and we have a day game tomorrow.

"Do me a favor," Robinson suggests. "Come over to my house for coffee."

Jackie lives in a residential area of Queens called St. Albans. We get there in a half-hour and his wife, Rachel, is waiting for us. We go into the kitchen, sit down for coffee, and begin talking about Jackie's latest storm. Even though he isn't as furious as he was in the dressing room, he still refuses to concede the point to me; he wants in the worst way to send the letter to Giles. My point is that Jackie has to take two steps backward before he can take one step forward. To that he tells me, "goddammit, Irv, you can't take crap from *anybody*. You've got to fight for what's right." By this time Rachel, a magnificent woman, has left the room, but it is obvious that she hears all of our dialogue.

Just then a voice from the next room calls Jackie. He excuses himself and returns a few minutes later. He looks sheepish. "Rachel tells me I've been rough on you tonight."

"No," I say, "you're being rough on yourself. Do me a favor, Jackie, and put that letter in a drawer for a week. Better yet, tear it up. Forget the letter. Sure you're right; but you're also wrong."

Robbie thinks for a minute, then picks up the letter and tears it to shreds. It is three in the morning. "C'mon," he says, "I'll drive you home."

I tell him it isn't necessary but he insists, and he drives me across Queens to Brooklyn at ninety miles per hour. Jackie drives the way he runs the bases. Make no mistake, that style of Robinson annoys some of the other black Dodgers as much as it does some of the whites. That's why Jackie's relationship with Roy Campanella isn't all that strong. Jackie can't understand why easygoing Roy isn't a standard bearer for the black cause the way Robinson is, and it eats at Robbie's insides. There isn't any bad blood between these two black superstars, but as personalities Campy and Robbie are worlds apart.

If you want a simple description of Robinson's baseball personality, you can always get away with calling him hotheaded. Likewise, Roy Campanella is just the opposite. Somewhere in between there is Don Newcombe, alias "Big Newk," one of the best pitchers ever. I know that people find him difficult and that he's gotten himself into a couple of jams—once punching out a needling fan after losing a World Series game at Ebbets Field—but I've never had any trouble with the big guy.

Quite the contrary; before I joined the Dodgers, Newk and I developed an interesting relationship, but not on the baseball diamond. We became partners, so to speak, in the wrestling arena.

Newk is riding high, wide, and handsome with his great arm, and many requests are coming his way. One day Newk calls me up and says, "Hey, meat!"—he is always calling me "meat," for some reason—"I want you to be my manager."

"Manager for what?" I ask.

"Contracts. Lotsa stuff comin' in."

Turns out that everybody's after him with deals for endorsements. So I become Don Newcombe's personal manager, and I get him about $10,000 worth of endorsements, which in those days is a lot of money. I get him Jeris Hair Tonic, and a hat company, and all kinds of cockamamy products.

Once the big guy and I hit it off I start thinking about other ways Newk can make money in the off-season. One day I get an idea. My man runs about six foot five and weighs way over two hundred pounds. If you didn't know better, you'd think he was a professional wrestler. "Newk," I say, "why don't we make you into a wrestling referee?"

He is interested enough for me to talk to some people I know in the business. I lay the proposition in front of wrestling promoter "Toots" Mondt. He likes it. Then we approach Branch Rickey, who is still running the Dodgers at the time. He says okay to the idea but adds, "I'll go along with this but I reserve the right to call the tour off at any time."

Now we are in the wrestling business. Newk and I head for a gym, where a fellow with cauliflower ears teaches the big guy what's supposed to happen in the ring. Then they get inside the ropes with a couple of young wrestlers and Newk begins to learn. They tell him that one of the tricks is to stay near the head of the guy who is down, so that nobody accidentally lashes out and kicks the referee. They show Newk how to hit a guy on the shoulder and back away as he comes off the mat.

Right off the bat Newk takes to refereeing, and in no time at all we have our first match. For $500 we're booked into Washington, D.C., and guaranteed a percentage of the gate. What I keep asking myself is whether anyone will bother to come out to see Don Newcombe, Dodgers' pitcher, as Don Newcombe, wrestling referee.

The first time out, we pack the joint. Not only that, but every newspaper sends a reporter over to interview the big guy. He is a hit with the media and the fans—but not such a hit with the white Washington hotelkeepers.

118

Washington is still segregated, so Newk is forced to check into a black hotel and I have to check into a white hotel.

To that I say bullshit and check into the black hotel with Newk. I feel more comfortable staying with him at the black boarding house than I do going it alone at a big-deal white hotel. We are so flushed with success over our debut that the hotel episode hardly matters when we finally check out of Washington and learn that our act is in big demand. Just by looking at the papers I can see why. Newk's mug is on every sports page and everybody is talking about what fun it was to watch him in the wrestling ring. We are immediately booked into North Adams, Massachusetts, and then Boston. Offers are pouring in and it looks like we have a gold mine.

Finally we roll into Pennsylvania Station, where we have to change trains to get to North Adams. That means taking a cab across town to Grand Central Station, which means time enough to pick up the late New York papers and see what's what. Newk and I are riding on air. I pick up the papers as we rush for our train. Once the train starts pulling out of Grand Central and we unwind, I open up the *Daily News* and get a quick case of lockjaw when I turn to the sports page. There, in huge letters, is a headline with a quote from Newk: "I Won't Pitch For Less Than $20,000." Neither of us can believe our eyes. We read and reread the story and finally realize how we've been had.

One of the many Washington reporters who talked to Newk has totally misquoted him on the salary issue. It is true that he is making $12,000 at the time and that he deserves a raise, but Don isn't the kind of person who would go on record demanding $20,000. I am with him throughout the interviews in Washington and never hear him say anything of the kind. Some son of a bitch has distorted what Newk said, and there it is, in screaming headlines, for everyone at Montague Street to see and fuss about.

The main man we are worrying about is Rickey. He gave us permission to take the tour and he pays Newk's baseball salary. We know he is the tightwad's tightwad, but we like—and fear—the man. "Mister Rickey's gonna call me home!" says Don, as our train rolls toward Massachusetts. I don't argue with him because after the initial shock of seeing the headlines, I feel insulated on the train from any outside problems. I tell Newk what will be will be, and let's get on with our commitment in North Adams.

We arrive there without incident, fill the rinky-dink joint—all the while telling ourselves it *is* bucks—and look forward to the next night, when we figure to fill Boston Garden with more than fifteen thousand fans.

We get to Boston late at night, check into a hotel, and go straight to bed. So far, so good. Maybe we're going to escape Rickey's wrath after all. Next morning the phone rings. "Irving, this is Harold Parrott [of the Dodgers' high command]. Mister Rickey would like to talk to you."

I take a deep breath, expecting the worst. Two seconds later I get it. "Irving," says Rickey, "I realize what you're trying to do for the young man. You've handled yourself very well, but I told you when you first started out that if I felt I had to step in, I would. . . ."

I try to get in a few words, except I keep sounding like an old Jack Benny routine. "But . . . but . . . but . . ."—I am sputtering like a motorboat going upriver.

Meanwhile, I can tell that Newk is virtually peeing in his pants. He knows the boss is mad. "Damn it," Newk whispers, "don't argue with the man."

The big guy grabs the phone from me and comes on with Rickey like Caspar Milquetoast. All I hear is "Yes, Mister Rickey! Yes, Mister Rickey! Yes, Mister Rickey!"

With every "Yes, Mister Rickey" I see another thousand-dollar bill disappear. Here we have an entire contingent of Boston newsmen waiting outside for us, a guaranteed sellout at Boston Garden, and Newk is still making with the "Yes, Mister Rickey." I feel like grabbing the phone from Newk and offering to wrestle Rickey. If he wins we call the whole thing off.

It isn't going to be, because Rickey is adamant. Now comes the tough part. I call the promoters, Toots Mondt and Paul Bowser, and tell them that Newcombe can't referee tonight. I figure we owe them a couple of hundred for reneging on the deal. Instead of screaming me off the phone, Toots is terrific. "Irv," he says, "we'll charge it off to friendship. Just say nice things about wrestling whenever you get the chance."

As for Newk, he simply is a victim of unscrupulous reporting and worries about what a man of Rickey's power might do to him. The wrestling caper does nothing to affect my relationship with Don.

If anything, Don and I become closer friends and I come to understand his personality quirks, including a vein of anger that occasionally surfaces and gets him into some awfully hot water. The worst episode of all takes place during the final game of the 1956 World Series between the Dodgers and Yankees at Ebbets Field. This is the game in which Newk gets bombed right out of the box by a Yogi Berra blast. It is a bitter-cold October afternoon and Ebbets Field feels like a convertible igloo. The weather symbolizes the Dodgers: cold, dark, and gray. The Yankees pile up so many runs so early in the game that a fan feels very sensible picking up and leaving by the sixth inning. Which is what Newcombe intends to do. The difference, of course, is that Newk isn't a fan; he is merely knocked out of the box.

Being close to Don, I feel concerned that he might do something rash, so I head straight for the clubhouse minutes after Newk leaves the mound. When I get to the dressing room, there's the big guy looking like he's in a big hurry to leave the premises. And the World Series game isn't even over yet.

"You can't do that!" I shout at him like I have never shouted at a Dodger before.

"Don't you tell me nuthin'," he comes back at me.

"Don, listen to me," I plead, "you *can't* do that."

He is undressed; a huge, hulking brown figure. He can wrap me around his pinky and toss little Irving Rudd out of the clubhouse window if he wants to show me who's boss. Instead Newk heads straight for the shower and turns on the faucets.

He seems to think the stream of water has created a curtain between him and me. No good, Newk. I walk right into the shower, clothes and all. I get all drenched, but I must make my point: "You *can't* leave the ballpark!"

I have an ace in the hole. Don's father, Jim Newcombe, has come into the room. He is sitting there, quiet. "Don't let your son walk out on the team," I tell the old guy. Seeing his reaction, I am not hopeful. Newk walks out of the shower, towels himself, and, as if no one is around, takes his clothes out of the locker and begins to get dressed. I am convinced that he won't stay with the club.

Don finishes dressing, makes a phone call, and then starts out of the clubhouse. As he leaves I notice a couple of New York City detectives standing near the entrance to the locker room. Almost instinctively we form a vanguard around Newk. We are afraid that once the fans notice him, somebody will get snotty and Newk will belt the guy. That could mean a lawsuit and all kinds of bullshit like that. This we don't need. We walk away from the clubhouse, down the ramp, and out of the ball park toward a parking lot near Empire Boulevard, the big street two short blocks from Ebbets Field.

As we're walking, I am thinking that all is going too good to be true in terms of Newk's safety. Nobody has noticed him; no fuss, no bother. All of a sudden we pass a white guy leaning against a car. He recognizes Newk and must have known what has been going on inside the ballpark. There's a nasty sneer on his mug as he snaps, "Tough shit there, big fella!"

That's all Newk needs. If Don's eyes had arms, they would reach over us and make Wheatena out of the needler. Before Newk can make a move, the cops tighten the vise around Don and hustle him into his car before he can lay a fist on the man.

Like Jackie Robinson, Newcombe too often allows his minus side to surface before the public, while the plus part emerges in private. Time after time Don quietly takes expeditions to places like Sunmount Veteran's Hospital to cheer the sick. He is a sensitive family man and proves it one day when he and his wife adopt a baby. We get some photographers from the papers to take pictures of the Newcombes and their new kid. Somebody asks Don what his plans are for the future, meaning his baseball future, and Newk answers without hesitation, "My whole future is this little fella right here."

I am very big with babies and ballplayers. When Joe Black comes to the Dodgers I not only find him an apartment, I scrounge up a crib for his baby, Chico. I give him my daughter Susan's crib, and that's how the Rudds and the Blacks become good friends. The Blacks visit us in Sheepshead Bay and Gert and I visit them in Bedford-Stuyvesant. The kids play with each other like it is out of a beautiful interracial movie.

Likewise, the Brooklyn dugout—once such rednecks as Dixie Walker are gone—becomes the acme of racial harmony. For that we can thank our classy captain Pee Wee Reese and some of the black players who generate warmth wherever they are, on or off the field. In that sense, tobacco-chewing Roy Campanella is among the warmest and, in his own way, the most likeable of the Dodgers.

Once during the 1956 season Roy is in an awful slump, when he comes to bat with one out and men on first and third. Campy, who hasn't got a hit all day, swings hard and tops a miserable roller to short. Now, Roy isn't that fast but this time he is so desperate for a hit that he legs it something awful to first and makes it by a half step while the runner from third base scores.

Jake Pitler, our first base coach, can't believe his ears as Campy crosses the bag and the umpire flashes the "safe" sign. Pitler is determined to find out what Campy said and asks the catcher when he returns to the bag. "I said, 'Thanks for the base hit, Heavenly Father.'"

To some it may seem childish for a grown man to give divine thanks for a measly base hit, but you had to know Campy to understand him in that simple situation. This is a man who reads his Bible before retiring each night.

Yet Campy also has a touch of wiseacre in him, like the time we bring a twelve-year-old kid into the Ebbets Field clubhouse after the kid wins a Knothole Club contest. The kid says he wants to pose with Campy for a photo. The big catcher puts on a phony frown and says to the boy: "You want to pose with me, young man, you got to have a chaw of tobacco in yo' mouth!" Not realizing that Campy is putting him on, the kid almost faints on the spot. Right away Roy lets on that he is joking and everyone has a good laugh, the kid included.

Campy's approach is to be the "good nigger." The happy-go-lucky catcher figures he has taken enough shit riding the buses of the Negro National League for much of his professional baseball life, and now that he is at the top, he wants to relax and enjoy it. It's not that Campy is turning his back on his own people but rather that he doesn't follow Robinson's extreme route. At the same time, Campy respects what Jackie has done for black players; he has put money in their pockets.

Robinson is also putting principle in their hearts. The other black Dodgers, such as Campy, Don Newcombe, Jim Gilliam, and Joe Black, realize that there are times when a black must take a stand on an issue that is meaningful to him. This point is hammered home to me by Robbie one spring when we are on an exhibition tour of Florida.

The club is in training in Vero Beach. According to our plans, we will take a bus to Miami and then be driven in a motorcade to city hall, where they will receive the keys to the city. I make the arrangements, get a dozen convertibles, get members of the key club to act as drivers, and then drop by a sign painter's shop to arrange for placards to hang on the sides of the cars to identify the players.

To make things easier for the sign painter I leave him the Dodgers' roster with instructions to just copy the names off my list. At last the day of the parade arrives. Along come the Dodgers and the motorcade with the signs. Everything seems nice and neat until I notice the signs on two of the cars. They read: JACKIE ROBINSON, ROY CAMPANELLA, JOE BLACK, DON NEWCOMBE, JUNIOR GILLIAM. All of the black players are segregated into two convertibles as if the arrangement was planned by Jim Crow, himself.

I want to die when I see that. Jackie gets into the car, but you can tell he is mad. He sits there for a moment or two and then he gets out and mutters that he isn't going. He goes back into the clubhouse. Pee Wee Reese is a couple of cars away. But he gets out too and says that if Jackie isn't going, he isn't going either. Pee Wee goes back into the clubhouse.

Inside of a minute or two there are ten other ballplayers back in the clubhouse. Most of them don't know what is happening. All they know is that if Jackie isn't going, they aren't going either. It is a terrible thing and it is wonderful too. All these fellows refusing to go in the motorcade because Jackie isn't going. And it is my fault— mostly my fault, anyway. But I never dreamed that the sign painter would pick the names of the black players out of the roster and place them in one car on his own hook.

Now it looks as though the whole motorcade idea is going to be a giant fiasco. It is going to look bad, and it is going to look particularly terrible for me. I go over to Jackie and tell him, "Look, I'm partly responsible for this whole thing and I'm sorry as hell about it. But if you don't go it's going to hurt me badly."

Jackie doesn't hesitate after that. "Okay, I'll go," he says. Then he gets up and calls to the others, "C'mon, we're going for Irv." I don't have to tell you that Jackie is the most popular guy in the motorcade. Everybody comes over to him for his autograph—Southerners and Northerners—they all want to shake his hand. They go after Jackie nine to one over anybody else.

But that's not the thing. The point is that he showed me his greatness and goodness that day. He is badly hurt and stung, but—poof! just like that—he yields to an appeal by a little guy like me. For that I owe him an everlasting debt.

Right after the production is over I go back to the sign painter who got me into trouble in the first place and I ask him what makes him do a thing like that, painting all the black guys on two cars.

You know what he tells me, in all his Floridian ignorance and innocence? "Mister Rudd, I didn't want to create an incident."

= 9 =
Of Kings, Capers, and the "Joisey" Dodgers

Whenever there is a somber moment at Ebbets Field I always can count on any one of several characters to produce a timely laugh. One of them is Harold Burr, a crotchety but comic old guy who does a sports column for the *Brooklyn Daily Eagle*. Burr actually is a nice, warm person once you get to know him, and he has a needle-sharp wit. Once, Burr brings in a copy of the *Eagle* that carries a feature story about Gladys Goodding, the nice lady who plays the electric organ for every Dodgers' home game at Charlie Ebbets's old ballpark. Gladys is now in her eleventh year with the Dodgers, which is a milestone for any musician at any stadium. The

Irving Rudd and Stan Fischler

Eagle headline on Miss Goodding's story is "Gladys at Ebbets Organ for 11 Years." That afternoon Burr comes into the press box and holds up the paper, pointing at the headline and quips, "No wonder the poor man died!"

Another funny man is Tex Rickard, the fellow who handles Ebbets Field's PA system. Rickard has a congenital knack of taking simple sentences and making them complicated. He also knows how to make confusing things even *more* confusing.

One day I'm in the press box when I get a call from Tex, who is situated right next to the Dodgers' dugout. "Irving," says Rickard, "the Skipper [Walt Alston] wants to know who's pitching for the Cubs against Philadelphia today. Can you find that out?"

Sure I can. I go down the far end of the press box to the Western Union machine and I ask if they have any word of who is pitching in the Cub-Philly game. They tell me that Bob Rush is going for the Cubs.

Fine. I go back to my press box phone and ring up Rickard with the answer. The phone rings, Rickard picks it up downstairs, and I say, "Hello, Tex, it's Bob Rush."

Rickard comes back, like he is talking to a long-lost buddy, "Hello, Bob, how the hell are you!"

Tex has a million of them, some of them quite unexpected and some of them public, like the ones that actually come over the Ebbets Field PA system. One day a visiting team complains to the umpire about coats and jackets that are draped over the railing in the center field bleachers. The umpire walks over to Rickard and asks him to make an announcement over the PA system about the problem.

Rickard agrees, turns on the loudspeaker, and says, "Will the ladies and gentlemen in the center field bleachers please remove their clothing."

A few days later Tex goes one better when he attempts to find a parent whose child has drifted away from his seat. "Attention, ladies and gentlemen," Rickard solemnly intones, "a little boy has been found lost."

128

I always feel saddened that the average spectator is never privy to the kind of one-on-one humor that takes place on the ballfield between player and player, manager and umpire—or player and king.

One morning Jackie Robinson nearly gets me into a jam on a day at Ebbets Field when King Faisal II of Iraq decides he wants to see the Dodgers. His majesty arrives with very short notice and I am entrusted with showing him our baseball palace. To my surprise, I. Rudd from Brownsville does not get nervous at the sight of the king from the Middle East. I welcome him to Flatbush when he arrives. "Hello, Your Majesty. Come, let me escort you inside." I take him into the ballpark at about noon when the place is virtually empty, except for a slew of photographers and newsreel cameramen who are yelling, as only cameramen can, "All right, bring 'im over!"

My big muck-a-mucks—O'Malley, Buzzy Bavasi, Fresco Thompson—are not around. I'm the only "ranking" official of the Dodgers. I march over to the dugout to show the monarch where the players sit. The cameras, meanwhile, are rolling, and at this point, up the dugout steps climbs Jackie Robinson.

"Hey, Jackie!" I holler, "come over here. Say hello to the King of Iraq."

Robinson gives me a look like he thinks I'm half wise guy and half crazy. He doesn't realize that this *is* the legitimate bossman of a country thousands of miles away. Jackie thinks I've flipped. I make all kinds of not-so-subtle faces to persuade him that I am not kidding. Before anything embarrassing happens, Jackie gets the message and shakes hands with the little king, and the pair wind up doing a tape on Jackie's NBC radio show.

By the time the king gets through with Jackie we're the best of friends. "Your Majesty," I ask him, "what is your favorite sport?" Turns out that he loves cricket. "Your Majesty," I ask, "do you have a good googly ball?" That is a kind of dipsy-doodle pitch in cricket.

The king's eyes brighten at the mention of his googly ball. "Rather good," he says proudly, "rather good, you know."

King Faisal is a warm fellow, at that, and I am really saddened when I learn, a year later, that he has been assassinated.

Such serious moments are not the order of the day around Ebbets Field. Mostly it is laughs, like the manner in which little Don Hoak, our utility infielder, clowns with gargantuan Gil Hodges, who plays first for us, about Gil's size. They start off their "bout" with Hoak grabbing Hodges's immense hands—they look like gigantic hams—and saying, "You see these hands? They're registered with the police department as weapons." Then they move into the center of the clubhouse and start "boxing." The bout consists of Hodges sticking out his huge paw and covering Hoak's face with it until Don yells, "C'mon, Hodges, fight fair!" By this time the whole team—including Gil—is breaking up with laughter.

Among the many Dodgers who make my life a little more fun is our peerless center fielder and home-run hitter, Edwin "Duke" Snider. I like Snider—a lot. He not only is an outgoing, smiling kind of fellow, he has a nose for horses—a fact of life that I, unfortunately, learn one spring during training camp in Florida. Duke collars me in the hotel lobby and is in a big hurry, but not too big a rush to prevent him from pulling a fifty-dollar bill out of his pocket. Snider gives me the name of a horse, tells me "it's a sure thing," and asks me to hurry up and place the bet with Bing, the hotel's doorman-carhop.

I. Rudd is a nice Jewish boy who doesn't know from horses or courses. When the Duke gives me the money and the hot tip, I hustle over to Bing with absolutely no intention of doing any betting myself. "I gotta make a bet on a horse," I tell Bing.

"Why, sure, Mister Rudd," he says. So, he takes the money, thinking it is *my* bet. I don't give the matter a second thought until later that night, when I return to the McAllister. There is Bing, just returning to the front door after having parked a car. He looks up at me and grins, like I had just done something wonderful. (Well, I had—for the Duke.) Next thing I know Bing is counting out large amounts of money into a bundle. *Oy vay*, what I missed that day! "Hey, Mister Rudd," Bing yells over to me, "if you got any more horses like that, you tell Mister Bing, ya hear!"

Another grand pair of personalities are our Queens-born pitcher Billy Loes and a young writer from the same borough, Jimmy Breslin. Apart from being a hell of a good pitcher when he wants to be, Loes is also a character. His classic effort occurs in a World Series game against the Yankees. A grounder is hit back to the box and Loes blows it completely. After the game, reporters ask Billy how he can possibly have loused up an easy grounder. To which Billy replies, apparently in dead seriousness: "I lost it *in the sun!*"

Thus, Loes is the perfect magazine subject for Breslin, who calls me up and says he wants to pick my brain on Loes. I tell Jimmy to come up to the office, we'll talk a little there and then I'll bring him home and we'll talk some more. Remember, Breslin still is pretty much of a kid and doesn't have the reputation as a drinker that he later gets as a columnist.

These are the days when Lucky Strike cigarettes and Schaefer beer sponsor the Dodgers' games on radio and TV. As a result we get a carton of cigarettes and a case of beer as freebies from them each month. I have just brought my case of beer home, I feel safe about Breslin, so I phone my wife Gert and tell her that a young writer is coming over, and please put the beer in the refrigerator.

My Gert thinks she is dealing with a nice Jewish boy and puts three beers on ice, leaving the rest in the carton. (Breslin, she later learns, is not a nice Jewish boy.) We get to the house, unwind, and I say to Gert, "Please get some beer out." Gert opens a can and Breslin finishes it in about thirty seconds flat. Then the second and the third.

"Any more beer?" he asks, and poor Gert is horrified. We talk through the night, and don't you think Jimmy goes through my entire case of warm beer in my house while Gert remains paralyzed just looking at him.

Beer and booze affect guys in our business in different ways. We have a pretty good outfielder on our club named George Shuba, who is from Youngstown, an industrial city in Ohio. One day George and I are talking and Shuba pops up and tells me what he's going to do when he quits baseball. "Y'know, Irv," Shuba says, "the one thing I'll *never* do is open a gin mill."

This sounds a little strange to me. Ballplayers are always opening gin mills. Why, we even had one on Flatbush Avenue, a couple of blocks from Ebbets Field, called Hugh Casey's, which once was run by the Dodgers' famous relief pitcher. So, I ask George why he wouldn't want to run a bar of his own.

"Because," says Shuba, more serious than I've ever known him, "I don't want to be a ballplayer owning a gin mill in Youngstown, Ohio, on account of I don't want to see a hard-working guy from a steel mill who's busted his ass all week come into a place of mine and blow all his dough on gin and beer." True to his word, George Shuba winds up working for the post office and raising his kids as straight, ethical arrows.

Billy Loes epitomizes the daffiness of the Dodgers' personality. But as the years go by and the club gets better and better, we tend to get a little more serious, especially when we play the Yankees. Unforgettably serious is the afternoon when Don Larsen of the Yanks is pitching his perfect game in the 1956 World Series against us. The feat is unique in sporting history and the whole press box is rooting for Larsen with every pitch he makes on that fateful October 7. From the back of the press box I can see Roy Campanella coming to bat in a late inning. I break the press box silence and start to yell: "The hell with history, Roy, let's get on base and start something!"

He doesn't, and history is made that afternoon.

In retrospect such moments are always good for a laugh In fact, some of the funniest baseball stories that I tell on the rubber chicken circuit are about old-timers, such as Connie Mack, who runs the Philadelphia Athletics for so long that he becomes known as "the Grand Old Man of Baseball."

One time Mack pulls his great pitcher, Lefty Grove, out of a game at a time when Grove is certain that he still has good stuff. Grove is so beside himself with anger that he turns to Mack when he gets to the bench and says, "Fuck you, Mister Mack!" The old man turns to the pitcher. "Well, Robert, fuck you too!"

Mack has a wonderful sense of humor. I remember the time he has a first baseman named Ferris Fain. In this particular game the Athletics are in the field defending against a bases-loaded situation.

The batter drops a bunt down the first base line and Fain charges the ball, looking to nail the runner coming in from third. By the time Ferris gets the ball, the runner has crossed the plate, so he looks to third for a force there but he can't; then he pivots and looks to get the guy at second and sees he can't, and finally he goes to get the runner at first base and heaves the ball into right field over the pitcher, who has been covering the bag for him. Mack, naturally, is fit to be tied, and when the inning finally ends, he walks over to Fain and asks softly, "Ferris, what ever were you trying to do with that baseball?"

Frustrated up to here, Fain shoots back, "Mister Mack, what did you want me to do with the ball—stick it up my ass?"

To which Connie Mack replies, "Well, Ferris, it would have been a lot safer there, a lot safer!"

Another story I like to tell, especially at synagogues and Jewish center gatherings, is the "inside story" about how I wound up with the Dodgers.

O'Malley has become the boss of the Brooklyn Bums, and he wants to hire some Jews in the front office on account of the Dodgers having a reputation as an organization that is much too gentile dominated.

With that in mind, O'Malley hires Lee Scott to the staff. Lee is a nice man with flashing white teeth and a dark moustache who has been a fairly talented Brooklyn newspaperman. Anyhow, it is one of the few times O'Malley is faked out, because on Ash Wednesday don't you think Lee Scott is wearing a big ash cross on his forehead!

At first O'Malley figures Scott for a sycophant Jew who is trying to please the gentile boss. When O'Malley sees Scott he stops him and says, "What are you doing *that* for? You don't have to do that to please me!" O'Malley figures that Scott is kissing ass by wearing the ash on Ash Wednesday. That's when Lee tells him that he is Italian and his real name is something like Scottorigio.

Not long after that, Frank Graham, Jr., is promoted from executive secretary of the Brooklyn Amateur Baseball Federation to the Dodgers' promotional staff, so I call up Harold Parrott, who is the chief press agent with the ball club at the time, and ask him to recommend me for Graham's old job. A few weeks later O'Malley has his first real Jew on the staff, at a salary of $5,000.

The O frequently generates debates among the serfs at 215 Montague Street. One endless topic of debate is who is the more frugal boss, Branch Rickey, who preceded O'Malley, or The O himself. The consensus has it that Rickey gets the nod—but only by a few pennies.

O'Malley has a very firm policy on players' salaries, and he transmits it through his chief paymaster and loyal general manager, E. J. "Buzzie" Bavasi. It is O'Malley's *order* that Jackie Robinson *always* be the highest-paid Dodger— $1,000 more than whoever was runner-up. According to Buzzie, who is the man who knows, Robbie's highest salary is $39,000, which in 1953 is one hell of a lot of money, especially since we are playing in a bandbox of a ballpark.

It is Bavasi's job to keep the salaries down, and he does it with a mixture of savvy and humor. After Don

Newcombe wins twenty-seven games for the Brooks in 1956, he asks Bavasi for $35,000. "Look," Bavasi reasons, "if you get thirty five thousand, everybody will expect you to win twenty-seven games again."

Newk mulls it over and, like he suddenly sees the light, says, "Y'know, Buzzie, yer right!"

As hard-nosed as he is, Bavasi is stunned to the very core one day when our fine pitcher Joe Black approaches him early in 1953. Joe was named National League Rookie of the Year in 1952 and Bavasi decides to hike his salary from the minimum $5,000 up to $12,000. "That's too much," says Black. "I'm not worth that much."

Buzzie almost faints on the spot. "Yes," he insists, "you *are* worth that much."

Pee Wee Reese—the guy Buzzie figures *is* the most valuable Dodger—is another who never realizes his value to the club. "Pee Wee," says Buzzie, "is a patsy." It was the same with our superb catcher Roy Campanella.

"Roy," says Bavasi, "never knows what he's making, because he's always spending it. One day he buys a home for thirty-six thousand bucks and a boat for thirty-seven thousand on the same day. The thing is, Roy is only making thirty-two thousand!"

Another funny-with-money character is Johnny Podres, the kid from the Adirondack Mountains of New York State who pitches and wins the seventh game of the World Series in October 1955, bringing Brooklyn its first, and only world championship. Bavasi finds Podres as naive about finances as Black, if not more so.

One day Buzzie explains the Podres theory on fiscal affairs. "All Podres wants," says Buzzie, "is enough cash to play a few horses. He'll call me with a tip and I'll tell him to put a hundred bucks on it for me. He'll call back and say, 'We got beat by a nose,' but he'll never tell me the names of the horses. Once he calls me with a nine-to-one shot, but when I tell him to bet a hundred for me he says, 'Why don't you bet the two hundred you owe me?' I tell him all right, and when he calls back he says, 'It went off at fourteen-to-one but we just got beat at the wire.' I still don't know the name of that other horse either."

In many ways, Buzzie turns out to be one of the most important people in Brooklyn history. Bavasi is the guy who convinces The O to hire Walter Alston as the Dodgers' manager, and Alston is the guy who brings us our first World Series win. "Walter's trick is simple enough," says Buzzie. "He is fair, patient, and generous; he always gives the players the benefit of the doubt."

It proves to be the case in the year 1955, which turns out to be one of the most memorable of my life.

By this time Walter Alston is in his second year as leader of the Brooks, and he has a fine team: Jackie Robinson, Gil Hodges, George "Shotgun" Shuba, Roy Campanella, and a great pitching staff headed by Don Newcombe. This year we win the pennant going away. It all comes down once again to the World Series against our regular rivals from the Bronx, the Yankees. After six games the series is tied at three each.

There are some great games I never got to see the end of, except on TV, because I am down in the dressing room working. It's the top of the ninth and I'm already winding my way down to the Dodgers' locker room, because win or lose, the TV and newspaper people will be there for interviews and I have to get things ready. We're all in the room watching the game on TV and there it is, Gil Hodges catching the ball for the last out and the first-ever world championship in the history of Brooklyn baseball.

Bedlam erupts in the locker room as the players come in splashing champagne on everyone and everything. The word of the win spreads fast, and it doesn't take long before everyone in Brooklyn knows—everyone except Gil Hodges, Jr. When Gil gets to his house on Avenue K in Brooklyn after the game, little Gil comes up to his father and says, "Daddy! Where have you been? You missed half of 'Howdy Doody' today."

All of Brooklyn is as high as a kite over the win. Only O'Malley could burst the bubble.

The city of Jersey City, New Jersey, is just across the Holland Tunnel, under the Hudson River, maybe a half hour and five miles from downtown Brooklyn. But in 1955, "Joisey" City, as any Brooklynite usually calls it, might as well be located somewhere between Anaheim and Azuza, California. We don't know it at the time, but our leader, Walter O'Malley, is quietly humming a chorus of "California, Here I Come!" And then one day late in 1955, Irving Rudd discovers himself whistling a few bars of "Jersey City, Here *I* Come!" and it is all because of California.

After we finally win the World Series in October 1955, I find out that O'Malley is getting more and more unhappy with life at Ebbets Field. There are a couple of theories on this: One is that he perceives how the black population of Brooklyn is rising and that many whites are leaving the borough for Long Island. It so happens that, geographically, Ebbets Field is in the direct line of the black movement, southward from Bedford-Stuyvesant (one of the biggest concentrations of blacks in the world) across Fulton Street, then the hub of the black community, to Eastern Parkway in Crown Heights, and finally to Empire Boulevard and Flatbush, where the ballpark is situated. More and more black people are showing up at the games, and the feeling is, O'Malley figures, more and more whites will stay away because of the blacks showing up. This theory does not necessarily make O'Malley an out-and-out racist, but you can get that impression, listening to those who believe it. I am not one of them.

Another theory has it that "Ooom," as some of the Dodgers' front office people now call him, is just being his own crafty self and realizes he might be able to squeeze some money—like a few million—out of New York City by getting Mayor Wagner to build a new ballpark for the Dodgers. Ebbets Field, for all its virtues, is getting on in years, there are no parking facilities, the club is the world champs and deserves the best. Surely New York City can do something about it—like maybe build a new stadium in downtown Brooklyn, near the Long Island Railroad station (that way O'Malley can get all the affluent whites from Nassau and Suffolk counties to come in) and rehabilitate the Flatbush Avenue shopping area at the same time.

One way to get Wagner and the rest of the city fathers to approve such an idea is to put a gun to their heads. The gun is marked "Jersey City."

Late in 1955 O'Malley announces that the Brooklyn Dodgers will play seven National League games and an exhibition at Roosevelt Stadium in Jersey City. A cynic doesn't have to hear any more. Today Jersey City, tomorrow (the other part of) the world! California.

I. Rudd is both terribly worried and terribly happy. I am worried because (a) I don't want the Dodgers to move, and (b) I believe they might, and, finally, (c) I like Brooklyn better than California.

On the other hand I am tickled, because Jersey City is a hell of an opportunity for me. On December 12, 1955, O'Malley moves me into a one-room office in the Hotel Plaza, Journal Square, Jersey City. Thus I become the first and only general manager of a major league baseball team in the history of the great state of New Jersey. Of course, if you take into account the fact that the Dodgers are playing only seven of their regularly scheduled seventy-seven home games at Roosevelt Field, I guess this makes me the one-eleventh general manager of the Dodgers.

At this point the only things I know about Jersey City are that it is the first big stop on the Hudson Tubes going to Newark and it has one of the most colorful (and corrupt) Democratic machines this side of Boston or Chicago, made infamous by former mayor Frank Hague. I have to learn fast, and in order to survive, I do.

The first thing I learn is that Jersey City *is* as political a town as I thought it was. Shortly after I put my shingle up at the Hotel Plaza, a girl walks in and says she wants to be my secretary. Well, that is fine and dandy. I need a secretary (although I always prefer to choose my own), and I am quite willing to hear about her qualifications. But the first thing she tells me about her qualifications is that her father is a Democratic clubhouse captain.

That won't make the interview a tragedy if she can show me something in the way of intelligence. But her idea of spelling cat is k-a-t-e, she has no idea what a semicolon is all about, and her typing is so excruciatingly terrible that I decide to hold on to a specimen just in case anyone gets back to me and asks why I told her, "Don't call me; I'll call you!"

Other than that encounter, Jersey City turns out to be a pleasant experience, if not Utopia-on-the-Hudson. There are a lot of good people in the town, a good restaurant run by a fellow named Bruno Valeo, and a damn good ballpark for our eight games.

They know their baseball over in Jersey City, only it is Giants baseball or New York Yankees baseball. The Dodgers? They could be part of the Keystone Kops act the way they are treated.

I realize what a job I am going to have promoting the Dodgers the day we have a "booster rally" for the club at a local armory and the mayor of Jersey City brings along his young son—dressed in a Yankees' uniform. No matter, I can't let The O down. He has not only named me business manager but in the Dodgers' newsletter, with a big photo of I. Rudd, the boss touts me as an "irrepressible promotion man." So, as they say on Pitkin Avenue, I have to "irrepress."

The goal is simple enough: get people into "Joisey" Dodgers games. It takes a lot of planning, and mostly I'm doing it single-handedly, with a little help from the city fathers. The first of our eight games at Roosevelt Stadium is on Thursday, April 19, against the Philadelphia Phillies.

I want to get my best shot in for the opener, so I call

up the famous Brooklyn comedian Phil Foster and he says he'll do a freebie for me. Then I call New Jersey's governor, Robert Meyner, and he agrees to make an appearance. So does the Dodgers Sym-Phony Band.

Meanwhile, I'm fighting another battle on another front—O'Malley's office. At this point I know for a fact that the Dodgers are the richest team in big league ball. They are making more money than even the Yankees. So I decide to petition The O for a living wage. Prices are going up all the time, and feeding the family is getting tougher and tougher on a salary of $5,800 a year.

I send the boss a memo and then hold my breath. I ask for a thousand-dollar-a-year raise, up to $6,800. I know that the success or failure of my request depends on the Jersey City promotion.

Now, to promote. Right off the bat I get a couple of breaks. During our first rally at the Jersey City Armory in February 1956, a guy comes up to me and says, "Hey, you wanna meet Willie Mays?"

Naturally, I take him for a wiseacre and want to tell him to get lost, except I am still new in town and my job isn't to get people mad. "Okay," I say, "introduce me to Willie Mays!" Next thing I know the guy walks over to me with a little black kid on his arm, and sure enough, the kid's name *is* Willie Mays. I ask him for his address and phone number.

A day later a clean-cut kid walks into my office and says he's from a prep school and wants to borrow our World Series film to show at St. Whatever School. "Fine," I say, "but do you have a letter from your principal?" The kid gives me the letter and I give him the film and ask that he sign the receipt.

I look at his signature and nearly fall over backward in my chair. The kid's name is Bill Rigney, like Bill Rigney of the New York Giants!

"Is that your real name?" I ask, knowing damn well

that Bill Rigney happens to be the Giants'—and Willie Mays's—manager.

The kid tells me that he *is* Bill Rigney and how he gets kidded about his name all the time. I wave him good-bye and suddenly realize that I have a publicity bonanza in my hands—my first two ticket customers are Bill Rigney and Willie Mays; a billion-to-one shot falls into I. Rudd's lap.

This is followed by another long shot, courtesy of our master-dealer, Buzzie Bavasi. He does the impossible and brings the hated Sal Maglie from Cleveland to the Dodgers. The Giants fans in Jersey City—who loved Sal when he lived at the Polo Grounds—will go for that.

I am pleased with our turnstile count, but I am less than doing cartwheels over O'Malley's attitude toward me. He already has called me in the middle of the night to thank me for the crowds in Jersey City, at which point I remind him of the Rudd memo requesting a thousand-dollar raise. The O's response is forever etched in my mind: "Irving . . . I *don't* like to be pushed. . . ."

Whatever happens in Jersey City, I know the hand-writing is on the wall as far as my future with the Dodgers is concerned. Not that I'm about to quit. Jersey City is an exciting experience. What is even more exciting, in a perverse way, is trying to determine what The O plans to do with the team—keep it in Brooklyn or move it to Los Angeles, as the rumors suggest.

Personally, I'm convinced that the boss doesn't want to go to California, if he can get a good deal in Brooklyn. And he figures he can squeeze a bargain out of Wagner that will give him enough reason to stay. For a while it looks like there might be a solution when New York's notorious power broker, Robert Moses, offers O'Malley what now is Shea Stadium in Flushing, Queens, home of the Mets. O'Malley says that that would be just fine, providing the ballpark *belongs to him.*

Wagner and Abe Stark, the president of the city council, are afraid to go along with the deal, figuring that if they do, they will both wind up in the slammer. They nix the deal and now O'Malley looks in earnest at California. It is The O's good fortune that Los Angeles has a hockey puck for a mayor named Norris Poulson.

Poulson wants the Dodgers to come to Los Angeles so badly he is willing to sell out the city if he can swing the deal. The boss still is reluctant to leave New York, figuring that Wagner soon will knuckle under to the fan pressure to keep the Dodgers in town. Meanwhile, Poulson makes his overtures and The O responds with an impossible laundry list of demands. One of O'Malley's far-out demands is that Los Angeles *give* O'Malley the Chavez Ravine property as a gift for coming west. The O figures that such an outrageous demand will force Poulson to go away, and then O'Malley will hammer out some sort of an agreement with New York City.

But Poulson doesn't go away. Instead he says to O'Malley, "You want Chavez Ravine? You got it!"

How can a tough, money-mad man like O'Malley say no to an offer like that? All of his exaggerated demands are accepted without a whimper. He pulls off one of the greatest business coups since the Dutch bought Manhattan Island from the Indians for $24.

Now I am convinced the ball game is over for both Brooklyn and I. Rudd. The Dodgers (we hear from insiders at Montague Street) are going to leave New York City. Here we live and die with the guys. Brooklyn is a state of mind, not a place. It is our team, our game, and, we figure, our rights are being violated. It is the richest team in the majors and still The O is going to pull up stakes in the city.

By Hanukkah 1956 I know the show is over for me. I just have to tie up the loose ends. On February 16, 1957, the *Brooklyn Eagle* runs a four-paragraph story with the following headline that says it all: "Rudd Resigns as Dodgers' Publicity Man."

Part III

= 10 =
Hot to Trot

The separation between I. Rudd and the Brooklyn–Los Angeles Dodgers is amicable but painful. I love the guys—Pee Wee Reese, Duke Snider, and, in a rather perverse way, even O'Malley. But the idea of leaving Brooklyn for Los Angeles doesn't appeal to me until I suddenly realize that not only am I out of a team, I am out of a job.

I second-guess myself for a few days and then start checking the help-wanted columns in earnest. I don't have to wait long. A pal phones and tells me he needs a good press agent badly. I know I am a good press agent but I don't know whether I want what this fellow has to offer—

a job as publicity man for the Balmoral Hotel near Miami Beach, Florida. But the dough is so good it would make even The O blink, and Gert and me figure we'll try the moon over Miami on for size and give it a whirl.

For I. Rudd, working the hotel racket is like Henry Kissinger becoming a tennis pro; like I am really a herring out of the H_2O. The sun is great, the palm trees sway, just as they say in the songs, and yes, there is a moon over Miami. But it ain't sports, and sports is where I want to be.

The thing is, when I think sports I think of boxing, baseball, or if I'm really hard up, basketball or football. The one sport I don't think about in 1957 is horse racing. In my whole life I have been to the racetrack a grand total of six times. I do not know a fetlock from a furlong, and it is safe to say that I am not too hot to trot when a fellow named Lewis Burton visits me at the Balmoral one afternoon in May 1957.

Burton is living proof that people who leave the newspaper business get rich quicker than the guys who stay. Lew progresses from two-fingered columnist at the New York *Journal-American* to a fat-paying job as PR man for Yonkers Raceway, a popular trotting track just north of New York City. When he is a newspaper guy Burton impresses me as bright and innovative. As a PR executive he impresses me in another way; Burton is merely a millionaire.

When he comes to see me, Burton is recovering from a heart attack. (After working at Yonkers, later I can understand why.) Lew and me have known each other for a long time, so there is plenty of small talk to dispense with before he gets to the point.

"Irving, how would you like to come back to sports?"

On hearing that, I feel like a pinball that just bounced off a spring. Trying to hide a gulp of delight, I tell Burton I'm interested. He tells me there might be a job for me at Yonkers as one of the track's press agents. "You keep in touch," he says, "and I'll keep in touch and we'll see what happens."

What happens is that we correspond on and off for five months. One night I get home from the fights at Miami Beach Auditorium when I see a message from Gert: "Call Burton." The pinball spring is working again. I get on the blower and hear what I want to hear: "Irving, I want you to come to New York. The job is yours—except for one thing. You gotta meet Marty Tananbaum first."

"You mean I still might blow it?"

"No, no, Irving. But I gotta be sure the chemistry clicks between you and Marty. Understand?"

Not really. I have no idea what manner of tribal triumvirate I am getting into, what with the Clan Tananbaum. Besides Marty, the boss of Yonkers Raceway, there is to be brother Stanley and brother Al, their wives, and their friends. It is a group that would test the mettle of the Marx Brothers, the Ritz Brothers, *and* the Three Stooges. Very close to the inner circle are two other characters, Louis Kantrowitz and Sidney Roth, who between them could keep the aspirin industry in business for a million more years.

I arrange with Burton to fly up to New York and finally meet the next Great Man, Marty Tananbaum. Burton is worried about chemistry, but I can tell that it is impossible for a Tananbaum and a Rudd *not* to hit it off, and I am right. Marty hires me; I give my two weeks notice to the Balmoral and return to my homeland, New York, to learn the racing business. I am also relearning the people business. I realize that baseball people and racing people are not alike. At first I lean toward the former.

Right away I find one major hitch in the job: even though I am going to be publicizing Yonkers Raceway, the place is closed. A major reconstruction is taking place and it won't be ready for actual racing until August 1958. In a sense this is good, because it gives me a chance to get a feel for the place and some of the characters and intrigue involved.

By this time Burton was ailing and the "publicity director" is now a guy named Lou Niss, who once had been the sports editor of the *Brooklyn Eagle*. Peter Lorre should have played Niss. He is full of intrigue and, from day one, informs me about plots and counterplots within the high command. Don't trust this guy and don't trust that guy is his theme. I keep waiting for him to say, And don't trust Lou Niss.

Niss, I soon discover, is small potatoes on the pain parade compared with Sid Roth. Almost from the start Roth goes after my ass, and my survival instinct tells me that I must stand up to him if I am to last at the track.

Our first decisive battle occurs at a meeting between M. Tananbaum, myself, Roth, Niss, and Burton. We're working over promotion ideas to tie in with Alaska becoming the forty-ninth state. Burton wants to buy one thousand forty-nine-star flags and distribute them to anyone at a betting window when the closing bell for each race rings. I tell Burton that this could get us in trouble if the people who don't get flags start beefing that the bell rang too early or late. "We'll have fistfights," I warn.

Burton agrees. With that I tell them my idea: give the flags to every schoolroom in Yonkers, courtesy of the track. Burton smiles and I feel good for about half a second, when Roth pipes up: "If that isn't the dumbest fucking idea I ever heard!"

I shoot right back: "Who the hell made you a publicity expert?"

Roth reaches into his pocket and yanks out a wad of bills that could choke a horse. "*This* is what makes me an expert!"

To that I ask, "Sid, what are you worth—a million?"

"Could be."

"Look, Sidney," I snap back. "I am going to tell you

what to do with your million. Take all those dollars, one bill at a time, and shove them up your ass."

Out of the corner of my eye I can see Tananbaum bring his handkerchief up to his face. He is reveling in my blast at the supposedly almighty Roth. With that, Roth shuts up, Tananbaum smiles, and I. Rudd realizes he has won the first and most important round at Yonkers Raceway. It now is clear that Marty not only likes me, he will pay attention to what I have to say in the future. Strategically and physically it is good to have *any* Tananbaum on your side. They are, I realize immediately, a very volatile bunch. Once, during a board meeting, Marty, Stanley, and Al have a disagreement. They each rip a telephone off the wall and brandish them at each other's heads before cooler heads prevail.

The Roth-Rudd episode makes it clear that if I am going to save my job I must produce enough gimmicks to get us ink. Before the track actually reopens, my aim is to publicize construction of the new grandstand and clubhouse. To that extent, everything works out well.

Bill Roeder of the *New York World-Telegram* does a feature on operating a crane that is putting up parts of the grandstand. Dick Young of the *New York Daily News* writes a column on touring the track site while flying over it in a helicopter. But from the press agent's viewpoint, the big prize always is *The New York Times*, and I come through on those hallowed sheets when Bill Conklin runs a story about how he "dined" on a stone slab in the middle of the uncompleted clubhouse.

The best stunt of all is yet to come. It is June 1958 and the horses are just arriving at the track. Everything is shaping up and we can see completion ahead of us. The time has come to erect the gigantic "Yonkers Raceway" sign on the side of the grandstand, which will be visible to the hundreds of motorists who pass by on the New York State Thruway every few minutes. They're putting the huge letters up on the eighty-foot sign when suddenly I get this flash. I ask one of the workers, "Can you change the letters around?" "Sure," he says. That's when I make my move. Next day, people driving down the Deegan see the biggest misspelling in the world: YONKERS RACEWYA.

Oy vay, did we get calls. "Don't you idiots know how to spell Raceway?" While they're yelling and screaming, we're getting ink like you wouldn't believe. The deliberate misspelling becomes an instant hit all over the country. Wire service photos give us coverage and everyone from the *Times* to the *Toonerville Tribune* writes up the phony faux pas.

Such triumphs are all the more important considering our greater war with the enemy-that-shouldn't-be-the-foe, Roosevelt Raceway. One of the first facts of life I learn at Yonkers is that Roosevelt is to Yonkers what Syria is to Israel.

At first I am naive about such matters. It seems to me that the two trotting tracks—they are in Nassau (Long Island) and we are in distant Westchester—have so much in common that we should pull together for the good of harness racing. That, however, is tooth-fairy stuff. The reality is that we are at war, and my very special enemy sniper is one weasel-like character named Joey Goldstein. He answers to a bigger boss, who reminds me of Sidney Greenstreet, one Nick Grande.

Working against this duet is like nothing I have ever experienced before. In the baseball business our common enemies were the Giants and the Yankees. But that, fortunately, was more on the field that anything else. Our relationship with the front office guys was always very friendly and aboveboard. Yet I immediately learn that in the Yonkers-Roosevelt war, sabotage is the order of the day.

The first inkling I get that I am being sabotaged by Goldstein (Roosevelt) comes on a visit to the *Daily News*, where I am hustling some Yonkers photos. Working for the Dodgers, I never had to go to the papers because the papers always come to us. But the trotters are not in the same class as big league baseball teams. I have to hustle for my client by actually knocking at editors' doors. In this case the editor is one J. Howard Knapp, who runs the *News* photo department and, as such, can make or break a press agent simply by using or rejecting a publicity guy's pictures.

I have known Knapp for many years and find him a surprisingly civil guy, considering his position of power. The word in our business is that Knapp is so temperate that he wouldn't say shit even if he had a mouth full of it. Upon entering his office, I feel more comfortable than I do in more alien territory.

Knapp nods at me and I notice it is less than a friendly greeting. Next thing I know he asks me if I know Joey Goldstein. I say sure. Then Knapp stuns me with a comeback: "Y'know, Irving, anyone who can't get along with Joey Goldstein can't get along with anybody."

Now I'm really worried. Knapp is supposed to be my pal; I'm wondering what Goldstein is pulling on me. I leave the photos with Knapp and return to Yonkers, where I meet Marty Glickman, our announcer, a sweetheart of a guy who has been in the sports broadcasting business for years. Maybe Glickman can clear the air for me. "Marty," I ask, "when I went up to the *News* I was sized up like some kind of monster. Knapp asked me about Joey Goldstein as if someone already had put the zinger into me."

Glickman smiles wryly. "Irving, welcome aboard; you are now really working for Yonkers Raceway."

The message is as explicit as it is implicit. As long as I work for Yonkers, I have to expect all forms of guerrilla retaliation from the gang at Roosevelt Raceway. There will never be peace with Joey Goldstein. It is me against him, Yonkers against Roosevelt.

As wars go, Yonkers is not in a favorable position.

Grande and Goldstein have a much bigger budget than we do. That means they can be freer doling out gifts to newsmen who are on the take. The Tananbaums are willing to spend money, but not nearly as much, and Marty Tananbaum has a distorted idea that if he gives a writer a gift, he automatically owns the writer.

This buy-'em philosophy is all pervasive with the Family Tananbaum. One day Al Tananbaum is sitting in the Yonkers clubhouse with his wife when a photographer from the *News* comes in and starts shooting pictures. Al calls the guy over as if the photographer works for *him* and not the newspaper. He demands that the guys take a photo of his wife at the clubhouse table. "If you don't," snaps Al, "I'll fire Rudd!"

The photographer, an old-timer named Billy Klein, isn't going to take any of Al Tananbaum's crap. Billy blows his stack and warns Al that he'll go to his managing editor and let him know what a jerk Tananbaum is. After Klein cools off and walks away, Al calls me over. "Irv," he says, "buy the guy a drink."

Instead of having the decency to apologize, Al figures he can buy him off with a drink—via me. This is typical Tananbaum thinking, and it doesn't take long for it to get around the newspaper business. Yes, the Tananbaums have clout, but they use it like a boomerang and it inevitably returns and bops them in the head.

The perfect—or imperfect, as the case may be—example is Marty's relationship with the *New York Daily Mirror*. At the time, the *Mirror* is a flourishing Hearst tabloid in New York City. Dan Parker is sports editor and columnist and one of the few crusading sportswriters around.

One day word filters up to us that Parker is writing a column ridiculing Marty Tananbaum and his brother Al. Marty gets wind of it and calls his pal Charlie McCabe, who just happens to be the publisher of the *Mirror* and, therefore, Parker's boss. Tananbaum urges McCabe to overrule Parker and kill the column.

Now that takes a big pair of balls on Marty's part, but he's got one of the biggest pairs I've seen, and damned if McCabe doesn't agree and the column *is* killed. It is, however, a Pyrrhic victory, because by enraging Parker, Marty has enraged an important man in the New York media.

Such shenanigans don't make my job any easier; nor does the limited prestige of harness racing among the various editors. When it comes to doing a feature on the trots there is always one problem: you cannot interview a horse. With Yonkers there is an additional problem: the Tananbaums.

They are like a lighted match to gasoline. If they are not taking a rap at a newspaperman, they are getting locked in a stockholders' suit. Meanwhile, I am trying to get them ink, and I finally persuade the *Sunday News* magazine to run a big photo layout, in color, of Yonkers Raceway. The *News* goes ahead with the story. The pictures are taken, the type is set, and the story is sitting in the editorial office ready to go.

I am feeling very good about it until I get a call from the photo editor. "Sorry," he says, "we can't use the Yonkers stuff."

"How come?"

"Somebody just told me that there's an investigation going on over the construction of Yonkers," the fellow explains. "Sorry about that."

It doesn't take me very long to figure out where he learned about this "investigation." The initials of the guy who told him are J. G., as in Joey Goldstein.

Like the Hundred Years War, the conflict between Yonkers and Roosevelt never ends. Victories—and they do come from time to time—are short-lived, short-circuited by some kind of clever counterattack.

One of the most damaging attacks ever launched by Goldstein involves one of Yonkers' biggest coups. In 1960 we hope to top Roosevelt by bringing in a superb New

Zealand horse named Caduceus. Sure enough, we get the horse and a hell of a lot of publicity. This infuriates Goldstein and Grande. So what do they do? They fly a bunch of officials and press people to Moscow, ostensibly for Soviet horses, and steal a lot of our space and newfound thunder. They never did get any Soviet horses to race at Roosevelt.

That isn't half as bad as another blow Roosevelt levels at us in 1964 when we sign Cardigan Bay, a terrific horse that we have been trying to get for two years. Now, we get him in Australia, getting ready to bring him back for the biggest bonanza Yonkers has come up with in its history. Then one day, while we still are in Melbourne, we get a call from our people in New York. They tell us that there's a story in the *Daily News* that Cardigan Bay's first start is going to be at Roosevelt Raceway.

We know for a fact that this is impossible, but Goldstein and Grande are determined to take the fuzz off our peach right away. Here we pull off the greatest coup in horse signing in twenty years and the paper says the horse will start at Roosevelt, not Yonkers.

Cardigan Bay does start at Yonkers, but Goldstein's land mine already has exploded in our faces and we have no choice but to remove the shrapnel and look ahead to the next battle—on the road to the U.S.S.R.

═ 11 ═
To Russia—
with Lox!

At the start of the 1960s the idea of bringing trotters from the Soviet Union to the United States is comparable to the notion of importing geldings from Venus or Mars. But in an era when men are flying in spaceships and the moon becomes an eventual vacation retreat just like Miami Beach, Russia suddenly turns into a possible source of racing talent for American tracks. Not only do we realize that fact of trotting life at Yonkers but our sworn foe across the county line in Long Island is aware of that delicious possibility too.

Inevitably, Joey Goldstein and his czar, Nick Grande, intercept our brainwaves and take a planeload of newspapermen to Russia. Goldstein's angle is that Roosevelt is getting a leg up on signing Soviet horses to race in the States. It is good copy and makes for lots of columns and headlines. It also makes Marty Tananbaum mad. Compounding the problem is our conviction that they have absolutely no chance of signing Russian horses. We are right. They get ink but no Soviet trotters.

What they do is get I. Rudd's head spinning. Sure, Russian horses coming to the United States would be a terrific promotion plus. Marty and I agree that a Yonkers expeditionary force must be organized to land on the steppes of the Soviet Union. The question is, how do I swing the miracle? I explore some ideas but none pan out, and I am beginning to fear that I'll never get to Russia— with or without lox—and bring back some horses.

At last, in 1962, the break comes. I am in Paris on trotting business when I meet one of France's leading racing writers, a guy named Roger Nataf. We get to talking about the Russians and he tells me that the Soviets have raced some horses in Paris recently. "You should bring those Soviet horses to Yonkers," Roger tells me. "When the Russians were in Paris, Irving, it was a cold January day, but you have no idea how large the crowds were to see them. We couldn't find enough seats for all the people."

If I needed any convincing that I *had* to land the Russians, Roger's conversation does it. When I get back to Yonkers I tell Marty about my talk with Roger and how well the Russians have drawn crowds in Paris. I figure he'll be enthused.

"Irving," he rages, "you blew it! You should have gotten on the phone right away and invited them!"

Oy vay. How do I explain to Tananbaum that you don't snap your fingers and bring the Russians galloping to Yonkers. "The Russians are mysterious," I tell Marty, "and hard to penetrate. I need time to make it work."

Grudgingly, Marty agrees, so I decide to keep my eyes

and ears open for all possibilities. In January 1963 I notice an article in *Life* magazine about a couple of photographers who are allowed into Soviet Mongolia.

"*Mazel tov*," I shout. A letter from the publisher precedes the article, telling how a big travel agent in New York City helped get the photographers beyond the Soviet travel barrier. "Listen," I say to no one in particular, "if he can do it for them he can do it for us."

I phone Gabriel Reiner at the Cosmos Travel Agency and tell him of my plan. Reiner has me meet one Nicholai Reznichenko, an enthusiastic horseman and first secretary to the Soviet Embassy in Washington. "He," says Reiner confidently, "can make it work."

After sending off a letter to Reznichenko, I get a call back from the Russian, asking me to meet him at the Soviet Mission on East Sixty-third Street in Manhattan. This is the first time I will actually be face-to-face with any citizen of the Soviet Union on a business deal, so I am more than a little nervous as I approach the huge apartment building across the street, ironically, from a shul on the Upper East Side of New York.

"Irving Rudd here," I announce to the security and nonsecurity types who fill the mission lobby. "I am here to see Mister Reznichenko."

After a reasonable pause, a short, sandy-haired gentleman arrives. It is Reznichenko himself. He speaks English with a heavily salted Russian accent, and he escorts me to a posh restaurant, Le Voisin, which is just a few blocks away. Already I can tell that the man has good taste.

Apparently my paranoia is surfacing, because I eye Reznichenko like a CIA operative instead of a racing press agent. Although I don't mean to do it, I notice how he removes his glasses to look at the menu. I spend the first half hour sizing him up. The ice finally breaks when I tell him that I have just read Harrison Salisbury's *900 Days* and how I am impressed with the Soviet citizens and soldiers for having lived through the three-year Nazi siege of Leningrad during World War II. *Now* it is time for business, so I lay out Yonkers' proposal for bringing Soviet horses to the States.

We will pay transportation for the horses and the men and guarantee $25 per diem. We will extend racetrack and dining privileges and extend the same courtesies as we do for all our guests—that is, give them Broadway show tickets, sightseeing trips, anything they want.

With that Reznichenko tells me that I have to strengthen the muscles in my typing fingers. "Comrade, you are going to have to write lots of letters. Lots."

So I write. I write to a man named Matskevitch and another named Georgei Petrov, the minister and deputy minister of agriculture in the Soviet Union. Then I have to write the same letter to Ambassador Anatoly Dobrynin at the Soviet Embassy in Washington. After that, all I can do is wait.

Finally the coveted call comes in from my buddy, Reznichenko. "If you please," he says, "come to Washington. I want you should meet Dobrynin and some agricultural counselors."

Who could resist an offer like that? I fly to Washington and meet Dobrynin. He wants to know what I have in mind, and I tell him. While I'm talking, they have copies of my letter in front of them. They peruse it, point by point, as I go on. When I get finished they ask a few questions. Then, with my letter in his hand, one of the Russians rises from his seat and says, "Would you please, Mister Rudd, write us a letter."

I nearly fall over in a dead faint. "A letter? About what?"

He doesn't blink an eyelash. "About what you want to do with the horses."

Now I'm wondering whether I'm being cast as the marble in a game of Russian roulette. Or is this a Soviet

replay of *Catch-22*? What can I do? You want another letter, Dobrynin, you'll get another letter.

I return to my office and dispatch the same letter,
word for word, that they read when I appeared for my
first interrogation. "I don't know what this is all about," I
tell an impatient Tananbaum, "but I'm doing exactly what
they're telling me."

The Soviets don't tell me how long I will have to wait,
but I have no choice. It is now Dobrynin's move, or maybe
Reznichenko's. I wait. Winter comes and goes and now it
is spring, and I'm still waiting. Tananbaum has taken off
for Sweden, where he is working on some kind of elec-
tronics deal, and I'm alone in the office one afternoon
when the phone rings. It is Reznichenko.

"Irving Rudd," announces my trotting comrade, "the
horses are coming!"

Before I can ask, What? When? he goes on: "They left
Moscow today. If you please, be ready to receive them."

I am so confused by the avalanche of news that I beg
Reznichenko for time to clear the daze in my head. I say I
will call back in a few minutes.

Could it be that I am succeeding at last, or is this more
Soviet confusion? I don't have to wait for an answer; the
phone rings again, and this time it's the State Department. "What do you know about three Russian horses
coming to the United States?" somebody on the other end
of the blower asks me.

I explain and ask them to give me the number of the
American Embassy in Moscow. The guy gives it to me,
and now I know I have my work cut out for me. The Soviets have, in fact, come through, but I realize that they
also have, typically, done things *their* way, and unless I
cut through a hell of a lot of red tape, all the great publicity value we might obtain—not to mention the horses—
might get lost. It is urgent that I talk to some American
in Moscow, pronto!

Getting through to the embassy at 2:00 P.M. New York time is like expecting a two-hundred-to-one shot to come in. Since it is 9:00 P.M. Moscow time, people are not likely to be hanging around the American Embassy waiting for a call from I. Rudd. People tell me that getting calls into or out of Russia usually takes a day or two, sometimes forever!

Anyhow, I dial. And pray. Mostly I pray. At last my prayers produce results. The call goes through in only five minutes and I get someone at the embassy. Not only does he know about the horses coming to Yonkers but he also knows the names of them and tells me all about each trotter. There are three trotting mares, he informs me, and they are going to leave the Soviet Union by train, due to arrive in East Berlin on Friday night.

"Oy, oy, oy!" I moan to myself. I don't want to rely on shipping agents to get the horses here; not when it involves taking them through East Berlin, of all places.

Pow! My Yiddish cup is working. Marty Tananbaum already is in Europe. All he has to do is get down to East Berlin from Sweden and we're in business. Meanwhile, I can fly there and greet them. So I phone Marty. "Good," he says. *"You* go to East Berlin!"

God has spoken. What can I do but go?

Picture this. It is now three o'clock on a Wednesday afternoon and I have to be in East Berlin sometime on Friday. I start peeling off the phone calls. First I call our shipping agent for horses, John J. McCabe, who tells me that a fellow named Joop Von Tienofen is *his* shipping agent in Hamburg, Germany. I call Joop. Right away he takes ten years off my life. "If the horses are arriving in East Berlin on Friday," Joop tells me, "you have to be there on Thursday, Mister Rudd, you must arrange to leave immediately, if not sooner!"

Sure, Joop, getting to East Berlin is as easy as hopping on the Broadway IRT subway. All I need is a token, right?

Then Joop adds a postscript: "And please bring along a bottle of good American bourbon for me, will you? That stuff is hard to get over here."

Now I'm not only worrying about getting a fast flight to Germany, but this meshuggener is breaking my chops about bourbon, no less. (I later discover that it is all worth it; without Joop we would wind up with nothing.)

My next call is to our travel agent, a commodity I put in the less-than-dependable category. He has screwed up in the past, so my hopes now are no higher than when I tried to phone through to Moscow. I tell him I *have* to get a flight to Hamburg—*"Tonight!"*

The one and only remaining flight takes off at 7:00 P.M. It is getting late and I am still stuck in Yonkers. I have no papers, no clothes packed. On top of that, I have no money! Between calls for a flight ticket I phone Yonkers' bookkeeping department to get some cash for the trip. Instead of giving me an okay, these tight sons of bitches give me nothing but static. "You can't have any money without Mister Tananbaum's approval." (Tananbaum is still somewhere in Sweden.)

Thank heaven the plane ticket comes through—but the money doesn't. I have one more ace in the hole to produce the cash, something I learned from Brownsville vegetable peddlers. I start running around like a beggar, borrowing money from typists, stenographers, even my secretary.

I phone Gert. "Make me a cream cheese and lox sandwich; I'm running off to Europe."

Quick-like, I drive home, get my passport, throw on some after-shave lotion, kiss Gert good-bye, and hustle off to Idlewild Airport. My luck, the staunch anti-German I. Rudd is booked on Lufthansa Airlines. But who can quibble. I break several personal speed records and manage to get on the plane just as the attendants are pulling the steps away. For the first time in four hours I feel as if I have the right to exhale. I am feeling better already, and by the time we land in Hamburg it is noon Thursday and I feel twenty years younger. The trick now is to find the very vital Joop, the man who is supposedly making all the red tape disappear for me. Joop is there at the airport, all right, a behemoth of a Dutchman. I present him with his bourbon and, from the look on his face, I realize that I could not have done better by him if I had handed him the Hope Diamond.

"Come," he says with the enthusiasm of an official greeter, "let us have lunch."

I don't want lunch, I want horses. We repair to Joop's office, where he phones East Germany, Russia, and, after quite a hassle, West Berlin. Joop eventually discovers that the train carrying the Soviet horses is still passing through Russia. We still have time, so he sends me to a hotel for some rest. "I'll pick you up in two hours," Joop promises.

Joop's enthusiasm convinces me that all will be well in a relatively short time, and I am tempted to phone Yonkers and tell the boys that we will pull off the coup of the decade and get Soviet horses. But a rare conservative streak overcomes me at this moment of journalistic orgasm. I. Rudd decides that it would be foolish to announce that we have the horses until the horses actually *are* in our barn. The next morning Joop books us on a plane to Berlin. "The train with your horses," he explains, "will be arriving in East Berlin around midnight." Up, up, and away we go and then down onto the strip at Templehof Airport. So far Joop is hitting all home runs. He tells me we are to make contact with a driver at the airport. I wait to see if he hits another homer. Sure enough, he does.

Our aide-de-camp is a twenty-three-year-old German who is waiting for us at the airport with an Audi. The trick now is getting into East Germany. Since Joop and the driver are not Americans, they are compelled, by regulations, to formally pass through the Brandenburg Gate. I have to go via Checkpoint Charlie. We arrange to meet on the other side once I've been passed through the red tape.

The kid behind the Audi drives me up to the checkpoint, where I can clearly see the four zones being militarily covered by Americans, Russians, British, and French. I walk up to the guardhouse and show my passport. The MP asks me my business and I tell them I'm here to see a German man about a Russian horse. The guard does a double take.

Then he hands me a card that says: "To the American citizen crossing into East Berlin . . . be aware that the East German government doesn't have any treaties with the American government; so you may be spat upon, reviled and jailed . . . and the U.S. government cannot guarantee your safety. . . . You enter on your own free will."

Just then I remember a conversation I had with Gert before leaving. She asked me if I had plans to go to East Germany and I told her I had no intentions of visiting the place. She was worried that I might go behind the Iron Curtain, and lo and behold, here I am about to enter dismal and deadly East Germany. When the MP looks me up and down and says, "Walk down that corridor," I feel as if I am a supporting actor with Orson Welles in *The Third Man*.

Anyhow, I start down the corridor, pass a big car marked "Polizei" where a bunch of cops are packing tommy guns. I walk beyond them, past a gray-colored line, in complete darkness. Now I'm in no-man's-land. Finally I come to some steps that lead up into a shack. I walk into the shack and discover that I have misled Gert—I am now officially in East Berlin. *Achtung!*

The first item I see in the shack is a photo of Vladimir Ilyich Lenin, then Fidel Castro, and then Walter Ulbricht, the boss of East Germany. Then I notice a fat, chunky dame behind the counter, carrying a tommy gun.

She is wearing a khaki army uniform and is built along the generous lines of "Two-Ton" Tony Galento.

She asks me if I have any gifts to declare. I say no. "Empty your pockets," she demands, "and let us count your money."

I can't believe it! I only have a little money, but they take it all and give me a receipt. Then she gives me a piece of paper with the number eight on it and tells me to wait to be called.

Now I'm starting to think. I remember that the guard at Checkpoint Charlie asked me when I expected to return to his station and I said three or four in the morning. And he said, "If we don't see you again by noon, you'll be declared a missing person."

Oy vay!

Before I can get any more constipated, someone calls out my number and I am admitted through the door, down some steps, and over to the other sentry. He looks at my passport and lifts the gate.

"This is it, Irving," I say to myself, "just what you always *didn't* want to happen."

I walk into a darkened East Germany and see nothing but rubble to the left of me and rubble to the right of me. Half-demolished, bombed-out buildings seem to be the leitmotiv. I don't mind, because the scene is brightened by the appearance of Joop and our German driver.

We begin driving past the rubble when my eyes are hit by a beautiful boulevard with high-rise apartments like I would expect to see on Fifth Avenue in Manhattan, and neat, well-lit shops. "This is terrific!" I say.

To which the young German shoots back, "Bullshit!" then adds, "I'm going to show you something." And he drives a few more blocks, takes a left turn and a right, and once again we are amidst the same kind of devastation we saw at the checkpoint. The driver explains that the short strip of luxury street I have seen is strictly for show and a select few potentates.

By now we've reached the East Berlin railroad station where we are to meet an East German representative. Sure enough, he is right there, wearing a seedy-looking suit and shoes that appear to be made of clay. After a brief dialogue in German, Russian, and English, the rep allows me into the station, where I feel extremely self-conscious.

There are lots of people in the terminal, considering that it now is 11:30 P.M., and all of them seem shabby and shopworn. By contrast, I. Rudd is strutting through in his brand-new cashmere coat (which I, personally, thought was the cat's meow), a dark homburg hat, my classy-looking Brooklyn Dodgers World Series ring, and my wedding band.

I don't know why I do it but I suddenly slip the Dodgers ring off my hand and put it into my pocket. I begin wishing that I didn't look so affluent; the self-consciousness at the moment is unbearable. For the first time in my life I'm the best-dressed guy in a roomful of people. Just then a loudspeaker blares an announcement that a train is arriving. Joop gives me the signal; it *is* ours. Whistles blow, engines hiss, and any minute I expect Joel McCrea to walk out of the mist in his *Foreign Correspondent* outfit.

Instinctively I dash over to the freight car that smells the horsiest. Just as I get to it, a railroad worker pulls open the huge, sliding door and I notice three or four people and some horses inside.

I point at myself and shout, "Rudd. Rudd. Yonkers!"

The men smile. *"Da. Da."* The Reds climb down from the freight car and the bunch of us automatically form a big circle on the platform, jabbering a mile a minute, when a couple of German military types appear out of the fog. They demand papers, which, fortunately, my new Soviet friends promptly produce.

Meanwhile, the multilingual merry-go-round is spinning faster and faster and we all seem to be on a treadmill to bedlam. Joop and the gang are alternating their dialogue between Russian and German, while I. Rudd is zigzagging through his Brooklynese. I am beginning to feel uneasy about our lack of progress. The Communists on the German side are making like they want to send the horses back forty miles to the Communists on the East German side. The time has come to introduce some good old Brownsville chutzpah.

Using my buddy Joop as an interpreter I demand of them, "Why are you giving these poor Russian fellows a hard time? They are good Communists just like you. They are your allies. If you want to give someone a hard time, give *me* the hard time. I'm an American. Chase *me* back to Berlin."

The Germans whisper to Joop that this American must be a lunatic. Thoroughly exasperated, the senior German official shouts, "Get those goddamn horses out of here. I've had enough of all of you." The Rudd strategy has worked. The official signs a document assuring us that the horses will be towed to the border by the train, then reattached to a West German locomotive and pulled into the West German freight yards, where we will finally get them.

We hope.

We realize that we are in the homestretch, but Joop and I also sense that this homestretch run will be the hardest. Our plan is for Joop and our driver to go back through the Brandenburg Gate. Meanwhile, I will return through Checkpoint Charlie and the East German official will stay with the train until the car rolls onto West German tracks. If everything goes according to plan, we will rendezvous the next morning with the horses. If it doesn't, I will die of a heart attack for sure.

Joop and I have no time to celebrate. A young, chunky guy approaches from the other end of the platform and walks officiously up to us, speaking Russian. The guy turns to me, yanks out his business card, and announces in

English, "I am Yuri Kornakow, third secretary of the Soviet Embassy to the People's Republic of Germany."

He wants to have *my* credentials. Instantly and with equivalent officiousness, I pull out my card and reply, "I am Irving Rudd, Yonkers Raceway, Public Relations–Publicity Director."

Kornakow is militantly unimpressed. "No," he insists, "your credentials. What aspect of government do you represent?"

"No government," I reply. "Private enterprise. Yonkers Raceway; a hippodrome. I am here to greet these people." I whip out a copy of the contract and show it to him.

Again he shakes his head. "But sir, where are your government credentials?"

"I work for His Lordship Martin Tananbaum, emperor, president, and chief commissar of Yonkers Raceway. This is the only government I represent."

To break the stalemate, we agree to conduct an orderly retreat to the station restaurant. There, over stale cake and ersatz tea, we both relax and Kornakow agrees to remove his verbal obstacles. With that I make arrangements with Joop and the Soviet house delegation to meet at the railroad yards to be sure that the horses are properly quartered.

Enroute to our ultimate rendezvous, I stop off at a chicken barbecue eatery in West Berlin and order six chickens, french fries, and eight bottles of beer. I pack them for my trip to the railroad yards and present them to my Soviet friends on arrival. They are tickled, but no more so than I. Rudd, who ecstatically watches the freight train squeakily rolling in with our horses. I feel like kissing the ass of each trotter as I realize that at last we have gotten them out from behind the Iron Curtain.

Consummately tired but happier than a pig in shit, I return to my hotel room to phone the ultimate communiqué to Leo Doobin at Yonkers, telling him that we have met the horses and they are ours.

When Doobin answers the phone and finishes jumping for joy, he tells me that at this precise moment he is having dinner with members of the enemy high command, namely Alvin Weil, president of Roosevelt Raceway. Turns out that Weil and other members of the Roosevelt board of governors have come to Yonkers for the races.

Doobin mentions to Weil that he should wish all of us at Yonkers good luck.

"For what?" asks Weil.

"We got the Russian horses."

Later he tells me that Weil turned a ghostly white. In fact, the Roosevelt boss man is so pissed at the news, he doesn't eat a piece of food in the five-course dinner. For a change, Yonkers comes in first and Roosevelt a dead last. The Commies have inadvertently made a hero out of me.

= 12 =

O Tananbaum, Stanley Tananbaum, You Are a Pain All Over Town

Despite the laughs and international kudos, Yonkers is becoming less and less fun for I. Rudd. I don't have to look very far for reasons. The name is on the door right down the hall—Stanley Tananbaum. Brother Marty, with all his quirks, I can handle, but Stanley is another brand of *noodnik*.

Stanley and I have had our problems over the years. Once, when he is in Europe supposedly scouting horses for us, I get a call from brother Marty. He is moaning because after three weeks, nothing is happening with Stanley's expedition. No horses, no nothing. "I want you

169

to go to Paris and lock the whole thing up," Marty tells me. "In fact, I want you there tomorrow."

A day later I am in Paris, and two days later I am at the track in Milan, Italy, where I learn that Stanley is hot after a horse named Alfredo, a beautiful brown horse with a white face and stocking feet. There is one big problem, though. His driver, Willie Casoli, tells me that the horse is no damn good anymore. "He wants to go into a break all the time," says Willie.

With that I start asking myself why Stanley Tananbaum is still after this horse. But I want another look, so we wait until Alfredo gets on the track and then give it another look-see. Sure enough, the horse is *galloping* around the track (something trotting horses are absolutely not supposed to do). Not only that, but Alfredo is constantly breaking, he is off-stride, and he obviously can't be controlled.

I can't believe that Stanley Tananbaum is unaware of the horse's flaws. Finally I say, "Stanley, how can you stick yourself with a horse like Alfredo? Can't you see what is wrong with him?"

From the puzzled look on Stanley's face, I can tell he doesn't know Alfredo from Count Fleet. "Which one are you talking about?" he asks.

"Stanley, the horse *that is breaking. Six times around and he is galloping!*" Just then Alfredo goes by and I point to the horse. I can see the color drain out of Stanley Tananbaum's face.

"That," he blurts, *"is Alfredo?"*

I say to myself, as Alfredo's derriere shines up at us, That is Stanley Tananbaum.

I can never get Stanley Tananbaum out of my hair. My final rupture with Stanley (and, eventually, with Yonkers) occurs at a press conference we are holding at Sardi's East Restaurant one afternoon. Marty Tananbaum makes an important announcement about our new international field and now we are really under the gun to get the captions and photos to all seven of the New York papers.

In the middle of the madness I notice an old driver named Charlie Martens, from Belgium, who has asked me and Stanley for a trot driver's helmet. Martens wants to give it to his son. I promised him that yes, he will get the helmet, and now make a special mental note not to forget.

We should leave well enough alone, on account of we got important stuff to do in a hurry, but not so with Stanley Tananbaum around. A few minutes later Stanley reminds me not to forget to get Charles Martens the helmet for his son. "Yes, Stanley, I remember," I say, "but let's get the friggen captions done first."

Now the luncheon is over and we are really busting our asses on the captions, when Stanley calls out from his table, "Irving, this is Charles Martens here. He'd like to know about his helmet."

I shout back, "No problem. It's all taken care of; the order was placed this morning." With that I get back to work.

Five minutes later it is Stanley again. "Irving, what about the helmet?"

After the ninth nudge about the helmet I say, "Stanley, can I see you for a minute, please?" So he comes over to the table while a messenger is standing there.

"Stanley," I say, my decibel count rising by the second, "about the helmet. How would you like to go fuck yourself?"

Astonished that a boss would be so addressed, Stanley replies, "What did you say?"

"I said go and fuck yourself, and I'll stick the helmet up your ass if I hear the word *helmet* again. Stanley, I don't know about you, but I got work to do."

"You don't like working for Yonkers Raceway, you can quit!" he snaps.

"*You* are telling me to quit? Remember this, Stanley, I take my orders *only* from Marty Tananbaum."

Eventually Marty and I and Stanley work it out and a truce is signed. For the moment there is peace on the

Rudd-Tananbaum front. But I can read handwriting on walls pretty good and I know my time is running out with the Stanley Tananbaums of the world. I decide I will stay at Yonkers until such time as a good offer comes along. Eventually what I *think* is a good offer does come along.

In 1969 Murray Handwerker, an old pal from my Brooklyn Dodgers days who just happens to be boss of Nathan's Famous hot dog and fast-food chain, sings me a Lorelei song about how I should come and work for him as a PR man. What's more, Murray warbles a tune about I. Rudd getting "rich" in the process. I like Murray and I like his money tune even more. With that I bid my au revoir to the Tananbaums and the horses—not in order of importance.

After nine months in the world of fast-food business, I. Rudd realizes that Nathan's Famous hot dogs are great to eat but a pain in the ass to publicize. However, one good thing comes out of the stint in Coney Island. I resume acquaintances with Pat Auletta, who I originally met in 1951 when I was with the Dodgers and Pat ran a Coney Island kids' baseball league. Auletta is a warm, congenial guy, a mensch in the best sense of the word. Apart from that, Pat is the father of one Ken Auletta, who has become a big deal in New York State politics. In fact, Ken is such a big deal that he is generally regarded as the brains behind Howard Samuels, one-time candidate for governor of New York State.

Although Ken is twenty-two years younger than Samuels, the kid is the one who runs the show at Howard's ballpark. Ken screens every call, every letter—including solicitations for magazine subscriptions—and okays every single appointment for Samuels.

I am still at Nathan's Famous when the phone rings one day and it is Ken Auletta on the other end. Auletta still is Samuels's rabbi, but Samuels now has a new congregation. He is "Howie the Horse," because Samuels now is head of the newly formed New York City Off-Track Betting Corporation. Samuels was appointed early in July, and now it is the middle of September 1970. "How about lunch?" says Auletta. "I would like to talk with you about working for OTB. My dad says you're great."

What can I say to that but accept the lunch invitation. We meet at the House of Chan on Seventh Avenue and hit it off pretty good. Now we are on dessert and the check flutters down to the table. It lays there and lays there and lays there. I say to myself, Irving, you have met another of the great short-arm specialists. I figure that if Ken Auletta ever picked up a check, a massive double hernia would result.

So I grab the tab and, no doubt, earn a big brownie point with Auletta. "How would you like to come with me right now and meet Howard Samuels?" Ken asks.

Why not? We go over to 72 West Forty-fifth Street, where the remnants of Howard Samuels's campaign headquarters are located. This handsome guy with a shock of silver hair, no necktie, and rolled-up shirtsleeves comes out from behind his desk. His hand is extended but for some peculiar reason his body is turned sideways, like someone does when facing an opponent in a fencing match.

The interview goes smoothly. He asks some questions. I ask some questions. The chemistry apparently clicks and we seem to hit it off. He tells me to come back in a few days. During this second meeting we talk money. I ask Howard for $30,000.

Sorry, I am told, but our budget won't permit so much. I have just been paid by Nathan's Famous, so I produce my check. "Look," I tell Samuels, "here's my check. I'm getting $25,000 a year. Give me the same for the OTB job."

Samuels mumbles something about "city money" and economies. "How about $23,000?" Howard offers. "You know, Irving, money shouldn't be the only guidepost. A man should give his time and service to his fellow man by working for government."

Sounds good and noble. I am fifty-three years old. I am willing to serve the government. I take $23,500 and Howie the Horse seems tickled that I am with him. He is even more tickled the next day, when my appointment gets a big play in the sports pages.

I am supposed to start work on Monday, September 28, although my appointment is announced ten days earlier. I don't know very much about OTB at this juncture, other than the fact that at this stage I am the only bonafide racetrack guy to be hired with racetrack management experience. Auletta is pleased with my background. He tells me that OTB is planning a big press conference to announce how the outfit will use a space age computer. "We'd like you there," says Ken.

Fine. That's a good week and a half away; it will give me time to wrap things up at Nathan's Famous. A few days later I get a frantic phone call from Auletta. "Could you come by," he pleads, "and help us set up things for the press conference?"

Who could say no? I report to OTB headquarters in the old Paramount Pictures Building at Times Square figuring that Auletta, at the very least, has the foundation for a big press mailing. After all, the upcoming media conference to hail the OTB computers is a biggie and deserves a massive PR assault.

But when I get to Auletta's headquarters I discover that there isn't a single press mailing and not even a single media contact list. On top of that, there isn't even a detailed biography of Howard Samuels. When I tell Auletta and Samuels that in the upcoming days and weeks the press of the world will be descending upon us, they just don't believe me.

With the help of a couple of gals and many phone calls, we whip that first press conference into shape. It is 1:15 P.M. on September 28, 1970, when Mayor John Lindsay is standing in front of a mock-up wagering window at an OTB outlet at 49 Chambers Street in downtown Manhattan opposite City Hall. The press is there about a hundred strong. Cameras click, pencils fly as Mayor Lindsay demonstrates the placing of a bet via telephone on horse number seven in the first race at Belmont Park.

Lindsay's mythical $2 returns $32. Other bets are made and the computer spews out tickets one after the other on command for the mayor and other dignitaries.

Among the bigwigs there is a group from an outfit called Computer Sciences Corporation, the outfit that supposedly is behind this magic machine that will do it all for OTB. The Computer Sciences people are here to explain that wagers can be accepted until thirty minutes before post time and that all sorts of bets—including daily doubles, exactas, round robins, and parlays—can be handled. The tickets will each have an individual code number, making counterfeiting impossible. Speed of transmission between branch offices and the main computer will be instantaneous.

Superficially we put on a very impressive show. The computer keeps spitting out tickets, *kaboom! kaboom! kaboom!* This is Buck Rogers at the racetrack. There is only one catch—*the* catch of catches. There is no computer anywhere at OTB! Not only is there no computer, but there will not be any for months and months, and yet there is Howie the Horse telling the world that OTB will begin operations in less than four months. *That* is my initiation to the world of OTB, which to me means Off-Track Blundering. Every day, in every way, I discover incompetency of the very worst order.

No sooner do I start work officially than I find myself surrounded by political hacks. There are $35,000-a-year executives floating around who haven't even seen a horse race. I was suspicious the day of our first demonstration. The tickets coming out of the phony computer terminal were really handsome but all botched up, like the entire operation.

Out of the computer comes tickets for Roosevelt Raceway. At a glance the tickets are impressive; they show two thoroughbred horses with jockeys sprinting across the face of the ducats. The only thing wrong is that Roosevelt is not a thoroughbred track. It happens to be a harness track, where the horses are hitched to sulky wagons and they use drivers.

All of which makes one wonder why the geniuses behind OTB ever decided to hire an unknown outfit like Computer Sciences Corporation for this very important breakthrough in racetrack betting. (To the everlasting credit of Howard Samuels, he had absolutely nothing to do with choosing the system.)

The OTB big shots had a lot of possibilities other than Computer Sciences Corporation. For instance, anyone who has been within fifty miles of a racetrack knows about the Automatic Totalisator System. Or if you are talking computers, even to a World War II Jap soldier holed up in Mindanao, the answer just has to be IBM. Yet here comes a completely unheard-of company with no track record around a racetrack, making outlandish promises to set up a system within months when the best experts say that there is no way it can be done earlier than a year to eighteen months, and they get the whole ball of wax.

Somebody is making a bundle somewhere. Computer Sciences Corporation stock doubles when they announce the OTB contract. Some pretty smart investigative reporters make a run at the stink behind the story but get nowhere. Likewise, there seems to be another story in why OTB ever moved to 1501 Broadway, the old Paramount Building, in the first place. For five years it has been a buyer's market for office space, especially in the Times Square area. Does OTB go looking for such a new building? No, it spends heavy dough to make its headquarters in a dirty old ramshackle building that is full of malfunctions.

They say we moved into 1501 Broadway because the main computers are housed on the ninth floor there. But I remember a big gun at Gulf and Western, which owns racetracks around the country and shopping centers and a piece of Madison Square Garden and also the Paramount Building. I figure if OTB doesn't rent the many floors of office space that it does in the Paramount Building, the building has to close, because no other company housed there comes close to renting the square footage we do. Then I find out that the big shot at Gulf and Western and Howie the Horse are pretty chummy and I don't even want to guess what was involved, but if renting space in the Paramount Building comes under the heading of "sound business approach to government management" (which Samuels constantly brays about), then all I can say is *oy vay!*

Within a few years OTB expands all over the building, with hundreds of thousands of dollars spent for renovations, paint jobs, equipment, carpeting, and furnishings. Fancy wood paneling, thick rugs, and electronic gadgets go into the offices of middle-management employees. One guy actually has his suite painted an egg-shell blue to coordinate with the manila folders in his filing cabinet.

This is not surprising when I review some of the jobs OTB is creating and the characters peopling these alleged jobs. We hire a vice president of marketing for $35,000. How does "director of productivity analysis" grab you? Or "director of affirmative action"? In addition to the nonessential job of marketing vice president, OTB shells out $120,000 ($10,000 per month) for "external marketing research." In the marketing field there also is a "director of marketing service" who gets twenty-two big ones *and* an advertising director paid $27,918. The last is a no-hoper who wouldn't know a horse if Secretariat reared up and kicked him right in the ass.

By January 1971 Samuels has hired more than two dozen hacks who had previously traveled the gubernatorial campaign trail with him. These characters comprise more than 10 percent of OTB's employees. Meanwhile, sixty thousand applications—never to be opened or examined—come in the mail. Personal and telephone applications from many persons with good racetrack backgrounds never get a shot. I figure that Howie the Horse studies Emma Lazarus every night and then modifies her plaintive lines to suit OTB: "Give me your tired old hack, your experienced no-show, your nonproductive stiff yearning to earn taxpayers' bucks. . . ."

Not that Howie the Horse is such a bad guy. He is a decent boss and a nice human who doesn't take himself too seriously. A great handshaker, Samuels is always ready with a congenial "Hi, I'm Howard Samuels" opener. Howard has incredible stamina and he tours OTB's operations starting at eight in the morning and going as late as midnight. If he sees things are going wrong, he never hollers but rather explains softly to correct the matter. Never does he demean even the lowest OTB employee.

Which doesn't mean that he doesn't take any crap; he does, and plenty of it, for the shoddy manner in which OTB has gotten off the ground. He is cursed by union leaders and is villified by such respected newspapermen as Red Smith, Dick Young, and Bob Lipsyte. Instead of getting all pissed off, Howard reads the raps and says to me, "I guess since they are the sports experts they have a right to knock my brains out. And maybe I deserve it."

He does try in many a one-on-one meeting to give his views to leading writers. My job is to stave off any bad-mouthing of Howie, if this is at all possible. In the beginning I try to bring him together with leaders of the racing industry and try to make allies of the racing people who put on the show—the owners, drivers, and jockeys.

We get a chance to reveal our platform when Howard is invited to speak before one thousand luncheon guests at the annual Brooklyn Chamber of Commerce meeting. Samuels agrees to let me write the speech. The theme is that if the racing game is to suffer injury because of OTB, then maybe it is better to scrap OTB altogether. Samuels talks about the people on the backstretch and their financial plight. The speech is well received and gets great sports page coverage.

I am very pleased with Samuels and very pleased with myself. I figure that I have the boss's ear and that, despite all the political crap going on around me, I can do a good job for OTB. But a few weeks later—just when I figure everything is going along smoothly—Howie calls a staff meeting and I nearly shit a brick when I hear what he has to say. Our goal, Samuels tells us, is to knock out organized crime.

OTB is a fledgling outfit, I tell them, and we should be thinking about straightening out the computers and let the FBI worry about straightening out the Mafia. That bit of candor does not endear I. Rudd to Auletta and I can see that the first bark of harmony between me and Samuels's slobs has been peeled back a little.

Not long after that our rift widens when I protest that the OTB office is being used for political purposes. First one of Auletta's secretaries hands me some notes regarding the candidacy of some guy in Alabama and tells me to get up a release. Of course, I refuse. Then there is the matter of a fund-raising tribute to Samuels designed to defray campaign costs after he got licked by Arthur Goldberg. Tickets are going for fifty a rap, and the arm is being put on OTB employees. I protest that, and I yell and scream when a list is submitted for me to contact big-name racing people like George Morton Levy, president of Roosevelt Raceway, and S. Harvey Fosner, vice president of Roosevelt, trying to milk them for fifty bucks a ticket for Howard's party—and at a time when the racetracks want to drink our blood. Imagine what a laughing stock Samuels and OTB would be if Levy and Fosner received a letter of solicitation. (Fosner is quoted in *New York* magazine as saying, "Howard Samuels is an unadulterated political whore.") I tell Auletta that what he and his OTB cohorts are up to is no less than a shakedown. Of course, he doesn't like what I tell him. Forget about politics, I tell him, and worry about getting OTB off the ground.

By December 1970 OTB is overloaded with problems. Our magnificent computer still isn't working; we have legislative problems, union problems, racetrack problems, employee problems, and just plain problems. Even worse is the realization that on January 4, 1971, we are supposed to begin operation with Yonkers Raceway.

Just before Christmas 1970 Auletta gets a bug to start planning for an opening, even though OTB still has no agreement with Yonkers Raceway; nor do we have an understanding with the Yonkers pari-mutuel clerks' union; nor do we have a working computer. Auletta's brainstorm is to take Mayor Lindsay on a pre-opening inspection tour of the two existing OTB facilities in Brooklyn and Queens, which are little more, at this point, than stores with betting windows.

I can't take it anymore, so I go to the mat with Auletta. Storming into Samuels's office I shout, "Look! On Sunday, January third, *The New York Times* and the *Daily News* are reserving huge headlines and lots of space heralding the beginning of OTB in New York City. You can't lie about starting up and not be anywhere near ready to begin!"

As I bellow at Howard, he blinks. He knows I am right and he agrees that a false start could open every can of computer-contract worms we have and close shop for OTB before it ever really opens. I prevail over Auletta and convince Samuels that we should take a straight-arrow stance. And he agrees. So we call a press conference and

Howard announces that there will be a delay in opening OTB. He comes off looking like the business genius he is touted to be by pointing out that the computers, while functioning at 98 percent efficiency, are not working at 100 percent. Therefore, if the computer isn't perfect, Howard Samuels is going to straighten it out before opening OTB to the public. As a result we get a great press.

What we don't get is a computer that works. Weeks go by and still our magical machine isn't working perfectly. At board meetings I tell Howard to get rid of Computer Sciences, go manual with the bets, and open new bids for a new computer company. Meanwhile, test after test with the Computer Sciences computer fails horribly and everybody at OTB is running scared.

Harvey Fosner at Roosevelt Raceway really puts us down when he says, "OTB is like a guy who has built a big airplane in the basement of his home and now he can't get it up the stairs."

We get another scare when George Levy of Roosevelt hints in a letter to OTB that he thinks we don't even have a working computer. That does it; Samuels decides that OTB will go manual, and to hell with the grand computer.

Of course, Joe and Jane Bettor have no idea just how screwed up our operation really is, because nobody has yet to really get the story. In fact, it is just the opposite: we are feeding appetizing stuff to the papers across the country and they are biting. For example, no less a newspaper than the *Chicago Tribune* runs a piece on the supposedly effective OTB security force. "Security at the nerve center is tight," says the *Tribune*. "Visitors must sign in and sign out, stipulating where they live, whom they represent and whom they want to see."

What the *Tribune* doesn't see is an in-house OTB memo listing "the unusually large amount of thefts from various departments, including mini-calculators, typewriters and personal property."

Sooner or later the real sleuths among the newsmen

are going to get on our trail. Finally we get nailed by Sam Roberts, the political reporter for the *Daily News*. He breaks a story with the headline: "Campaign Horses in Samuels' Stable at Offtrack Corp." Roberts writes that "More than two dozen veterans of the political campaigns of Howard Samuels have been hired by the city's Offtrack Betting Corp., which Samuels heads, a survey by *The News* disclosed yesterday. They represent more than ten percent of the corporation's 200 employees."

The *News* story lists guys making as much as $25,150 a year down to a $13,000-a-year community relations specialist. There are some embarrassing revelations. One of the characters mentioned is Laverne Newton, who is getting $13,000 a year in the "community relations" area. Newton not only gets nailed in the *New York Daily News*, but there's also a story in the Columbus, Ohio, *Evening Dispatch* about Newton being in Washington, D.C., to "take complete charge of the 1972 Democratic National Convention." Here we are at OTB with the Preakness just two weeks away, we're up to our withers in work, and the OTB community relations specialist is down in the nation's capital advocating new politics.

Another one mentioned in Roberts's piece is Ricki Conn (or, as the late fight announcer Harry Balogh would have called her, "better known as Rhoda Cohen"). Conn jumped from a $17,000-a-year employment manager to a $35,000 job as OTB vice president of personnel. Ricki's greatest claim to fame at OTB, as far as I. Rudd can discern, is that she and a few other staff women inspired Howard to say the word *fuck*. When the grand accomplishment finally transpired they shouted, "We finally did it!" as if Mount Everest had been climbed. And indeed they *had* done it, because ever since then, that lovely expletive has become an ingrained part of the never-to-be-governor's daily speech and was never, but never, deleted.

Needless to say, Auletta is quick to defend the Samuels appointments against critics. "We feel," says Ken, "that we were very fortunate that the need to build an entire new corporation came at a time when we had the opportunity to bring in people who did not work a normal nine-to-five day; and they're talented people who worked with Howard and know how to get things done."

I'll say they don't work a normal nine-to-five day. Every one of them racks up a big financial score by filling in completely unsupervised time sheets. Within the first year of OTB's operation, some of Howard's henchmen and women are already owed as much as twelve months' compensatory time.

I am stuck with one such malingerer, who was foisted on me as an "assistant public relations director." He keeps his own hours—and earns $16,000 a year—and every time I complain to Auletta about the twerp I get nowhere. Meanwhile, this assistant is using my office and the telephones and other facilities to work with Vic Gotbaum of the State, County, and Municipal Civil Service Employees Union. Finally I go right to Samuels and tell him either this "assistant" goes or I go, simple as that. Finally they move him into another division called "customer service." This is a short-term deal, because the guy soon is released when his accounts come up some six or eight thousand bucks short. Is he fired? Don't be silly; they let him resign and get a hell of a nice severance check.

Meanwhile, the papers are still after us and the *New York Post* has a piece saying, "At least 21 former political campaign workers are on Howard Samuels' Off Track Betting Corp. payroll drawing salaries that add up to $371,600 a year."

The press begins referring to OTB as "the Samuels Stable" and Auletta is busy running up the denials left and right. One of his best—in response to the *Post*—is simply: "It's not true; Howard has no plans at the present time to run for political office."

My disenchantment with the scene grows by the

month. Everyone, it seems, is milking OTB for what they can get out of it, while I can't even get paid for the work I did on the very first panic press conference, when Auletta called me over from Nathan's Famous. When I remind Ken that he never paid me for that, he shoots back, "Irving, we were trying you out." (Oh, well, Samuels did say that a guy should serve his government, didn't he?) With it all, there is some satisfaction. In time OTB manages to surmount the many gremlins and does begin to grow, and I am tickled to help build the organization in some way.

Eventually Auletta leaves—walking out with about $35,000—and then has the balls to write to Mayor Abe Beame about what is wrong with the city's politics, when he had people around him stealing and he knew it. When Samuels decides to run for governor he asks me to come along with him. I tell him thanks but no thanks, and I also tell him what I think of the people around him.

"Howard," I say, "if you rely on these same guys you've had at OTB, the only way you will get to Albany is in a Trailways bus."

So Howard tries to be governor and Irving tries to keep his sanity at OTB under the new boss, one Paul Screvane, an erstwhile commissioner of sanitation, who makes Howard Samuels appear like a Socrates by comparison.

Screvane needs me for the first few months he is on the job, only because I have too much smarts being around OTB from the very start. But as I case the guy up and down, I sense he is not good for me and that, worse yet, he is terrible for OTB. Right off the bat Screvane shows what kind of man he is by putting restaurateur Toots Shor on the payroll for $150 a day, two days a week as a "consultant."

Oy, do we get blasted for that. Ed Comerford, writing in Long Island *Newsday*, opens with: "Who was the New York Off-Track Betting Corp. genius who suggested putting Bernard (Toots) Shor on the payroll at $150 a day, plus expenses, to do a job for which Shor admits he has no particular qualifications?" From there Comorford gets tougher and tougher. "What timing," he writes. "The unemployment offices are clogged with carpenters, engineers, auto salesmen and teachers who don't know where their next meal is coming from. The city is shutting down firehouses and threatening to lay off cops. It's like ordering ice cubes for a party on the *Titanic*."

Like a pinball bouncing from pillar to pillar, Screvane commits blunder after blunder; but his biggest boo-boo of all involves a scheme where OTB would try to buy Madison Square Garden. When the news of OTB's intent (actually Screvane's crazy idea) hits the papers, every muckraking journalist in town, from Jack Newfield of the *Village Voice* to Jerry Izenberg of the Newhouse newspaper chain, gets on Screvane's ass. As Izenberg puts it in the *Newark Star-Ledger*: "Why, if OTB, which by law was set up to funnel desperately needed dollars into the city's General Fund, was making so much money it could talk about buying a building which paid interest rates which would have made Richard the Lionhearted's kidnappers blush, wasn't that money going to be spent in the interests of the people of the city?"

The best and the brightest columnists jump on Screvane. Dave Anderson in *The New York Times* reams him, mocking OTB for really meaning "Our Town's Broke." Newfield runs wild in the *Voice*, and Izenberg winds up running a three-part series ripping Screvane from here to there and up and down.

By the time the dust has cleared, Screvane's name is mud in the Big Apple. "Anyone who respected the city's citizens," says Izenberg, "wouldn't have dared propose such a monstrous misuse of money which could eventually have reached the city's general fund."

As publicity man for OTB, I am up shit's creek without a paddle. The boss needs a victim. Or, as Izenberg puts it: "Humiliated, embarrassed as only a politician can be (not over what he planned but over not being able to do it) Screvane blamed everyone from Sun Yat Sen to Alexander The Great for the TKO to his vanity. Apparently, Rudd shared in the blame."

Sure enough, Screvane calls me in to his office and tells me I am through.

"These are your final words?" I ask.

"Yes," he says, "although I hate to do this to a man of your age."

"Well," I come back, "it's your ball game."

I turn and head for the door. Just as I am about to walk into the hall, Screvane looks up and shouts: "And if I made a mistake about the Garden, that's *my* fucking business!"

The letter of dismissal says I am fired for budgetary reasons. My friends in the newspaper business know the real story. Screvane got caught with his Madison Square Garden pants down and he wasn't going to fire himself. I like the words of Izenberg best. He does a whole column on my firing and says: "Rudd was—and remains—a consummate publicist. He has done a great many things over the years. Impersonating Harry Houdini is not one of them. No publicist on earth could have undone what Paul Screvane did to himself in the Great Madison Square Garden caper."

Part IV

= 13 =
From Champs
to Chumps

After I left OTB I free-lanced for a while. I did some racing publicity work for CBS and also worked for a publisher's distributing company. I let it be known that I was looking and one day got a call from John Condon, who was at Madison Square Garden. He said, "Irv, how would you like to make a comeback in the fight game?" I wouldn't be sitting here, working for Top Rank, today if it were not for John Condon.

As far as I. Rudd is concerned, the difference between a champ and a chump is a good press agent. Never is this point better proven than during my Don King adventure, which begins shortly after the Ali-Norton fight. Muhammad and Ken already have collected their million-dollar paychecks and gone on their own way, while I am out of a job. Such is the nature of the business, but after a brief respite, handling Norton and Ali provides a splendid entrée back into the boxing mainstream. My work is known again, and one person who finds out about it is Don King, erstwhile numbers runner, ex-convict, and boxing promoter extraordinaire. How, you may wonder, do I wind up in King's entourage? Mostly thanks to the incestuous world of boxing. I will explain.

While I am still handling Norton and Ali, King promotes a doubleheader boxing card in Florida featuring George Foreman and Roberto Duran. Turns out that Duran's trainer is Ray Arcel, one of my oldest and closest buddies in boxing. Arcel is pissed as hell over the lack of publicity generated for the Duran-Foreman program and he makes no bones about it to King.

"What," says King, "would you like me to do about it?"

Arcel tells him straight out that he should hire a professional public relations man who knows what he is doing, and not try to do it all by himself. "The man you want," Arcel tells him, "is Irving Rudd."

Meanwhile, other people mention my name to King, so by November 13, 1976, when the phone rings in my home, Don has a pretty good idea about who I am and what I can do for him. Arcel is on the wire: "Don King wants to see you at his office—eleven tomorrow morning!"

I know what that means. Between Arcel and the other guys in my corner, plus the successful job I pull off on the Ali-Norton fight, *plus* my boxing background (after all, I *started* my career working for Al Douglas, a black promoter), there is every reason to believe that King is going to offer me a job. The question that I have to decide is whether I. Rudd wants to go to work for Don King. To help me come up with the answer I do some research on this mystery man of boxing, a guy who is making daily headlines but six years ago nobody (except the cops) knows about.

What I discover is both bad and good. On the minus side is the fact that he once was thrown out of school in Cleveland; became a numbers runner, and eventually became the top numbers man in the Cleveland ghetto. Next, a street fight over some owed money ends with Don smashing the other guy to the pavement. Nine days later the guy dies, and Don is convicted of murder two.

For the next forty-eight months King is a resident of the Marion Correctional Institute in Marion, Ohio. ("Where only hatred and oppression existed," he once tells me.) From these ashes, Don's phoenix begins to develop, and from that point until our meeting, his life turns more plus than minus. He becomes a voracious reader (even gets an offer from the Harvard School of Business while still at Marion) and, upon his release, winds up working for Louis Stokes, brother of Carl Stokes, then mayor of Cleveland.

Soon after that there is a hospital crisis in Cleveland and for a time it looks like four hospitals will close in the city. Taking a long-shot hunch, King makes a call to Muhammad Ali asking him to fight a benefit in Cleveland. The Champ's answer of yes launches King's boxing career. The exhibition (on August 28, 1972) raises more than $80,000 and, as King likes to put it, "the jailbird becomes a phoenix."

Ali and King hit it off immediately and the Champ tries to interest Don in going into boxing promotion, but Don says he isn't quite ready for it. But after George Foreman fights Joe Frazier in Kingston, Jamaica, King decides that the boxing business is for him. ("The enthusiasm," he tells me, "was electrifying. The spectacle was enormous and I felt that I had to be a part of it.") Pretty soon he is handling Ray Anderson (a light heavyweight), then Earnie Shavers and Jeff Merritt.

It isn't that easy for King, because he doesn't have a top fighter yet and he is having problems with other promoters, not to mention the biggie of biggies, Madison Square Garden. Just when it looks like he is set up for a knockout, Ali phones him, offering help. "If you really want to help," says King, "let me promote you in the biggest fight ever held in the world—Foreman and you. First you're gonna knock out Frazier, then I want to match you against Foreman. I want to prove once and for all that you're the greatest!"

King promises Ali $5 million to fight Foreman. When the Champ hears that, he swallows for a second and then says, "Hey, nigger, you crazy!"

Crazy, no. Crafty, yes. Don pulls off the fight, even if he has to persuade Bula Mandunga, an emissary for the government of Zaire (formerly the Belgian Congo) to hold the fight in his country. From that point on, whether Madison Square Garden likes it or not, Don is King of fight promoters.

So I. Rudd, who broke in with a black man in 1936, finds himself forty years later breaking in with another black man, but a significantly different kind in many respects. Al Douglas was a cultured man with a refined wit and never a day in prison. Al read and spoke French yet worked in the middle of Harlem. I don't remember Don King setting foot in Harlem. Another difference is that Douglas always put up his own money for promotions; King puts up other people's money.

With all this background in my head, I go over to King's office in the upper reaches of Rockefeller Center. By no means have I rejected him in advance but by no means have I decided to take the job no matter what.

I know little about the man and even less about his operations. But I can see it's a very close-knit deal, strictly one-on-one. He goes to the Philippines and talks to the people *in person*! He goes to Zaire and he is up front talking to the people in Zaire. Don King doesn't run by committee; he doesn't come back to the office and take a consensus. He runs by Don King and Don King alone.

The meeting turns out better than I expected. I impress him by remembering that he had been in Earnie Shavers's corner on the night he got flattened by Jerry Quarry. He likes the idea that I know all about his numbers-running background and that I am able to finger the point when he appeared down and completely out of the boxing picture before Ali came along. We talk for an hour and discover that our promotional ideas move along the same tracks.

"You come to work for me," the big man says. We agree on a price ($400 per week), shake on it, and one day later I. Rudd's big adventure of 1977 is underway. Within a week I find myself totally awed by my new boss; I mean, he really boggles my mind. Up until then I figure that I'm a pretty good idea man—in fact a *very* good idea man—but when it comes to ideas, I'm to learn, King is even better than me. In that first week, I also learn that in addition to promoting fights he is an importer of Red Chinese products and owns a fishing fleet. (It should be known that Don's "fleet" consists of two boats that nobody, to my knowledge, ever sees.) On top of that he is involved in the entertainment world, looking at scripts, books, plays, everything! In that area he is as impressively fallible as he is successful in boxing.

One day a man by the name of Sylvester Stallone comes to Don with the script for a fight movie called *Rocky*. Stallone wants King to back the film but Stallone is unknown and has some unusually big demands for a nobody, so King chases him away. Not that I fault Don for that, because he is only one of many smart people who tell Stallone to get lost. Don isn't willing to risk money on an unknown quantity.

But that really is the essence of King's operation; he is always using other people's money. As the days begin flowing by at Don's office, I get a good idea about his operation; it is a numbers operation all over again, except that instead of operating on the streets of Cleveland in the middle of a ghetto, he is high atop New York City in a lavish Rockefeller Center suite. Still, the glossy trappings don't fool those who are right on top of King. One of the insightful black people in his organization sums up Don perfectly when he describes the company: "King runs a ten-cent nigger operation!"

Could be, but I'm still gung-ho enough not to worry too much about it. Don is paying me pretty good and the checks aren't made of latex. Besides, a lot of exciting things are happening, like fights. One of them is George Foreman going up against Jimmy Young on St. Patrick's Night in San Juan, Puerto Rico.

One day I get a call from Don, who tells me to get the hell over to Philadelphia. It is three weeks before the fight and Young is doing a prefight taping for ABC television. Don is worried about Young. "He's too soft-spoken; talks with his head down. It makes him sound like a bad-ass black guy, surly, and that ain't good. See what you can do down there!"

So I'm off to Philly on the Metroliner. The word is to check in at the Ben Franklin Motor Inn and find his manager, Jack Levine, and another fellow named Ray Kelly, as well as his trainer, Bob Brown.

No problem, until I get there and meet Levine. Right away he tells me that the crew from ABC-TV wants to take Young to see the movie *Rocky*. He figures we will get some inspiration and he wants me to come along.

I am instantly and instinctively suspicious of these TV types. This I don't need any more than I need a case of gout. The next day we're supposed to start with roadwork and I want a good night's sleep so I can be up for the business at hand. "Irving," Levine persists, "you should come to the movie." I don't want to argue; I might as well see what he has in mind.

Up to my room I go; I splash water on my face and go down to the lobby. Next thing I know I'm being introduced to the ABC-TV crew headed by a young kid named Terry O'Neill. I don't like what I see. They are all wearing neat blue jackets with the "ABC" logo under the pocket and looking like they were just packaged by Abercrombie and Fitch. Looking at them, I *almost* get to like Howard Cosell. I say to myself I must beware of Terry

O'Neill. Along comes Jimmy in his big Lincoln and now we're off to the movies

To a certain, limited extent, I am impressed by Stallone's film *Rocky*. Stallone is a good actor and Burgess Meredith comes off okay as the tough old fight manager. But when all is said and done, *Rocky*, for all its raves, isn't real. And I tell young producer O'Neill so. "I can't buy what that ham-donny [Rocky] is able to do to the champ. It is way too phony."

My instant review doesn't go over too big. Anyway, we're back at the hotel, ready to split for our rooms, when O'Neill says, "Irv, why don't you sleep late tomorrow? No need for you to hang around for roadwork." It sounds phony to me.

Hmm, I'm wondering, why the hell shouldn't I be around the fighter I've come down to Philly to see? In other words, what is this O'Neill kid up to now?

I turn to Levine. "Jack, what time is our meeting tomorrow?"

"Roadwork starts at six."

(I want to be sure to anticipate O'Neill.) "Okay," I say, "downstairs in the lobby we meet at five-thirty A.M." (This is just in case O'Neill and his TV buddies try to pull something off.) Now I feel a little better and head for the sack.

But I. Rudd isn't so smart this time. At 5:30 A.M. the next morning I am in the lobby, but nowhere do I see Jimmy Young. I only see Levine. "Where's the fighter?" I ask, fearful that the ABC-TV boys already have faked me out of my jock.

"Oh," says Leving, "*they* took him."

"Where did they take him?"

"I don't know; they just *took* him. For roadwork."

"But Jack, he's your fighter, not theirs. You let them take your fighter for roadwork. Are you crazy?"

Now he's fussing and fuming all over the place and I can see how the crafty hand of ABC-TV is working.

Thinking back to my experiences with Ali and Norton and now looking over at Levine and O'Neill, I realize that I have gone from the champs to the chumps.

"Well, gee, Irving, we need the exposure," Levine pleads.

Roadwork, my ass. I know what these TV guys are up to; they want Young to run up and down the Philly Museum steps the way Stallone does in the movie. That, to me, is not roadwork; that is pure bullshit.

"What your man needs," I tell Levine, "is *real* roadwork, 'cause if he loses, all this 'exposure' ain't going to mean shit. Now where's that fucking museum?"

Levine gives me the information. I grab Young's trainer and we cab over there. Sure enough, just as I figure, running up and down the steps like a goddamn puppet is Young. Up and down he's running while the cameras grind away.

"Cut it!" I yell from the bottom of the steps. *"Cut it!"*

The whole crew stops and stares at me. I run up the steps, right at O'Neill. *"What the fuck do you think you're doing?"*

"Who are you talking to? We're doing . . ."

"Never mind the explanation. This kid is fighting on the seventeenth. The bout is just around the corner; what happens if he slips on these steps and breaks a leg? Then everybody is up shit's creek without a paddle. Let's go back to the hotel and caucus." Now they are impressed with my decibel count; I win my point and get them to stop. We then go back to the hotel to argue whether Jimmy Young should be Sylvester Stallone or Jimmy Young. "The way we look at it," says O'Neill, "Jimmy is from Philly, so is Rocky. We want to take shots of Young working out in the same places that Rocky did."

"In other words, tomorrow you wanna take Jimmy to the Philadelphia meat market, like they did in the movie," I say. "And you're gonna have Jimmy punch sides of beef with his bare fists like Stallone did. Is that your plan?"

"Yeah!"

"No, my boy. Not while I, Rudd is around here. And I'll tell you why: Apart from the fact that the fight is just three weeks away and Jimmy can hurt himself in some stupid way, like punching a carcass, this whole aping *Rocky* shit is demeaning to our fighter. Remember, in the movie Rocky is nothing but a shylock's helper, a head breaker, a goon, a never-was.

"Jimmy Young is *not* a never-was. He went to high school. His father is a welder; his mother works. He knows nothing about welfare or docks or streets or hooliganism. More important, he may be the next heavyweight champion of the world. I think it is an embarrassment to have a possible champion portrayed this way."

I know I am getting through to at least one guy in the room: Levine. "Irving," the manager finally pipes up, "you're right. He ain't no Rocky!"

The network jock sniffer O'Neill doesn't like that, but for the moment nothing more is said—until I go back to my room. The phone goes and it is an ABC man on the other end. It seems that I have angered the network. The sports TV honcho of honchos, Roone Arledge, is pissed. His flunky is on the other end. "Irving," he says, "I suggest you back off. Terry O'Neill happens to be a very competent producer."

I agree but also disagree. "By TV standards I'm sure he is; but *I'm* standing pat. He's not gonna have Jimmy Young punching beef carcasses."

"How about some roadwork on the docks?" Arledge's man pleads.

"Okay," I concede. "If it'll make you happy to have roadwork on the docks, we'll have roadwork on the docks. But if he so much as punches a side of beef in the Philly meat market I'm gonna punch Terry O'Neill right in the fucking mouth!"

A truce is worked out between I. Rudd and ABC. I'm

not unhappy about it and leave Philadelphia confident that I have done the job right.

When I get back to Don King's office I tell Don about the whole episode with O'Neill. "Did I do right?" I ask.

"Irving," he says, "you're right. Jimmy Young ain't no Rocky." Then he laughs his head off.

I'm pleased that Don has backed me up, but the best is yet to come. We go to San Juan, where Young beats Foreman in twelve rounds. After the fight I'm in the dressing room, when Jimmy Young walks in and spots me.

"Man," he says, "you were right. I ain't no Rocky!"

I say to myself, True, and you ain't no Ali either. There is, in fact, only one champ and, as I am rapidly learning, only one King. Right now I'm with the hottest promoter in fighting, with all the top talent. I figure I'm set, maybe.

As long as Don King has Muhammad Ali in his pocket, I figure that Don (and I) will be riding high. Whether he is the actual champion or not, Ali still is *the man* as far as the fight game is concerned in 1977. Aging or not, the Champ still has charisma and great drawing power. Unfortunately, King's ties to Ali are not quite as strong as the Champ's punches. A behind-the-scenes dispute between Ali's adviser Herbert Muhammad and King causes a split. Don is getting all kinds of ink and Herbert Muhammad apparently doesn't go for that stuff. A whispering campaign begins, no doubt stirred by some of the lackeys around Ali, saying to Herbert Muhammad, "Hey, that Don King is getting more publicity than your fighter." Herbert Muhammad finally decides to take Ali back to promoter Bob Arum, head of Top Rank, a closed-circuit TV organization, and Madison Square Garden. So Don King's biggest money card is pried away from him. As Don aptly puts it, "Now my rear is scraping the sand." He is right and I am wondering what kind of miracle he will pull off to get himself out of the slide. What King eventually does proves his brilliance as an idea man and convinces me that he is one human who never, no matter what the odds, should be counted out.

He decides to stage a running, cross-country boxing show aimed almost exclusively at the television networks. He calls it the "U.S. Boxing Championships Tournament" and almost instantly gets a good reception. "I want to bring back the days," he says, "when people knew smaller fighters. I want to recapture the days of Willie Pep, Tony Zale, and Ray Robinson."

The concept is brilliant. He will have a sixteen-week series of bouts to produce "American champions." Since all titles but the heavyweight championship are held by foreigners, it is figured that the extra clout of the title will persuade foreign champs to fight Americans, which they aren't doing.

Next Don works a deal with *Ring* magazine, the so-called bible of boxing. *Ring* agrees to establish bouts according to a seeding plan: number one vs. number eight, and so on. *Ring* will set up a "committee" headed by James A. Farley, Jr., chairman of the New York State Athletic Commission, which appoints the officials. Everything about the planning appears shrewd, especially when the ABC network comes in and tells Don that it will back the tournament to the tune of $1.5 million. To me it looks like King is building himself another stairway to the stars.

What the network doesn't realize, and what will prove to be the weakening sand in the foundation, is that Don King is not developing the organization to match the scope of his ideas. In time that failure will bring Don King and his "U.S. Boxing Championships Tournament" to its knees if not produce a technical knockout.

= 14 =
Long Live
the King—
We Hope

In July 1976 Don King seems to be sitting on top
of a mountain of potential money. He has contracted with
ABC-TV to stage his "U.S. Boxing Championships" and
the network has agreed to pay Don King Productions $1
million in purse money and $40,000 per show for produc-
tion costs. Typically inventive, King decides to stage the
bouts in the most glamorous and unusual places imaginable—on board the aircraft carrier U.S.S. *Lexington* at
Pensacola (Florida) Naval Base; at the Naval Academy in
Annapolis, and at the Marion (Ohio) Correctional Institute, where Don did four years for manslaughter. Brilliant! The first bout, on January 16, 1977, goes off nicely

on the aircraft carrier. King's idea is predicated on building new faces and new heroes, and, damnit, it turns out that I am watching some of the best fights in all my years in boxing.

Right after the aircraft carrier escapade I head for the Fontainebleau in Miami Beach to make sure everything is hunky-dory for the title fight featuring Roberto Duran against Vilomar Fernandez.

When I get there I find it ain't. In fact things are screwed up beyond belief. For starters I have to deal with the father-and-son owners of the Fontainebleau, Ben Novack, Sr., and Ben Novack, Jr. King wants me to deal with Junior, so I find him in his office, and after ten minutes of dialogue I can't make up my mind whether he is an idiot or a genius; all I do know for sure is that he has an agonizing stammer and he calls all the shots at the hotel. Just the guy I need to get the fight on the road.

King tells me that the grand ballroom should be checked out first, on account of that is where the fight will take place. When I ask Junior to show me the ballroom he says nix. "You don't *have* the ballroom," says the kid. "King never closed the deal on that." Then he tells me that King never closed the deal on the free cars for the press or anything, for that matter. The fight is coming up and I have no cars and no ballroom. All I have is a surplus of grief.

Here we are, staging the lightweight championship of the world, and we don't even have a place to stage the damn thing. I phone King and put Novack on the wire, but all Don gets is a verbal commitment to put the fight somewhere—but not the grand ballroom. Novack offers me the Fleur-de-lis room, which happens to be a restaurant, not particularly suited to boxing. There's only room for 750 people, hardly respectable for a championship. Adding to my troubles is an unexpected discovery that King is partners with Chris Dundee, a big fight promoter in Miami Beach who is in some sort of trouble with the local boxing commission. That, however, is a piddling matter compared with finding a good site for the fight. Dade County Junior College makes me an offer to have it at the school gym, but the school can't make the cash package promised us by the Fontainebleau. Right after that I learn that the Miami Boxing Commission has fined Dundee and taken away the exclusive rights he has to promote fights in Miami, a deal he has had going since 1950. When King hears about this, he phones me and says he has been granted a license to promote fights in Miami Beach and that I should accept on his behalf. This sounds fishy, since it isn't like Don to stay out of any spotlight.

King must be figuring that this will antagonize Dundee, and I ask myself whether Don's move means that he no longer plans to work with Dundee in Florida. Apparently Miami sportswriters are thinking the same thing. Ed Pope, a writer with the *Miami Herald*, pumps me on the question of what Don is trying to do to old Chris. What can I tell him? "We're not going to throw an old pro out," I say. "We worked with Chris before and we'll work with him again. We didn't come to Miami to knock anybody off." (Unfortunately, I am convinced that King *does* want to dump Dundee.)

Meanwhile, the Fontainebleau management tells me I can use their tennis courts for the fight. What still puzzles me is how we are going to get enough seats into the hotel to have a decent crowd to show the TV audience. I don't have the answer, until one night I am in the hotel room watching the tube when a tennis match comes on from Boca Raton and I notice that they are using bleacher seats for the gallery. Why not use them for the fight? I ask myself. So I give the tennis people a quick call and they tell me where to rent the bleachers. I rent the bleachers and get the tickets printed—$40, $20, and $10 tickets. These are outrageous prices, but that is what King wants and that is what he gets.

Next comes the detail work—setting up the ring, roping off the sections, and numbering the seats. We are running out of time and running out of hope. If the show doesn't go on and it is looking more and more as if it *won't*—King forfeits a bundle and is out of the fight business for good; no major network will deal with him again. Meanwhile, Don is staying in New York, seemingly oblivious to all the crises in Miami. One of the biggest crises involves the junior Novack's inability to understand that I need a press row because I have fifty legitimate requests for press credentials. I tell Ben that the press has to be seated at ringside and I'll need another row of seats. I win that fight, but it isn't easy.

Now it is two days before the bout and it is brought to my attention that we could have problems with automobiles pulling up into the driveway of the Fontainebleau and tying the hotel in knots. We could get screwed if a lot of people arrive, see the traffic jam, and turn around and go home. An idea comes to mind: rent minibuses and lug the ticketholders from the municipal parking lots to the hotel.

I check out a local bus company and they tell me I can rent fourteen-seat minibuses for $160 a day. I figure that with two minibuses ($320 for the day) I can get twenty-eight people at a time to the bout and clear up any parking problems. With ads on the radio and in the papers we can handle everything. So I phone Don in New York and tell him what I want to do. A long silence follows.

"Don? *Don?*"

King's pause is pregnant times ten. Finally King blurts: "Irving, you don't understand this business of promoting. *You gotta make a deal!*"

"Whadaya mean?" I ask.

"Trade off, man! Don't you understand, Irving? You gotta go to them bus people and trade off stuff that we got for stuff that he got. If he wants three hundred and twenty-five dollars, don't ever give him the money; trade off!"

"Trade off what, Don?"

"Trade off the back of the round cards. We get pretty girls to wear little tights and a sweater and they walk around with cards after each round is over and the bus company's name'll be on 'em. Tell 'em their bus company'll get mentioned on national TV."

"Don, can you guarantee that?"

Of course he can't. And he won't budge; will not go for the lousy $320. So I go to Novack and tell him about the parking problem. I really lay it on about the potential traffic jam tying up the valet parking service until I get him terrified. Novack figures that he will get blamed for the entire mess, not King.

"I'll go for the three-twenty bills," Novack says.

Right down to the fight itself we have trouble. I practically have to install the ring by myself, and when we get to the weigh-in there is a question about the authenticity of the scales. Then Fernandez's manager bitches about the time of the weigh-in and Ray Arcel takes me aside and says we are very close to losing the fight. But I get the ring up; the scales are okayed, and as I fly by the seat of my pants, everything falls into place at the eleventh hour. After all is said and done, Don King realizes that it cannot happen without Irving Rudd. But no sooner am I leaning back, resting on my laurels, when another bombshell explodes in our faces, and this one is a lulu.

On February 13 we're at the Naval Academy in Annapolis, and that's where the shit really hits the fan. On the heavyweight card we have a bout between Scott LeDoux, a not-bad but not-good journeyman, against Johnny Boudreaux, who is no better. As far as I'm concerned, watching the fight, LeDoux punches the hell out of Boudreaux and deserves to win the fight.

But they give a "unanimous" decision to Boudreaux, and let me tell you, when the decision is announced it is really a shock. Why they give Boudreaux the edge I can't

say, but apparently LeDoux can—and does. He throws a
fit, tries to grab the mike from Howard Cosell, and in the
process knocks Cosell's toupee off.

After the fight LeDoux unleashes the first meaningful
barrage against King and our "U.S. Boxing Championships." "I was warned about this a month ago," shouts
LeDoux. "I was told that there was no way I could win in
this tournament controlled by Don King, Paddy Flood and
Al Braverman." (Flood and Braverman manage boxers in
the tournament but also are consultants to Don.)

At first LeDoux's blast is treated as sour grapes. In
fact, it is something of a joke, since the knocking off of
Cosell's hairpiece gets him the kind of notoriety (and favorable publicity) he couldn't buy in a lifetime.

Don is suitably indignant when he hears about the
LeDoux blast. "I am subject to the cruelest and most unfair castigation," he says in rebuttal. "Emotional invec-
tives and absurd charges are broadcast to a continent.
When tempers cooled, apologies are made, but they are
made in sequestered rooms, away from the camera. I am
shattered. My thoughts are covered by dark clouds. Is
this the end? Has what I worked for been sabotaged? Will
ABC abort the program?"

For the moment, no. LeDoux's bitching notwithstanding, Don still is riding high. *Newsday*, the huge Long Island daily, gives him tremendous space; a full page and
then a runover on another page. The blaring headline runs
right across the top of the page: "The King of Boxing Promoters."

Bob Waters writes the piece and King tells him, "I
have been reborn once more after I have been slaughtered
and I have been slaughtered so many times I've lost
count."

One place where King has been slaughtered is the
Marion Correctional Institution, and that's precisely
where we wind up on March 6. The former resident in
Room 10, Cellblock 6 has, for the moment, regained all of

the cool he lost after the LeDoux bout. He strides around the prison wearing a gold-encrusted jacket and waistcoat. Red Smith of the *Times* says, "Don's brown pants had a crease that could draw blood."

Red Smith is great to us. He goes along when King visits his old cell. Warden Perini is standing alongside King when I say to Red Smith, "Don came in about the time Warden Perini became a warden. You have to admit that Don went further in life than him. He's out and the warden is still here!" Well, Don just broke up, because he *does* have a sense of humor.

When Don enters the ring, he is greeted with placards that at least show that the inmates have a sense of humor: "KING'S BACK WE TOLD YOU SO!" Another reads: "SOME DUDES YA CAN'T CHASE AWAY WITH A CLUB, WELCOME BACK, DON KING."

That an alumnus appears to be doing so well while they are still incarcerated does not seem to bother the prisoners. And certainly it doesn't bother Don. "I look around," he says, "and see many familiar faces. I am one of you." With that a cheer goes up around the gym. "It is with mixed emotions that I am coming back to what was a trauma in my life. Wherever I have gone outside, I have never tried to hide Marion CI. I never forgot number 125734."

Time and again Don is cheered, although a few boos are heard when he introduces Walter Hampton, head of the parole board. Half-serious, King scolds the inmates: "Hey, that's the dude that sprung me."

Then come more laughs when Howard Cosell is introduced and more placards go up: "FINALLY, HOWARD IS WHERE HE BELONGS" and "HOWARD GOT IN—WILL HE GET OUT?"

Cosell gets out of Marion okay, and so, for that matter, does King. Once again he is smelling like a rose. The *Times* not only gives us a column (by Red Smith) but Deane McGowen does a nice piece on the fights themselves. "Success only follows travail," Don likes to say, "I should have realized I had some travail due me."

King doesn't know it at the time, but more travail is coming—fast. On March 24 Kenny Weldon, another boxer beaten in our tournament, cries foul. It turns out that Weldon is *Ring's* tenth-ranked lightweight. His gripe is that he paid George Kanter, an agent, "a lot more than 10 percent" to compete in King's tournament. Hearing that, reporters begin to ask questions, like how come fighters have to pay for being in a tournament they qualified for on merit?

We move on to San Antonio, Texas, where more storm clouds appear. *Sport* magazine has this college professor named Sam Toporoff doing a story on Don's tournament. At the time Toporoff seems to be doing an innocent enough piece. He spends an entire day following Don around and, finally, asks him how he manages such a grueling pace. "I never get tired," says King, "because it ain't *my* energy that's being dispensed. It is *God* speaking through me." For the moment, at least, it appears as if the professor is snowed by King's bullshit. Unfortunately, the same cannot be said for a federal grand jury in Baltimore.

LeDoux isn't content to merely knock off Cosell's toupee and scream highway robbery. He pursues his beef to the authorities, and in early April a Maryland grand jury begins investigating the tournament. Compounding our problems is the fact that a crew from rival CBS has been filming a segment for a puff piece on King for *Who's Who* (which I helped place). They are at Annapolis when LeDoux blows his top and get all the footage they need for a special "investigative report" on the championships. CBS labels King's championship a "house" tournament and suddenly the dirtiest word in boxing—*scandal*—begins appearing again in all the papers.

I have now reached a point in my professional relationship with Don where I no longer can be a docile employee. I cannot work for a guy who is dishonest and I want King to at least come clean with me privately. I have to know he is clean; we have a heart-to-heart and he tells me he is clean.

Naive though I may be, I am willing to believe him. That means that I am sticking with King, no matter what is to come of this ever-growing mess. It means that I. Rudd must devise some strategy like I have never done before in my life. It's obvious to me that King isn't his usual self-assured big shot self. He needs help and he comes to me for salvation.

What is happening began with a trickle of negative publicity in February 1977, when Scott LeDoux started his babbling. But by April 1977, when the federal grand jury gets into the act, Don is drowning in a torrent of negative publicity. Worst of all for us is the fact that the New York media, which has more or less laid off the minus side of King, suddenly pounces on him with a vengeance. It now is open season on Don and everyone wants to get a piece of his Afro.

Since I am committed to rescuing his ass it behooves me to work out a complete battle plan, starting with the man himself. I know that we will be ahead of the game if I can persuade Don to keep his big mouth shut. But this is like wishing that February would follow March. As the spokesman for King I have to make myself available to the media every hour of the day and I must give them the truth and nothing but the truth, so help me, Don! I have to return every phone call regardless of whether it is from friend or foe and then sit back and hope for fair-mindedness. One thing is certain, Don is a different man. He borders on contrite. Where once he listened to me with half an ear, now he is sitting on my every word. He is paying attention because he knows that I. Rudd can save his ass.

Even when I am thousands of miles removed from the man he is tuned in. As it happens, on April 15, 1977, I am working for him in Miami Beach when another anti-King bomb goes off. A member of the King entourage corners me, very agitated, and tells me that the word is out three months and twenty-seven bouts after we start the "U.S. Boxing Championships," ABC is canceling the whole shebang.

I hustle back to the hotel because I know that Don will be after me for advice. Sure enough, the phone rings. "Irving," King says, "I'm flyin' down. When I get to the hotel ya better have a statement for me."

At this point I realize by the sound of his voice that I am talking to a madman. What the hell kind of "statement" can I pump out at this point with so little facts at my command? I try to get more information from him but all I come up with is noise. "Dammit, Irv," he screams, "don't fuck with my mind. Get a statement ready. *Get a statement ready!*"

Don is now like the guy at the carnival, with his head sticking out of the hole while people are throwing baseballs at him. Many times he appears to be flinching and a couple of times he staggers, but still he never goes down.

After a little more thought I realize that only one course is available to pull King out of this hole, and it is based on the original idea he hammered out with *Ring* magazine and Nat Loubet, the publisher and editor of *Ring*. This was when the whole idea for the "U.S. Boxing Championships" was hatched; Don wanted to make the tourney legitimate by having *Ring* handle the selections. It looked smart to bring in Loubet and his assistant, Johnny Ort. In terms of authorities, these men were as good a collection of boxing men as King could obtain—on the surface, at least.

But as the fighters, such as LeDoux, began beefing about the results and the seedings, it dawns on me that *Ring* may not have been all that legit and that the magazine was in the position to push well-connected fighters up in the rankings at the expense of those who are not well connected. That, I decide, will be the thrust of my counterattack. My plan is to blunt the initial attack on King by pointing the finger at the real culprit, *Ring*. But how do you take on a power such as *Ring*? The Rudd theory is that if unqualified fighters are getting high ratings from *Ring* and good fighters are not getting high rankings because they don't have a rabbi, it isn't Don King's fault, it is the fault of the outfit that he is paying seventy big ones to. In other words, I tell Don that he has to say that *Ring* stinks.

He agrees, and a day later Don launches his counterattack with an announcement that the *Ring* ratings were suspect. That is our handle and it is a good one. King charges that Nat Loubet doesn't know a damn thing about boxing and that Don King is the innocent victim of "thieves and vipers." He insists that *Ring* is "shoddy as hell in its policing of the thing." King tells the world that all the problems with the tournament are a result of foul play in the *Ring* magazine ratings.

Now the war is on for real and it is hard to tell friend from foe. Right away the ABC network wants to look like Mr. Clean, so they hire a "special investigator" and turn "evidence" over to the U.S. attorney in Maryland. Meanwhile, our blast at *Ring* effectively turns the heat on the magazine and Loubet conducts a very disorderly retreat.

While all this is going on, believe it or not, King is busy putting together another fight, this time between Muhammad Ali and some stiff from Spain named Alfredo Evangelista. As it happens, ABC already has paid $3 million for the rights to televise the match, scheduled for May 16. Considering the flak we are dodging on April 16, the Evangelista fight seems several light-years away.

Our put-the-blame-on-*Ring* ploy works, but only to a point. Although the media has turned its guns on the magazine and away from Don, it is only for a few days and it by no means removes all the heat from our office. In fact, I soon feel surrounded by the enemy on every side as the sniping begins in earnest. One of the biggest guns is leveled at us by Pete Hamill, the *Daily News* columnist.

Unlike most of the other stuff that is written, the Hamill piece appears *not* on the sports pages but right up in front of the paper, which just happens to have the largest circulation in the country. Hamill kicks the living hell out of Don and thereby makes it imperative that I try to bail out King. I phone Hamill and say, "I'm not the one to argue with you about what a guy should or shouldn't write in his column, but you never once called my man, King. You wrote that stuff without ever getting King's side of it. That ain't exactly kosher."

Hamill accepts my logic and agrees to have lunch the next day, and out of the meeting with King he writes a second column on Don that is considerably toned down from the first.

Then Milt Richman of UPI writes a column that absolutely kills us. Richman's column goes out to five hundred papers; he is one of the most powerful sportswriters in the country. I phone Richman, who is a nice Jewish boy who doesn't usually make waves. "Milt," I say, "is this what your parents taught you, to pass judgment on a man without even talking to him?"

Richman, I know, is blushing. "Okay," he says, "get me an interview with King."

An hour later they meet at Don's offices, now located in a townhouse on the posh Upper East Side of Manhattan, and out of it comes a pretty favorable piece, all things considered, titled "Don King Tells His Story."

Little by little I feel I am recovering a lot of lost ground for King. Meanwhile, *Ring* keeps getting blasted but good. ABC-TV releases an affidavit from boxer Ike Fluellen, who puts the zinger on *Ring* magazine, claiming that it rigged the ratings. Although Fluellen hasn't fought a single fight in 1976, he is ranked third. On top of that, the *Ring Record Book* lists two fights that Fluellen allegedly fought in 1976 in Mexico. Both are phonies. In his affidavit Fluellen says he never even fought in 1976. Every day, in every way, *Ring* is looking worse. By contrast, King is looking better—until he disobeys my advice and goes off half-cocked about how the white men are responsible for his troubles.

King doesn't hear. Or he doesn't listen. He meets *privately* with the black newspaper publishers from around America and they come up with a statement that "the white press conspired to discredit Don King in the boxing world, and therefore restore white promoters to the control of boxing."

I nearly shit when I discover what Don did, because (a) he is supposed to lay back; (b) he is supposed to stay and meet the regular press; and (c) we had agreed to lay off the antiwhite crap.

Naturally Don winds up with mud on his face. On May 6, Dick Young leads off his *Daily News* column with a terrific blast at King. "I would expect such a brash untruth from Don King in his moment of desperation," Young writes, "but not from eminent leaders of the black community." Then as a postscript Young adds that the press conference suite "was arranged by Don King Productions, if that is 'upholding the tradition of the free press.'"

I know from years of experience dealing with the man that Dick Young is hypersensitive on the race issue and that it is downright stupid to let him grab hold of it by forcing a black-white confrontation. I have the feeling that Young isn't through with King after the blast at the black press conference, but I have absolutely no idea about the next salvo to head our way.

The Saturday before Don's Ali-Evangelista fight I pick up the *News* and Young has a column saying that Evangelista has cataracts on his eyes! Meaning, of course, that there is no way the fight can come off this year.

Right away, I smell a rat. First of all, we all know that

this Evangelista is a guy who Ali can whip with his eyes closed and one arm tied behind his back; and now Dick Young is saying that Evangelista can't even see straight. Right away I am reminded of another stiff Ali once fought, Jean-Pierre Coopman. After the first round Ali is winning so easily that he comes back to his corner, looks over the ropes, and sees Pat Summerall and Tom Brookshier, the TV blow-by-blow guys, looking very sad. "Oh, boy," says Ali, "are you guys in trouble! This guy's got nuthin'!" Well, if Coopman had nothing, Evangelista has minus nothing! And now Young is making matters even worse for us. Which means that I. Rudd must quickly go to work and disprove Young's column.

No problem. I hustle Evangelista over to an eye doctor; he gives my man a complete examination and, just as I suspected, the verdict is 20-20 vision. Perfect.

My eye doctor gambit amuses Bill Nack, the Long Island *Newsday* columnist. He writes, "At least Evangelista will be able to see who is hitting him in the ring, and not fall up the steps getting there."

Why did Young write that cataract item in the first place? My theory is that ABC-TV planted the item with him because ABC is pissed at Don King and wants out of the fight. But the network is tied in by the contract and guaranteed $2.5 million to Ali. The way I see it, ABC figures that the cataract crap, if given enough ink, will force a cancellation. But I know that Evangelista has cataracts like I have two heads, and the eye exam proves I am right. The fight comes off and Evangelista, whatever his vision, puts up a good enough battle to make the bout respectable.

The Ali-Evangelista fight is a tonic for Don. He needs some kind of psychological momentum and this does the trick. "I needed a win real bad," he says. "Don't bother me if I don't make a dollar on it. It is just the idea of putting it on." And he is right on this count. I can see by the way his eyes light up that King is counterattacking in earnest now.

"Nobody gave me a chance in this one," Don boasts. "ABC was out, out, *out*! When that story broke that Evangelista had cataracts on his eyes, that's all the excuse ABC needed to pull out. I had to go up there and talk to the bosses at ABC and get them back in."

But not all newsmen are snowed by Don's latest frontal assault. One of the skeptics is Paul Zimmerman of the *New York Post*. He hits King with questions about *Ring* and the ongoing probes. Don brushes it off as "a lot of talk, a lot of investigating . . . seems that everybody's investigating everybody these days . . . don't know where one leaves off and the other begins."

King is right, in a sense. ABC makes a grandstand play, bringing in Mike Armstrong, the guy who investigated the New York City Police for the Knapp Commission. Hiring Armstrong is a joke to those who know our business, because Armstrong knows nothing about boxing. In fact, the first thing Armstrong does after he gets the ABC job is phone Jerry Lisker, the sports editor of the New York *Post*. Armstrong wants Lisker to teach him all about boxing—over lunch.

When Armstrong's "investigation" begins, he gets Al Braverman, the fight manager, in for a grilling. One round with Braverman, and Armstrong himself looks like a victim of a TKO. Before Armstrong can open his mouth, Braverman says, "How much is ABC paying *you* to run this investigation?"

Right away that upsets Armstrong. "What the hell business is it of yours?" Armstrong comes back.

"Aha," counterpunches Braverman, "you are going to ask me a lot of questions that are *no business of yours*." By the time he gets through with Armstrong it is no contest. Al wraps him up and throws him away.

Meanwhile, King and ABC-TV are 180 degrees apart. The network is sniping away at King, and King is still shooting back. At the same time Don realizes that if he loses ABC he will have trouble keeping fighters in his camp. By mid-May of 1977 his empire is tottering. "Perhaps," says Paul Zimmerman of the *Post*, "the Evangelista fight will prove to be the last hurrah for Don King and his travelling circus."

Now I am protecting our flanks, our center, but not our rear, and sure enough, that is where we get it next. That professor, Sam Toperoff, who we figure is doing a nice piece on Don King, comes out with a devastating article in *Sport* magazine titled "The Death of the Don King Tournament." Worse still, *Sport* prints a big cover picture and cover line rapping the living shit out of King.

"The King boxing empire appears to be in serious trouble," writes Toperoff. He goes on to say that there are reports of defections among fighters important to King and that the investigations continue. Anyone in his right mind figures that Don is dead as a boxing power broker.

But anyone foolish enough to harbor such thoughts just doesn't know Don King. Not only isn't he dead, he is very much alive, and I. Rudd is doing his damnedest to keep him alive and kicking. Will King survive? Since I am working for him I also am betting on him coming through, although he is rapidly becoming one of my least favorite people in the whole wide world.

= 15 =
From Chumps
to Champs

Watching Don King bob and weave his way through all the verbal blows of the spring of 1977 has provided quite a lesson in the art of survival for I. Rudd. I am truly amazed that the man appears, in the summer of 1977, to emerge unscathed from all the barbs being hurled by ABC, by the media, and by the so-called investigators.

As I study Don King I hope that somehow all of his problems will have a cathartic effect on the man. I realize that I am probably naive to expect any change. A slumlord may lie on a hospital bed for six weeks, deathly ill, with plenty of time to think about how he will become a new man if he survives. But once he is out of the hospital he is *still* a slumlord. Likewise, Don King is never humbled by his troubles of April and May 1977. Watching him in June 1977 leaves me with the conclusion that he is nothing more than a big, affable phony.

His traumas have taught him neither compassion nor understanding. After watching Don closely for several months I come to the conclusion that he simply thinks he can con everyone, from ABC's Roone Arledge on down. But he and I discover that King can't bat 1.000, because the law of averages is against him. We both learn this one day when Don discovers that I know Bob Tisch, then head of the Loew's Hotel chain and later postmaster general of the United States. "Hey, Irving," he says, "why don't you call Bob Tisch and offer him one of my good fights—at his hotel in Monte Carlo."

It sounds like a hell of a nice idea, romantic Monte Carlo and all that, so I call my pal Tisch and he gives me a big "Hello, how are you?" I am feeling optimistic.

"Bob," I say, trying not to sound as hesitant as I feel, "I was talking to Don King and I'd like to talk to you about putting a fight in your Monte Carlo hotel."

There is a hesitation and my radar tells me that something isn't kosher. Finally Tisch says, "Irving, hasn't Don King told you that we've spoken?"

Don is sitting only five feet away at that moment. "No," I say, "not that I ever know of."

"Well," counters Tisch, "we have. There's no use talking about it, Irving. Don wants *everything*. And I can't go for that."

We say good-bye and I hang up and look across at King, feeling lower than a sidewalk curbstone. "Hey," I say to Don, "what the hell are you tryin' to do to me?"

"Come on, man," he says, "I was just jivin' you. I figured . . ."

"Whadaya mean, you 'figured'? It's one thing if you tell me you tried to work with the guy; then, maybe, I take a different approach. But don't let me come on to Tisch like I'm just discovering something."

Only then does King reveal that he talked to Tisch *ten times* about the deal and Tisch told him to get lost on account of Loew's was going to wind up with zip dollars and King would get everything.

Which is not to suggest that King is a totally bad guy or that he and I. Rudd do not get along. The fact is, we do get along, because I understand his mountainous ego. Don is a crass, arrogant man, a self-centered egotist. But with all this there is an insatiable desire on his part to be loved and publicized at the same time.

Once, he is being interviewed by a newspaper guy and I happen to be along with him. In the middle of the interview a thought comes to mind and I excuse myself with an interruption: "Don, I'd like to tell a little anecdote that is illustrative of what you just said." Then I tell a story about King, an anecdote that I know he rather likes. As I am telling it I can hear his voice starting in a low tone and then rising with a delightful crescendo: "Go, man, go! Make me big! *Make me big!*"

Well, he is bigger than big in June 1977, even though the probers are to the left and the probers are to the right and it seems that everybody wants a piece of his hide. Nevertheless, in the midst of all the hassling and the bad headlines, Don gets on a plane, jets to the West Coast, and pulls off a miraculous coup.

First, he negotiates with Bob Biron, a guy against whom he has a lawsuit pending. Biron, who is Ken Norton's manager, negotiates with Don for four days around the clock. When they are through they have worked out the lawsuit *and* a deal. Norton is going to fight Jimmy Young in Caesars Palace, Las Vegas, on November 5, 1977, for the right to meet Ali sometime in 1978.

There you have it. At a point when most other men would have hopped a slow boat to China and changed their name because of all the heat in the papers and on TV, King not only has his head through the hole in the carnival game but he is the one throwing the baseballs, instead of catching them in the face. And if that isn't bizarre enough, King lines up ABC-TV to televise the damn thing! *Pfft!*—just like that, Don and the network have forgotten that they hate each other. It's like ABC doesn't even remember that it once televised a disclaimer about Evangelista's ranking before the fight went on the air. How, you have to wonder, did King ever make such a remarkable comeback so fast? Don himself has the answer: "Muhammad Ali has been the matchmaker. This marvelous match has been ordained by the king, himself. 'Let them fight each other,' Ali ordained, 'and I'll fight the winner.' Truth prevailed, and reason and logic." At least King's version of it prevailed.

By clinching the Norton-Young bout, Don has launched a successful comeback with the media. Phil Pepe of the *New York Daily News* hails the event with a column and the headline "Don King's Coup." The man now is seeing the light at the end of the tunnel; his confidence is rebuilding. "Only in America," Don says, "can a man come back to get a second opportunity, as I have done."

No doubt about it, the heat cools and King begins freewheeling as if nothing ever happened between him and *Ring* magazine or him and ABC-TV. Despite all the probing and all the magazine and newspaper articles, Don and ABC are back copromoting again. "King," says the *Daily News*, "is a super salesman."

News columnist Norm Miller asks the question, "What kind of irresistible charm does Don King have?"

The answer is that nothing can be legally proven that is damaging to Don. Sure there is that gray cloud overhead—the phony *Ring* ratings—but the network remains hungry for major fights and boxers who will boost their ratings. Since King continues to prove that he can come up with the fighters, ABC keeps coming to him with the bucks.

Eventually ABC completes its so-called investigation of King's U.S. Boxing Championships. When ABC's "probe" is published it is clear to me that I earned my money when I persuaded Don to go ahead with my strategy of pointing the finger at *Ring*. "It is plain from our investigation," the report says, "that at this time *Ring* lacks the credibility necessary for it to carry out its assigned role in the tournament."

As for King's involvement, the report goes on, "We were unable to find any evidence that King himself was involved in kickbacks, false ratings or other similar irregularities. The most disturbing action by King for which we were able to acquire direct evidence of personal involvement was his clearly improper payment of $5,000 to John Ort [associate editor of *Ring*] which seriously compromised the integrity of the selection process."

How serious are the findings? The answer appears in Dick Young's *Daily News* column. If we are going to get clobbered, that is the place. Instead Young pats King lightly on the behind with the following commentary:

> They decided that while ABC-TV and Don King had done some unethical things, there was nothing criminal in the conduct of the television series known as "U.S. Boxing Championships."

> I'm not so sure of that, but I'm happy it came out that way, because now maybe the show can get back on the tube for the fall season. From what I've seen of some TV previews, this fall season can use it.

> A resumption of the tourney would be good for the unemployed boxers, good for the fans, and good for Don King, who makes things happen in the murky world of boxing. Roone Arledge of ABC makes things happen in the wide, wide world of sports, although I never will forgive him for having spawned Howard the Shill, nor will millions of fans.

> King and Arledge are drawn to each other. Both play the game on the principle that anything can be made all right if you rub enough money onto it. Buy people. Roone learned that at Columbia University. King learned it in the slammer.

The shady ethics, the padding of boxers' records, the booking fee kickbacks, the mythical ratings of contenders, "fell into the business judgement area," according to Mike Armstrong, the private eye who conducted the investigation. And the business judgement area, of course, "was beyond the scope of our investigation," according to the arrangement by which ABC-TV hired the investigator.

That is ludicrous. Call something business judgement, and it can stink to high heaven, but remain outside the scope of an investigation purportedly designed to uncover a stink.

Anyway, it is good that King and Arledge can go back into partnership. It is also good they got caught the first time. Now they will know they are being watched.

Beautiful. The King has regained his throne and is jauntier than ever. Almost immediately he announces a new European "boxing alliance" and discloses that he has formed a partnership with Umberto Branchini of Italy, a European promoter and manager, for an exchange of ranking boxers.

It is like old times for Don—almost.

As the summer of 1977 unfolds, King does something he has never done before with I. Rudd: he stops coming up with the bucks. On July 8, 1977, Don advises me and everyone else in the office that the whole kit and caboodle is shutting down, "indefinitely until further notice." No severance pay, no health insurance, no hospitalization. Nothing but a good-bye Charlie! Don hastens to add that he will invite us all back, presumably when business picks up again in the fall. But who needs that kind of applesauce? Who needs such ingratitude? Without further adieu, I decide to get away from this guy as quickly as possible.

I talk it over with Gert and we agree that it is foolish to hang around waiting for King to start paying me again. So I return to the East Side offices and clear out my desk. As I walk out of the brownstone for the last time, I wonder whether I am the only one who remembers Don

King's deathless cry for help on that bleak night in April when he was flashing his SOS.

"Dammit, Irv, don't fuck with my mind. Get a statement ready. Get a statement ready!"

I got it, all right, got it but good—even though King privately tells one newspaper friend of mine, "I owe it all to that little guy, Rudd. He saved my ass."

Unfortunately, you can't cash those quotes at the bank, so it is time for I. Rudd to accentuate the positive and eliminate the negative; or, to put it another way, get away from the chumps and find the champs again.

There is only one escape hatch—the telephone. I scan the horizon, realize that my pal Muhammad Ali has just signed to fight Earnie Shavers, so I call John Condon, the boxing boss at Madison Square Garden, and lay it all out. "John," I say, "Don King has closed down—who knows for how long—and I'm on the beach."

I figure I'm going to be greeted with stony silence, or some pallid prose about how it's too bad and don't call me, I'll call you. "John," I repeat, "I'm on the beach."

"Irving," says Condon, "I'm tickled to death!"

The son of a bitch says he is tickled to death, and I am out of work. With friends like that who needs Joey Goldstein? "John," I wonder, "how can you be tickled with me outa work?"

"Because I want you to work for *me;* I need you on the Ali-Shavers fight. In fact, what I'd like is for you to head right out to Ali's training camp. We're having a press conference tomorrow all about the fight and you can start working immediately. You and Ali are buddies, right?"

Right. But my press agent's mind is working on a different frequency. Sure, me and Muhammad are buddies, but that is precisely the reason why I should *not* work his camp. "John," I insist, "you don't want me in Ali's camp; you want me to work with Shavers. Do you know why? Nobody knows Shavers; everyone knows Ali and his act.

Shavers will be a challenge for me and I'll hype the guy like he's never been hyped before."

Condon is stunned by my response. Obviously, everyone would like to be with Ali. The Champ generates his own publicity; it's almost like not working being with him. "Look, John," I say, laying on the convincer, "Shavers is the guy we have to build up, not Ali."

John is convinced, and he is delighted that I would want to go to a place called Calcutta, Ohio, where Shavers is working out. There may be a black hole in Calcutta, India, but I guarantee that this Calcutta, on the borders of West Virginia, Pennsylvania, and Ohio, has to be the black hole of North America. The tip-off is that the nearest "big town" to Calcutta is East Liverpool, and the local Jaycees have the balls to call it "the pottery capital of the world." So be it. I take off for Calcutta and wind up in the only decent hotel, fifteen miles away, in Chester, West Virginia. Earnie Shavers is nearby, staying at a friend's farm.

Since we are in *yenevelt*, it means that I. Rudd has a lot of time to think and figure out a way to get Earnie's name in the newspapers. So I think and think and think. Finally I come up with an idea: why not try to measure the velocity of Shavers's punch, since he owns one of the highest knockout percentages of any fighter who ever lived? It was a takeoff on a stunt I once pulled with the Brooklyn Dodgers at Ebbets Field. We brought a machine to the ballpark that could measure the speed of a pitched ball. Our great reliever Joe Black was tops at 98.6 miles per hour. Now we want to find out how fast our Earnie punches. So I put out a press release—really a plea—calling for anyone to come forward with a machine that can measure the velocity of a punch. While I am at it I claim that Shavers's punch is the equivalent of the driving force of an auto smashing into a wall at three hundred miles per hour. The results are good and bad; we get a lot of ink out of the stunt but we don't come up with a machine.

Good old Red Smith comes up with a big column in the

Times along with a photo of Shavers. Red likes Earnie and says, "Ali could wind up with his comely nose buried in resin." On top of that I connect with nonsportswriters. One of them is Sidney Fields, who does the "Only Human" column in the *New York Daily News*. I pitch Fields on doing a piece on Shavers, who stands six feet tall and weighs 210 pounds, and his wife LaVerne, who is only five feet and weighs only a hundred pounds. Fields goes for the idea and does a column on Earnie, his wife, and his daughters. The column gets good play with a neat headline and a photo of Earnie.

Camp with Shavers is a pleasure and, I am soon to learn, a big plus for I. Rudd. One day I am watching Shavers go through his paces in the ring when I notice a chap named Bob Arum enter the gym. I have known this Arum fellow from the fight game for several years. He is a fight promoter and entrepreneur, but I have only met him a couple of times.

Arum has his wife Sybil and one of his sons from a previous marriage along with him. Right away I notice something strange about Arum's behavior toward me. We talk for about fifteen minutes and then he goes his own way, but within the gym. Every so often I see Arum and I get the feeling that I am being watched. Sherlock Holmes I am not, and I don't think I am paranoid, but I keep wondering why this Arum keeps looking at me—or why I *think* he is looking at me. I get the answer the next day at breakfast. "What are you doin' after this fight is finished?" Arum asks me.

I smell a job offer. "What am I doing? I will be on the beach again, that's what I'll be doing."

Arum comes back, "Irv, I want you to give me a call a week after the fight is over. We'll have a little talk."

Little talk, big talk, who cares? If Arum wants to sit down with me I am happy; it beats talking to yourself when you are unemployed. For the moment, however, I am employed, and I am thoroughly convinced that I made the right move when I persuaded John Condon to let me handle Shavers rather than Ali. As I told Condon, the Champ is his own heat press agent. When he meets Shavers face-to-face before the fight, he does what he does best: he insults his foe.

"Your bald head makes you look like an acorn," Ali says. "That's going to be your nickname—Acorn. You look like an acorn that fell out of a tree, nigger.

"You should want me to win this fight, boy, just for the sake of boxing. You should want me to keep my title, 'cause if you win the title, Earnie Shavers, the title will die." On and on Ali goes: "I might just shine your head for you, Earnie. Yeah, and then teach you to talk; you gotta learn to talk, Shavers."

As usual, Ali produces columns across the country. Very accurately, Mike Lupica of the *New York Daily News* echoes my thoughts with this headline: "Ali's Act: Same Old Hype, But It Still Works."

The fight itself is a minor classic. Shavers nearly takes it away from the Champ, but Ali calls it all back from memory. Only Ali could withstand an attack in the last thirty seconds the way he did and almost put Shavers away. Ali wins the fifteen-round decision, and personally, I am proud of him. The next day, after the traditional postfight press conference, I meet the Champ. By now we are old buddies and he sits down with me. "You showed yourself to be one of the greatest fighters ever," I tell him, "but I think you ought to hang up the gloves once and for all."

"You really think so?" Ali asks.

"No hard feelings," I say, "but the time has come to quit."

Ali looks at me, quizzically but not defiantly. He shows me just by his response that my message has seeped through, but I also sense that there are other reasons— money, for one—that must keep him in the ring, at least for the immediate future. So we bid our adieus and I return to New York and the meeting with Arum.

= 16 =
Bobbing and Weaving with Arum—or Hitting the Heights with Top Rank

It is good to be back home. For one thing, I get a large pat on the back from John Condon (a real pal) and I get the invitation to have lunch with Arum at the Friar's Club. As soon as I am buzzed through the iron gates at the Friar's and greeted by Arum, I can tell by the firmness in his handshake that he is interested in more than simply lunch and small talk.

We sit down in the main dining room and within five minutes Arum says, "How much do you want to handle publicity for me?"

I waste no time either. "Gimme $500 a week and you got yourself a deal."

"You got it!"

Wait a minute, I say to myself What the hell is this guy doing? Why doesn't he at least go through the formality of bargaining me down a few grand like any other self-respecting promoter would do? But Arum says no more and I know I heard right, so I figure I am now working for a latter-day St. Francis of Assisi. How right—or wrong—I am will soon be known, but for the moment I am enjoying the moment. I am off the beach once more.

On October 10, 1977, I officially take over as publicity director of Top Rank. It is not all that unlike Don King's outfit, in the sense that Arum is in the business of making big bucks out of promoting fights. After that, the difference—excuse the expression—is like black and white. Instead of being treated like a piece of shit, the way I was by King, I am regarded by Arum with respect and paternal kindness.

If Arum and King have anything in common at the beginning it is their almost obsessive desire to cavort in chaos. For weeks after taking over the job I am without my own desk or telephone. When we move into our new offices on the nineteenth floor of 450 Park Avenue it is like a scene out of *Marat/Sade* or a Marx Brothers movie. Crates all over the place. Typewriters on the floor. Phones on chairs. "Boxing's Mad, Mad, Mad World" is a *Daily News* headline about our operation, and it is right on the nose. Not that I care; I am working, and I'm on my way to Las Vegas to handle the October 22 fight between a guy named Leon Spinks, whom I know very little about, and Scott LeDoux, the fellow who started the shit-hitting-the-fan episode with Don King and Howard Cosell.

Before I take off I check with a few boxing people to get a line on Spinks. "He's a surly bastard," I am told by one friend. "You're going to have your hands full." When I get to Vegas I am told that not only is Leon Spinks on the card but he has a brother, Michael, who also will be fighting the same night.

I waste no time looking up Leon and find him at the hotel with brother Michael. Any fears that I may have nurtured before arriving are immediately dissipated. We immediately dig each other and I am surprised how much I take to the brother. I love them both, but I especially find Michael a warm and wonderful kid. As for Leon, I come on very low-pressure with him. We talk a lot and he soon opens up, telling me that his father had repeatedly told him that he would never be any good, never would amount to much. As soon as I hear that, I realize that I have to make a point of building up Leon's self-esteem. Others had warned me that he was worse than a dope— that mentally he was somewhere in the vicinity of an idiot. Bullshit. This Leon Spinks, I discover, is a very street-smart guy who reminds me of a lot of fellows from my Brownsville–East New York ghetto. Unschooled, determined, tough, but basically a good chap.

As a fighter Leon impresses me, although I regard his brother Michael as the better boxer. In his bout with LeDoux, Leon comes out of it with a draw, which is not bad considering that LeDoux is so much more the experienced fighter and also that several ringsiders believe that Leon actually has outpointed LeDoux.

After the fight I head for Leon's dressing room and see him there on the bench in front of his locker. "Leon," I say, "I hope you don't feel too badly about the way this thing went. You did very well considering that the other guy has been around a helluva lot longer than you have."

I am impressed by the manner in which Spinks takes the verdict. "I don't feel badly," he says. "How else am I goin' to learn?"

Leon and I are fast becoming buddies. I handle his next fight, on November 18, against Alfio Righetti of Italy. This time, with a slam-bang finish, Leon wins a ten-round decision. Sitting behind me at ringside is none other than the Champ himself, Muhammad Ali. Every so often I turn to Ali and I notice that the Champ is practically salivating as he watches the kid, Spinks, deliver his lefts and rights. I wonder about that.

I know that an Ali-Spinks fight is as much a possibility as an Ali-Evangelista bout once was; and we both know what came of that. I also know that Leon has Ali on his mind. More and more, Spinks is talking about taking on the Champ, and after the bout with Righetti he meets with the media and tells them that he would like nothing more than to meet Ali. One of the newspaper guys comes back and asks what makes Leon think he can fight the great Ali.

"I'm thinking about that," Leon explains. "I've got a good couple of months to straighten out what I did wrong tonight and I'm gonna work on it. I know I have to learn how to cut off the ring on that man."

It is clear to me that he isn't the least bit fazed at the thought of going into the ring with the Champ. I admire the manner in which he handles his interviews and I secretly hope that the Spinks-Ali fight comes off as soon as possible. As a pal of Ali, I have mixed feelings. I still want him to retire as champ, but I also figure a bout with Spinks will be a piece of cake for Ali while giving the kid some excellent experience.

I think to myself, Why shouldn't Ali fight Spinks? He needs the cash; he should beat Leon, then maybe Alfredo Evangelista again, and then maybe Irv Rudd for three million a pop. Of course, at the time I don't realize how Ali's hand speed and general reflexes have eroded since the fight with Shavers. And I haven't much time to think about it, because Arum puts me on some televised weight-lifting exhibition that has me wondering for a while whether I am heading down the tubes again. I mean, weight lifting isn't exactly my bag. On top of that I have to buck the Norton-Young fight that is coming up a few weeks before my muscleman show. No matter. I produce a couple of gimmicks and get more space than Norton and Young put together.

Arum is not only impressed, he is very impressed. When I walk into the office and say hello to my boss, he reacts as if I have just recited the Ten Commandments. Then he tells me that he has signed Spinks and Ali and that he is raising my salary by 50 percent. And that I will have to take on staff. Now, at age sixty, I. Rudd is making more money than he did under Walter O'Malley, Marty Tananbaum, and Paul Screvane.

Working for those three I felt like Rodney Dangerfield, the comic who keeps moaning, "I don't get no respect!" Arum, by contrast, holds me in awe and gives me respect like I never had before in my entire life. In turn, I respect Bob because he is a doer, not a bullshit artist.

Meanwhile I have a lot of do-ing to do. The Ali-Spinks bout is set for February 15 and I leave for Las Vegas on February 1. Right away I got headaches—trouble of the first order. Spinks has been sent to the Borscht Belt for training at a big hotel called Kutscher's Country Club, situated on Sackett Lake near Monticello, New York. Unlike Ali, who always makes himself at home wherever he trains, Leon starts to piss and moan. His big complaint is that he can't get "soul food," the specialties of a black man's menu. I know we can always manage to get stuff, but Leon checks out of the place. What really bothers me, though, is how he expects to last against the Champ if he is only going to eat pork and ribs.

Pretty soon I realize that Spinks is a small problem compared to what is happening with Ali. A complete transformation is developing in his personality. Instead of the gregarious boxer always ready with a line, we find ourselves with a sphinx.

All of a sudden Ali doesn't want to talk to the press. He does not want to give any interviews, and he is not playing any favorites either. The turnabout is so remarkable that at first most of the newsmen are suitably skeptical about the Champ's reclusive behavior; they figure it for a stunt, and to tell the truth I don't blame them a bit.

But I know for a fact that Ali means it. Time and again I ask the Champ whether he will let down his barriers and be the Ali of old, but all I get is a shake of his head. A firm *no*.

With that I decide to lay low for a day or two with Ali and figure out some sort of gimmick to get ink. He is training in Miami; I notice that the Champ's birthday is January 17, and January 15 happens to be Super Bowl day in New Orleans. That means that there will be a ton of newspapermen from all over at the game and the potential for plenty of stories. So I let the word out to Ali's people that I want to fly some writers to Florida after the Super Bowl. Word comes right back to me like a boomerang that Ali will not talk to anybody. Period!

My ace in the hole is the Champ's private phone number. I call him up. "Champ, this is Irving Rudd."

I get to first base; he doesn't hang up on me. "What's up Irvin'?"

"Champ, I wanna celebrate your birthday and bring in some crippled and ghetto kids . . ."

"N-o. You get that? N-o!" Then a pause. "I don't want any of that shit. If they wanna come to see me work out, fine, but I ain't gonna do no talkin'."

"You got a deal."

Right away I sound out a few newsmen on account of I instinctively feel that I have a big, big story here: Ali, the world champion boxer and world champion talker, won't talk. But I realize that this is going to be a tough one to pull off, maybe my toughest assignment ever. How do you make a birthday party an event when the birthday man already has told you he won't talk to *anyone*? I visit Ali a few days before the party and he repeats his no-talking warning to me. I tell him that is fine with me.

"Champ," I add, "they're coming to see you on your birthday, and they respect your not wanting to talk as long as you're going to work out for them. You are going to work out, aren't you?"

"Yes, I am," he replies.

So I set up the party, first contacting an old PR pal named Hank Meyer, who handles a new Miami hotel called the Omni. Meyer agrees to hold the dinner at his place after Ali's workout. Great. I get hold of the hotel's pastry chef and we work out plans for a cake that will be the most spectacular imaginable. Lucky for me, the chef is an ace and produces a cake that is three feet by two feet in the shape of a ring, enhanced by a pair of boxing gloves and a crown. So good is his job down to the smallest detail that even the tiny gloves have the Everlast trademark and insignia on them, made of marzipan. There is not one piece of artificial decoration on the cake. HAPPY BIRTHDAY, MUHAMMAD ALI is the inscription.

Meanwhile, the Fifth Street Gym is jumping with spectators and newsmen waiting to see the Champ work out. The biggest, from Red Smith to Dick Young, are all there as well as guys from San Francisco, Chicago, you name it. They are now more curious than ever about Ali's strange behavior.

At last Muhammad comes out of his dressing room for the workout. To my eyes he is fat . . . bloated. He has not been training very hard, and it shows. He snorts and sniffs and appears to be in less than mint condition. I begin to worry about him. Finally I walk up to him. "Champ, I need a favor from you. I want you to go into the ring and pose with the cake. No talkin' to anybody, just pose with the cake."

He sulks for a second, mutters, "Oh, shit," but goes into the ring. Before I can even hand him the knife to cut the cake, everyone stands up and sings "Happy Birthday." He cuts a piece of cake and holds it for photographers. He is pleased by the scene and I feel no compunctions about pushing him a bit more. "Rather than serve the cake to the folks," I suggest, "why don't you let me send it to the Variety Hospital and Home for Crippled Children?"

The Champ loves the idea, so I take the cake, with one piece missing, and rewrap it. Then I phone the Variety Home and tell them that a huge cake is on the way, courtesy of the Champ. "You a good man, Irvin' Rudd," Ali says. With that he goes right back to his workout—and silence.

Sensing that Ali means business, the writers disperse and the Champ starts pounding away. But one newsman won't be budged. There is Dick Young of the *Daily News* who persists in hanging around. I have my eye on Young, but I know that I can't get rough on him because he is bird-dogging a story. That is his job, and now he is trying to catch Ali as the Champ leaves the ring. Muhammad remains silent as Young fires questions at him relentlessly, until Young finally blurts out, "So, you're not talkin', Muhammad?"

Ali just stares at Young and continues walking to the dressing room. I am worried because Young can make us or crucify us with a column. A split second after Ali gives Young the brush-off, I turn to the columnist. "Well, I'll be a son of a bitch," I say to him. "Dick, we now have a match—the Sphinx vs. Spinks!"

When Young hears that he stops in his tracks, turns to me with a grin, and then continues on his way. I knew I connected, and a day later I have my instincts confirmed when Young carries that very line in his column and, days later, it is picked up all over the country.

I was smart and I was lucky; smart to take the negative situation with all the dire consequences of Ali staying mum and turning it into a positive. But the fact that Young hung around and caught the spark of my remark is the turning point. That night Gert and I are invited to the dinner in Ali's honor at the hotel. Usually the guest of honor is one of the last to come, but not Ali. He is the very first, along with his beautiful wife Veronica. As soon as he walks in, he spots me and Gert.

"Where you sittin', Irvin'?" he asks.

I point to a distant table. "Uh-uh," says Ali. "You and your wife are sittin' with me and Veronica."

"Delighted," I say.

Now the newspaper guys are drifting in. They see Ali and head for his table. "How you doin', Champ?" they say. Ali smiles and he is generally amiable, signs some autographs, but adamantly refuses to talk boxing. At the moment he is more interested in having a very social conversation with me and Gert. "Mrs. Rudd," he says with apparent seriousness, "how long you married to that guy?"

"We're married thirty-five years," Gert replies.

The Champ does a double take.

"Mrs. Rudd," he half shouts, "how did you ever last that long?"

Gert rolls her eyes for a second and replies with a grin, "Irv's on the road a lot!"

That line sends the Champ into convulsions. When he finally stops laughing, Ali turns to me. "How old are you, Irvin' Rudd?"

I tell the Champ that I am sixty years old, whereupon he turns to his wife. "Veronica, when I'm gonna be sixty, our daughter, Hana, is gonna be twenty-four. She'll be out of college."

Now the birthday party is warming up and a smaller version of the original boxing gloves cake is wheeled out while a strolling violinist plays "Happy Birthday." At this point Ali once again demonstrates why he is a master of public relations. He takes a knife, deftly cuts the cake, and then takes one piece at a time and hands each to a newsman. With each serving he says, "If you're my friend, you're gonna understand why I'm so quiet." The party is a success in every way and we get worldwide coverage for it, although the Champ still is holding to his silence—no interviews vow.

Even the most cynical newsmen now realize that Ali is unequivocal about not talking, and a whole spate of reasons are given for his unusual turn. Of these, two get the most play. One is that Ali's sycophantic sidekicks have convinced him that Elvis Presley never had a publicity man, no press conferences, and look at all the money he made (Which is not all true; Presley did not always sell out his concerts.) The second reason is that Ali realizes that, pugilistically speaking, he is eventually going to die. He understands that all his momentary "friends" will desert him. Already, in Miami, some of them have disappeared. But there are still a few around who try to butter up Ali. One guy yells, "Hey, I just rubbed the Champ's left arm, stay away. . . . Hey, Champ, I just put the bag down there. . . . Champ, I cooked your eggs this morning. . . . I polished your shoes." Ad nauseum.

At last we move the entire entourage to Las Vegas to prepare for the fight that is only days away. Ali still hasn't talked, and there are some who figure he will stay mum until the bell goes to start the bout. But on the night before the fight I get a phone call from Harold Conrad, one of Ali's advisers. Conrad says the magic words: "The Champ wants everyone up in his room—he'll talk!"

Writers flee the pressroom for Ali's place as if the Champ has announced that gold was discovered in his room. Meanwhile, I chase all over the hotel just to be sure everyone gets the word. That done, I repair to Muhammad's room to see what there is to see and, more important, to hear if he really has anything to say.

The Champ holds court in vintage Ali style. For openers he wears a set of false teeth, purposely mimicking Leon Spinks's gap-toothed grin. Then he does a traditional Muhammad number about how he is still "the Greatest" and will give young Leon a boxing lesson. With it all, I am not convinced. Ali does not look right to me and I am worried for him. While he has lost weight he does not appear in prime fight condition. The Champ reminds me of Bummy Davis after Bummy got a furlough from the army to fight Fritzie Zivic the second time, and Zivic beat the

living shit out of him. From my angle it appears that Ali
has gone to the well one time too many. On the other
hand, the kid, Spinks, is oozing with determination. I tell
Will Grimsley of the Associated Press that the more I
watch Spinks the more I am reminded of another U.S.
marine of fifty years ago—Gene Tunney, who beat Jack
Dempsey and became the heavyweight champion. "Will,"
I say, "we could have an upset here."

I notice that several writers are down on the fight.
Hearing the downbeat talk, I tell them that they are being
unfair to Leon. Sure, the Ali of ten years ago would make
mincemeat of the kid, but the Ali of 1978 is another story.
I don't think he will hurt the kid, and who knows, the kid
could win. Anyhow, I am convinced that Spinks has a
right to be here.

The fight, in its own perverse way, is a classic. The
Champ opens by doing his I-don't-care routine, with guard
down, taunting the challenger. By the sixth round most of
us expected Ali to get down to business and get serious
with the kid. But Spinks is stubborn, and whenever it appears as if Ali is going to do some hard hitting, somehow
Leon gets out of it, counterpunches, and throws the
Champ off guard. Right down to the end, the diehard Ali
followers figure that he will pull out the fight in the
twelfth, thirteenth, fourteenth, or at worst, fifteenth
round. But it never happens. Spinks hangs in there and
manages to survive the distance and, perhaps, even win
the damn fight.

The instant the bell heralds the end of the bout, I
climb into the ring. My assignment is to see Ali to his
dressing room, determine how he feels, and ask him when
he wants to meet the press. When I finally get through
the ropes, I still have no idea whether the Champ is still
the champ. The decision has not yet officially been announced, but already there are some important clues. Ali's
face is puffed out of proportion and I notice him stagger
across the ring to congratulate Spinks, even though the

word is not out yet as to who won. Normally Ali remains in his corner to accept the decision.

I am worried because the crowd in the ring is unusually large and very intense. I holler to Ali's people to get him back to his corner and three of his aides form a human circle around Muhammad, sit him on his stool, and don't allow anyone within fifteen feet of him. Watching Ali on his stool, I see a thoroughly whipped man. This is officially confirmed seconds later, when the decision for Spinks is announced. Much as I am sad for Muhammad, I cannot let emotions overtake me at a time like this. I have a job to do as grandstanders are carrying Spinks all around the ring.

Suddenly Carlos Shibeck, head of UPI's photo department in California, yells, "Irving, Irving, turn Spinks around. Turn him around! We're not getting our pictures!"

I plunge headlong into the circle of well-wishers and confront Leon. "Champ!" I plead, wondering whether he will remember me in the euphoria of the moment. Before I can get another word out, Leon, as if we are running into each other on a street corner, blurts out, "Hi, Irvin', how are ya?"

"Leon," I plead, "they want you to look at them—over there!" No problem; I turn him around, and then Spinks does this beautiful thing—he throws his arms up in the air, makes with that delicious gap-toothed grin, and we get pictures all over the world. In one second Leon shows me as much PR poise as Ali.

That done, I leave the ring with Muhammad and follow him into his dressing room. Apart from myself, the only folks there are his wife Veronica, Angelo Dundee, a few Muslim officials, and Muhammad, sitting on a bare folding chair. For the moment he looks to me like a beaten old warrior. Contusions surround his eyes, his face is crossed with slashes, and his kidneys are bruised.

A television set is sitting in the corner and someone

flicks the switch. Just then they are showing a replay of the end of the fight and the decision. A few of the Ali people in the room start yelling that the Champ was robbed. They start chanting "Al-i, Al-i" and whip themselves into a frenzy that Muhammad got a bum decision.

Ali stares at them as if they are a collection of dumb little kids. "Look," Muhammad says, "we ain't gonna have any sore losers in here tonight! The boy whipped me and whipped me fair. That's it, hear? I don't wanna hear any more talk about they robbed me!"

One of those doing the we-wuz-robbed! number is Ali's brother, Rachman. When Muhammad orders everyone to stop beefing about the decision, Rachman does an about-face and blames Ali for training wrong. The Champ bristles at his brother. "You stupid man," Ali snaps, "make up yo mind. First you got me robbed; now you got me in no shape."

I notice Veronica in a corner. She is all alone and conspicuously ignored. Nobody has even bothered to get her a cold drink. I ask her if she wants anything and get her a fruit juice. Ali catches me.

"That Irvin' Rudd is thinkin' about you all the time," says the Champ. "That's my Irvin', always thinkin' 'bout others."

There is a knock at the door; one of Ali's men gets it, and who walks in but Leon Spinks. He walks over to Muhammad, puts his arm around Ali, and kisses Muhammad on the cheek. "You're always gonna be my champ," says Leon, "and I'm always gonna love ya."

Ali is touched. "Ya fought a good fight, boy," he tells Leon.

At that point Ken Norton enters. "Hey, Ken," yells Ali, "you got yourself a tough little nigger, if you wanna fight Leon."

Norton laughs. Meanwhile, the media is being held at bay, suitably pissed because they want to talk to Ali. But I know better; this is one time I am not going to rush him.

Finally, an hour after we walked into the dressing room, Ali stands up, steps out of his protective cup, and looks over at me as if he expects to hear some advice. I say to him, "Champ, it's entirely up to you, but I'd like you to come to the press area for a while."

Under the circumstances of the evening, I expect him to balk, possibly get pissed off at me. But this is a real champ. "Irvin'," he says, "if you think it's important."

"No," I reply. "Champ, if *you* think it's important, you go. I want you to go for only one reason—because I don't want anyone to say Muhammad Ali didn't show up."

A couple of the Champ's sycophants don't go for the idea of Ali making any showing. I hear, from the background, pissing and moaning and mutterings of "He ain't goin' nowhere," and Muhammad obviously is disturbed by them. He turns to me. "Irvin', they say I shouldn't go."

"Fine, Champ," I say, "I'm going down to tell the press that the men in your entourage feel you shouldn't talk to the press." I glance over at them. Then I tell these mooches in my sweetest tones, "And you can be sure, my friends, that I will tell them that."

The Champ tugs my arm. "Irvin', we go!"

Once down at the media room, Ali sits himself right down next to Spinks and instantly congratulates him. Nothing that Ali does from that point on could be considered less than the epitome of class. He is generous in his praise of Leon and he doesn't alibi one iota. To me and a lot of other people, he comes out of that episode a great man.

After all the grilling is over, Ali leaves early the next day for a prearranged trip to Bangladesh. As he leaves for the airport I catch him in front of his limousine, put my arm around him, and say, "Champ, we'll be seeing each other again soon. Have a good trip; I wish you well."

I mean it from the bottom of my heart when I wish him well, because I feel and fear for this man. Watching him agonize in the ring with Spinks, I can tell that he is a different fighter than he was just four years earlier.

Before he gets into the car I try to get him to listen to me, just for a couple of moments. I feel strongly enough about the man to want him to do right, and I tell him precisely what I think. "Champ," I say, "you talk about the Muslim faith. Muhammad, that is nothing more than an offshoot of the Arabic Moslem faith. So if you're so interested in it, why don't you go to Egypt for six months and live there? Go to the mosque every morning; get into it for real. Learn what the hell you're talkin' about. After six months of that you can really decide if this is the road you want to follow. Then come back and preach to the people. Not like Oral Roberts or Billy Graham, but only like you can do, armed with the knowledge of the Koran and the Bible. Champ, you can really be a healer for good."

I don't know whether I have made an impression or not, but it already has become clear to me that Ali, who spends freely, needs money and he sees his chances for making it fading fast. Norton wants a piece of Ali's head and Spinks will fight him again. I don't want to see Muhammad come back, because he is a shell of his former self and Norton will be looking to punish the Champ. For me it will only bring back the bad memories of the second Zivic-Davis fight.

So Ali goes his way and I. Rudd now must zero in on Spinks. We have tentatively set noon the next day for Leon to hold his first press conference as heavyweight champion. Noon sounds good to me because I can use a good night's sleep. But at six in the morning the phone rings. Australia calling. Next it is New Zealand, then New York. The usual start to I. Rudd's day.

I field a few more calls, have breakfast, and then get upstairs to launch Leon's press conference. Making sure to be ahead of the game, I corral Spinks before any of the

240

writers get into the room. "Leon," I say, "I want to straighten something out with you in advance. I know you are the heavyweight champion but I can't really call you 'Champ,' because in my vocabulary, that term belongs to Ali."

Of course I was chancing a belt in the mouth, but Leon is a good fellow; he understands. Spinks smiles and says, "Irvin', I'll tell you what—from now on call me 'Boss,' because I want to be your boss."

I tell him that that's fine, but when the press conference actually starts I want to be sure, so I lean over to Leon and say, "Well, do you want me to call you 'Champ' now?"

"No, man, I'm your boss. Just call me 'Boss.'"

"Boss" it is, but I soon discover that others are calling *me* "Boss." The Ali-Spinks championship went over so well, from the press viewpoint, that I am getting compliments all over the place. That, however, is not as much a pleasure for me as the reaction I get from *my* boss, Bob Arum.

After Spinks's press conference I tell Arum that I want to get back to New York for the weekend. I intend to pay my own fare. I haven't been home for more than two weeks and I miss Gert. Bob says I should bring Gert out to Vegas, or even to Beverly Hills, to unwind. "Of course," he says, "if you'd rather go home—whatever you like."

"Whatever you like." I hear it but I can't believe it. After spending years with the likes of Walter O'Malley, Marty Tananbaum, and others who said, Sure, of course . . . and then welshed on the deal, I can't quite believe that Arum means what he says. Tananbaum never gave me ten cents' worth of spit; never said to me, Irving, good job! Now I am working for a human being who says, Go home, I'll foot the bill! I have never worked for anyone like this Arum man.

It is not until I am back in New York, relaxing at my

daughter's house on Long Island, that I realize what has happened in the past month. Suddenly it dawns on me that I have handled the whole Ali-Spinks bout by myself. I. Rudd was *the* honcho. I have worked many championship bouts, going back to 1939, but never anything like this. The fight had five hundred visiting newspapermen from all over the world and I took care of the whole schmear.

I only allow myself a day to rest on my laurels; then it is back to work. Soon after I get back to New York, Leon and his brother Michael arrive in town and come up to our new office. Our headquarters is in shambles, even worse than when I first got there. The floor is littered with paint cans and cartons. It looks like it is ten years away from being organized.

When Leon and Michael stroll in I am eating a tuna fish sandwich at my desk. To me they seem more like a couple of overgrown street waifs than fighters. Just looking at them, I get the feeling that they haven't eaten for a while. "You guys want some lunch?" I ask.

Their eyes brighten and then I realize that if I had not asked the heavyweight champion of the world to have a bite with me, he would have starved that afternoon. "Hey," Leon says, "do you really mind?"

"C'mon," I tell him, "order somethin' or I'll bust you one right on the chin." The two of them laugh. Leon asks, half embarrassed, "Can I have a ham and Swiss on white bread—no mustard?" Mike orders roast beef. I get them two sandwiches each with tea, and the three of us sit on packing crates eating lunch.

More and more I realize that these are two very earthy, very sensitive, very appreciative kids. Leon is actually touched that I bother to worry about him, and a month later he mentions offhandedly to me that he appreciated my getting himself and Mike the sandwiches. By this time Leon is making headlines all over the place and we are trying to arrange a fight for him against either Ali or Ken Norton in Africa.

The proposed site is Bophuthatswana, and if that isn't going to drive me nuts teaching the new guys how to spell it, nothing will. One of my first "victims" is young Mike Lupica of the *Daily News*. For him I write out the phonetic pronunciation on a large piece of paper: "Bow-pu-tot-swana."

"First order of business," I tell Lupica, "is we learn how to pronounce the fucking thing."

I hand Lupica the release that says the fight will take place in Mmabatho, Bophuthatswana, in September. "Irving," he says, "remember to keep a straight face when you tell people about it."

It is hard to keep a straight face the way Leon Spinks is moving. He has left New York and landed in Detroit. No sooner does he arrive in Detroit than my phone rings. An AP sportswriter is on the other end. He tells me that Leon has a new lawyer and do I know anything about it.

"This is a new wrinkle you are springing on me," I tell the AP guy. "What did Spinks say?"

The AP fellow reports that Leon has signed nothing, that he has no agreement with anyone. I tell that to Lupica, who is sitting across from me. "Spinks," says Lupica, "is gonna wind up with more lawyers than Patty Hearst."

I tell the AP guy I'll get back to him and immediately call my boss, Bob Arum, and tell him about the Detroit report. "Very interesting," says Arum. "I'll do a little checking."

The other phone rings. It is Butch Lewis, one of Top Rank's bosses, who is close to Spinks. I tell him about the Detroit business. He says he will check. Then Arum calls back and wants me to repeat what I told him a minute ago. I repeat.

I turn to Lupica, who is too young to remember. "In

the old days it was easy; a fighter wouldn't go to the john without his manager."

Another ring. AP in Detroit wants more information about Spinks. I give it; then Chet Cummings, another Top Rank official, walks into my office. "Guess what, Irv, Spinks just got the keys to Detroit from Coleman Young, mayor."

"Fuck Coleman Young, mayor," I say.

I pick up the phone and call Arum. "Boss, I'll need about five minutes alone with you to discuss Spinks and what's happening in Detroit."

Lupica and I walk to the door, dodging the crates, the typewriters on the floor, the phones on the chairs, and the paint rollers. "We got here a Marx Brothers movie," I tell the *News* columnist, who can't be twenty-five years old.

"Would you have it any other way?" he says.

"Well, my mother wanted me to be a doctor; or, at the very least, a rabbi."

"Would you have it any other way?"

"It still beats digging ditches and driving a cab."

The next day I pick up the *News* and there, spread across the top of the sportspage, Lupica has a whole column about me.

". . . Irving Rudd, a little white-haired man with a fighter's nose and a Brownsville voice who has been taken directly from Central Casting to play the part of Top Rank's press agent . . ."

I think Momma would have been proud had she read these few lines.

244

= 17 =
Sugar and Spice
but Everything
Not Nice

The columns keep coming and so do the 1980s. Life isn't all milk and honey for me, but there is plenty of sugar and spice. The sugar comes in the form of Ray Leonard, one of the most unusual and gifted boxers I've ever had the pleasure (*and* displeasure, I might add) to work with. The spice is provided by Ray Mancini, Marvin Hagler, and Thomas Hearns.

I originally met Leonard at the Muhammad Ali–Ken Norton fight in 1976 and we ran into each other again in 1979 when he was fighting at Capital Centre in Landover, Maryland. I figure I have spent roughly a year of my life

245

with Sugar Ray, which includes all of the training camps I have worked in starting in 1979.

What marks Sugar Ray different from so many other boxers I've dealt with is his meticulousness. He strikes me as the quintessential fighter of the 1980s, in that he is acutely aware of the value of television and the other electronic and print trappings. He is a perfectionist who doesn't miss a trick, whether it is his satin black robe with gold block lettering that spells out SUGAR or his immaculately shined boots or his snow-white headgear. Let me ask you, how many boxers are there who would have the balls to wear a row of showy silver studs outlining his groin? Only Sugar Ray.

He has come a long way from the twenty-year-old fighting for an Olympic gold medal in 1976, when his primary goal was to get his parents out of the ghetto.

"I'm a diamond in the mud," is the way he describes himself. "I'm just different. I'm a nonconformist. Sure, I have detractors, pessimists. But hell, if everybody was a positive thinker, this would be one weird world."

Yes, it *is* one weird world working with Sugar Ray Leonard. What could be more weird than two fighters about to slug it out for a fat purse—and supposed to be hating each other—when one asks the other for his autograph? I kid you not, it happens before the Leonard–Larry Bonds fight at the Carrier Dome in Syracuse in 1981.

This is quite a production put together by the Syracuse Chamber of Commerce. You have to remember that Syracuse isn't known as the fight capital of the world. So when the upstate New York city gets a big bout, the merchants are going to do it up brown—which they do, with a huge press conference, the works.

Bonds shows up at the prefight meeting with the media accompanied by his wife. The place is loaded with television people, cameras here, more cameras there, writers from all over the world, and everyone is looking forward to a good grudge fight. How many times have we seen fighters coming into one of those about promotions practionally breathing are and spitting blood at each other in anticipation of the match? Hundreds. Sometimes they really are angry and other times it's hype, but at least they are conveying a feeling of fighting.

Not Larry Bonds. To this day I can't believe what he said, and at the time I *certainly* want to shake the wax out of my ears, because there is no way Bonds is doing what he is doing—and yet he does it. He walks over to Leonard, and instead of faking a punch to the mouth or at the very least seething at him, Larry pulls out four eight-by-ten glossy photos of Sugar Ray Leonard. (Bonds reminds me of *me* when I used to stand outside the players' entrance at Ebbets Field when I was nine years old and ask Babe Herman for his autograph.) "Ray," Bonds says, "I've got these four pictures of you. Would you mind autographing them for me, my wife, and my kids?"

I'm standing there, right between them, and still not believing what I'm hearing—but I'm hearing it. What I am concerned about most of all is that one of those dozens of TV or radio microphones will pick it up or one of the newspaper guys might hear it. Thank God nobody does, so I grab Bonds as unobtrusively as I can and say, "Bonds, put those fucking pictures away before I shove them up your ass! Are you crazy?" He hears me good and gets rid of them just in time. I spend the rest of the day shaking my head and saying to myself, Holy shit; in fifty-odd years of press agentry I never saw anything like that.

Being involved with Leonard's camp is distinctly different than with someone like Ali; like the difference between filet mignon (Leonard's followers) and garbage (Ali's followers).

The characters who followed Ali around were, for the most part, parasitical wise guys indiscreetly running with broads, shaking down storekeepers, and being smart-alecky with waiters in dining rooms.

Sugar Ray has no more than ten people, tops, in his camp, including his brothers. None of them are thieves, moochers, users, or shakedown artists. In Leonard's camp everybody has a job, and everybody does it—even if it means having one guy in charge of Sugar Ray's left glove and one for the right. Yet for all their professionalism, Leonard and his camp lack Ali's genius for dealing with the press—a problem that makes my job harder.

The general staff under Leonard consists of two interesting characters: Mike Trainer and Janks Morton. Although he is a lawyer, Trainer is always referred to as the champ's manager. I will say this about Trainer—as I used to say about my old Yonkers Raceway boss Al Tananbaum—if I ever need a heart transplant I want his, because it hardly ever has been used! Trainer is his own kind of man, a fellow, as they say, who marches to a different drummer. Except Trainer marches without socks—never wears them. He's the kind who will go on a business trip to, say, Montreal and take absolutely nothing with him, no socks, no papers, nothing. That kind of shtick.

Only once do I see Trainer shaken, and it involves a classic dumb move perpetrated by Janks Morton. In the pecking order at Leonard's camp Morton ranks right behind Trainer. Janks is a big, strapping black man who knows I distrust him and dislike him, although I'm still hard-pressed to tell you why. Anyhow, Morton is the guy who steered Leonard to Mike Trainer and in his own way has a lot to say about Sugar Ray.

With all due respect to Morton, he couldn't train his hair with Vaseline much less a fighter, and this episode proves my point. We are in Maryland for the 1980 Leonard-Duran fight. We have an opportunity to get a special photo session with *Newsweek* magazine, which for us would be worth one hell of a lot of money. If you get a cover from *Newsweek* or *Time* you're getting the best, not only in national coverage but also first-rate photography. In return you have to give them time, because *Newsweek* is the kind of outfit that likes to spend a lot of bucks on art. When they send a photographer, you figure he's good for at least an hour with your man and you're tickled to give it to him.

I arrange with the *Newsweek* photographer to touch base with Sugar Ray right after a sparring session. Everything is hunky-dory. I figure there's no need for me to stick around. I've seen about two thousand of these photo opportunities, and besides, I have some publicity work to do for Ray up in my room. I say my good-byes to the *Newsweek* man and go upstairs.

About twenty minutes later there is a knock on the door. To my amazement, who should be standing there but the chap from *Newsweek.* "Boy," I say, "do you work fast!"

The photographer isn't smiling, he's frowning, and I'm sure that if he could have growled he would have done that. "Fast, shit," he snaps. "That son of a bitch Janks Morton, he shut down my photo session!"

Steam is flowing out of my ears. I'm fuming. I pick up the phone and shout, *"Get me Janks Morton!"* The operator says, "I'm sorry, sir, he's checked out." I have a feeling he still is there but under a different name. He wants his name off the register; a little hideaway trick. I phone one of the hotel executives, Polly Moroney. "Polly, please," I implore her, "I want to talk to Janks Morton."

Polly is a lovely lady, but she shoots back, "I can't do that, Irving; it will be my job."

Now I'm wondering how the devil I'm going to find that SOB, Mike Trainer—that's the ticket! Now, Trainer is the kind of guy you don't phone at home. Matter of fact, it's harder to reach Trainer at his house than George Bush at the White House. But I reach Trainer at home and he says, "Irving, how did you get my home phone number?"

"I haven't got time for that shit," I bark. "Mike, that fucking Janks Morton, he shut down *Newsweek*'s photographer after only twenty minutes. *Twenty fucking minutes and he shut down* Newsweek! *No cover!*"

Mike Trainer, who doesn't shock very easily, nearly gets a case of lockjaw. I can't believe it—the man actually gasps. He knows that jerko Morton has really screwed us. Besides the fact that he has canceled the photo shoot, we have interviews and photo shoots set up for first thing in the morning. Here I am with interviews promised to several reporters, and no Sugar Ray—or Morton, for that matter.

Trainer gives me Morton's unlisted room number at the hotel and tells me to call Morton in the morning. Well, I am so steamed that I stay up till 3:00 A.M. and then proceed to Morton's hotel room. *Boom, boom, boom* I pound on Morton's door till he opens it, all groggy-eyed and half awake. "There are interviews first thing tomorrow morning, eight A.M.!" I don't slug him like I really want to do, but I sure as hell feel a lot better.

By this time, of course, the photographer, Ken Regan, is gone, so I just have to hope that something good will happen.

It happens a week before the fight. Regan phones. "I've been commissioned to shoot the fight," says the photographer, "but what I need is an apron space on the ring."

That is a mighty big order, and it won't help us sell any tickets because his fight photos will appear after our bout is over and done with. But I have an idea. "Ken," I say, "I don't like to play games, but I have to. You already have some pictures of Sugar Ray. I'll get you the space on the ring apron if you get me the cover [of *Newsweek*] a week before the fight."

We get the cover of *Newsweek* all right, and when Trainer sees it, the unflappable one permits himself a "Wow!" I look at him for a moment and then say, "Mike, look carefully at the photo, because if you do, you'll see little flecks of blood in the background. *They're mine!*"

* * *

Seven years later, after I have shed a great deal of blood out of the ring, as has Leonard in the ring, the great fighter gives it all up and tries his hand—or should I say his mouth—at broadcasting. He becomes a fight analyst for CBS, and a lousy one at that. He sounds like he is talking with a mouthful of mush. When he first gets into the broadcasting game Sugar is still being idolized as the great fighter that he was. He comes walking down the aisle to thunderous applause from the audience. But bit by bit the applause becomes less enthusiastic and pretty soon he is just a boxing announcer.

In my estimation, he simply can't live with that. For Sugar Ray Leonard, private citizen, there really is nothing to do, and pretty soon he can't live without the applause that he grew to love and expect as a boxer. That leaves him with one and only one thing to do: climb back into the ring.

When Leonard starts to train again at Hilton Head in 1987, Trainer, back in Las Vegas, asks my boss Bob Arum for "one last favor."

Little do I know that this one last favor will almost cause me to have a coronary (not really), if not some major migraines (really!).

"Bob," Trainer says, "I need one last thing of you. We want Irving Rudd to work Leonard's camp." Ah, well, Bob concedes and I end up at Hilton Head for a real roller coaster of an experience.

I arrive at the Leonard camp late in January of 1987. The fight, against the world champion Marvin Hagler, is to be on April 6. The day after I arrive Trainer calls a meeting of myself, Charlie Brotman (another Leonard aide-de-camp), and a couple of guys from hotel management. Trainer sits me down and says, "Look, Irving, we like you, we respect you, but you work for Arum and therefore you are a Hagler spy. You better listen to what we tell you and how to go about doing things or your ass is out of here in twenty-four hours." I am stunned.

Bob Arum has to beg me, *beg me*, to stay in that camp for even the next five minutes! Faster than the time it takes to blink there is a new rumor being spread and more mess being made.

One day I come back to my hotel room from watching Leonard train to a phone call from a panic-stricken Arum.

"Irving, what's with Leonard?"

I had just watched him box a few rounds and don't know what he's talking about. "What do you mean what's with Leonard?"

"He hurt his hand," says Arum, who was a few hundred miles away.

"What's the matter with you, Bob?" I answer. "I just saw Ray."

Arum goes on to tell me that some schmuck TV guy in Boston who always is looking for a scoop had a report on the air that Leonard injured his hand and our fight is in jeopardy.

Before I can inhale, Phil Berger of *The New York Times* is on the blower. "Hey, what's going on?"

"What's going on with what?" I reply in my best Brooklynese.

"I hear your guy is having trouble holding his weight."

Before Berger can say another word I shoot down that stupid rumor and Phil trusts me.

Bingo. Now it's the *Los Angeles Herald-Examiner*. "What's the matter with Leonard? I hear he's got blood disease." I knock that down too, but the next call scares the shit out of me. It's Lou Falcigno, the guy who provides the equipment for closed circuit in the Northeast. If he has any doubts about the fight coming off, then we're in real trouble. "Just hold on, Lou," I implore him. "I'll get right back to you and I'm sure everything will be okay."

I get an idea. If I can get myself ten or fifteen minutes with Sugar Ray, I know I'll get to the bottom of all these crazy rumors. Sure enough, Leonard tells me everything is A OK. Great, but the brush fires are blazing all over the country. That means there is only one way to put them out, en masse, with the outfit that covers the continent, The Associated Press. I figure if Leonard talks to AP for five minutes and tells them that he's in shipshape, all will be resolved. As usual, for some unknown crazy reason Leonard will not give the interview, so I get on the phone with AP's boxing editor, Ed Schuyler, and one by one demolish every one of the dirty anti-Leonard reports, without the help of Leonard, Brotman, or Trainer!

This is a case where my five decades of experience and reliability pay off. Schuyler knows me well enough to know that I wouldn't stiff him on a story. Without a second thought he runs a piece telling the world that all is well with Sugar Ray.

I say proudly that my word stands up. The next day Leonard is back in the ring and we are selling tickets again. And a few weeks later, Phil Berger, in a *New York Times* story, states in black and white that Al Braverman—a right-hand man for Don King—had spread the bloody rumors all across the country.

That's the Leonard camp in a nutshell: one fire after another starting up and having to be put out, all because these guys either don't know or won't bother to learn how to treat the media.

Brotman and Trainer are incapable of treating the press with courtesy, and they don't have the class to look out for the "little people," the way Ali always did. I've been told by bellmen, waiters and limo drivers that whenever the Leonard crew goes anywhere, they give the "lousiest tips." For example, a limo driver who is a regular at the Las Vegas airport, told a skycap he was waiting for the Leonard group to arrive. No sooner are the words out of his mouth, all the skycaps vanished from that side of the airport.

When we are at Hilton Head the Leonard frugality is

in full and embarrassing view. After twelve weeks at the hotel one would expect a guest party of such large proportions to at least dole out a hundred bucks to the head housekeeper. Not the Sugar Ray group. Instead, at the end of the stay a dinner is given where hotel workers can pose for a picture with Leonard and receive a typewritten letter of thanks. That's it. No tip, nothing. They get a picture of Sugar Ray to hang on their wall but no money to buy even a lousy picture frame with.

After nine years of dealing with Trainer and Leonard I still have to keep a gross of aspirin handy. I still get migraines thinking about the *tsouris* he gave me over the years.

I'll give you a for-instance. In 1989, during the Leonard-Hearns II fight preparations, Trainer has this habit of not being around when I need him most. On this occasion we are working in the Poconos with a nice young man named John, who belongs to an agency that is helping us with the fight. John has to get a simple okay from Leonard (via Trainer) for a release. If we wait for Trainer it will take a whole week, and we don't have that kind of time to spare.

I think I have a simple solution. I ask one of Leonard's guys to find a Fax machine. "Fax Trainer," I say, "and tell him to fax me back the okay."

Trouble is, I ask the wrong guy. All he wants is to preach about Jesus. That's all I hear is Jesus this and Jesus that. Finally, in utter exasperation, I say, "Y'know, I preach about Jesus, too, when I get pissed off. I say, 'Jesus Christ, can't you get anything right around here.'"

Since I am getting nowhere with him, John and I agree that we just have to get to Ray himself for about two minutes and say, Look, this is for John, would you sign this. And this other thing is for so-and-so, would you sign that so we can go back and get our work done without waiting a whole week for Trainer.

But, typically, we can't reach Leonard, and now the

buses with the writers and the radio and the TV people are ready to take off back to New York. We have no choice but to get aboard but I can see that John is so pissed that the veins in his neck look like they are going to burst.

I can't take it anymore, so finally I blow my stack in the bus, right among the media guys, one of whom is Wallace Matthews of *Newsday*. The next day I pick up the paper and there is a scathing—I mean *scathing*—piece under his byline about the high-handedness of Leonard and Trainer.

Matthews spares nothing, going on about the Leonard-Trainer shtick, the pair of phonies that they are, and their imperial tactics. There is no doubt where Matthews got that story—from me, of course—but there is no mention of this in the piece. Meanwhile, Bob Arum reads it and chews the shit out of me. "Bob," I explain, "I can't help it. There's just so far a guy can go. If this is the end and you want to fire me, so be it."

He doesn't, thank God, because I'm sure he realizes that I've spilled blood for him and saved him plenty, especially when his enemies fired torpedoes and I get in the way to deflect them out of harm's way.

It would be nice for me to say that I enjoy working with Sugar Ray, but that would brand me a liar. The fact is, I don't think Leonard is a nice guy. Period. And enough incidents have occurred in our relationship to make me think this chapter should have been titled "The Boy Next Door Is a Prick." Two nonencounters with Sal Marchiano and Shirley Povich of the *Washington Post* will give you an idea of what I mean.

Marchiano, with NBC-TV in New York, is an excellent reporter whom I've known ever since he graduated from Fordham. Not only is he a good guy but he is an important journalist in a big market, not to mention Povich, an eighty-three-year-old gentleman and an esteemed sportswriter. Under no circumstances should either of them be slighted, but with Sugar Ray you never know.

Before the 1987 Hagler fight, Leonard has this rule that Mondays and only Mondays are his interview days. And only at a special time on Mondays. On a Wednesday he will grudgingly consent to talk to some television guys. But the only closed-circuit TV guys he'll talk to are from the Washington, D.C., area, because that sweetheart Trainer has swung a closed-circuit deal for him and Ray in D.C., Baltimore, and Norfolk, Virginia. In Trainer and Ray's narrow minds it means that only media people from those areas should be able to interview Leonard on days other than Monday.

Ridiculous. Then, I get a call from Marchiano. "All I want is a few minutes with Sugar Ray," he explains. "I work until midnight on Sunday, so the best I can do is take a late-morning plane down to see him. Otherwise I would have to get back up at six A.M. Just give me fifteen minutes at three o'clock in the afternoon. I'll come in, do the interview, and shoot right out."

It seems reasonable enough, but reason is not a major force at this time, at least not with Charlie Brotman, who has become yet another pain in the ass between me and Sugar Ray. I plead Marchiano's case with Charlie and urge him to get an okay from Leonard. What the hell, it's NBC. We're not talking about Podunk.

Charlie returns a short while later with the message: Ray feels that he'd rather inconvenience Marchiano than have Marchiano inconvenience him.

Meanwhile, Shirley Povich, God bless him, drives down from Washington with his wife Ethel, and *he* gets frozen out. Next it is Nick Charles from the Cable News Network. Finally I walk up to Charlie and say, "I don't know what's gonna be, but I can tell you I ain't gonna stand for this shit. I'll walk out of this fucking camp. You can't treat the old man [Povich] like that."

Next thing you know, the old man gets himself an in-

terview with Ray, and after the workout, Nick Charles gets his. Obviously this is not the same Sugar Ray I had met when he was Simon Pure Golden Boy just out of the Olympics. What changed him? Who knows. I have been told for a fact by people who should know that his meeting with Don King on September 28, 1976, at Yankee Stadium (when Ali fought Norton) was pivotal.

They say King took Ray into the men's crapper and showed him a hundred grand in cash. At the time the kid was determined to go on with his schooling, but his wife-to-be, Juanita, was with child and he had to marry her and go to work to make a living. So he decided to go pro; and with that decision went his amateur status, his innocence, and his courtesy.

After the Hagler fight I handled for Leonard in 1987, I don't speak to him, Charlie Brotman, or Mike Trainer for two years. Not out of hostility, mind you; I just don't want any part of that group. If I see Sugar Ray show up at a fight—as spectator or as a broadcaster—I pay no attention to him. I never seek him out and I think he senses that.

Our paths finally cross in November of 1988, in Las Vegas. Leonard is set to fight the Canadian champ, Donny Lalonde, while my man, Thomas Hearns, will box James Kinchen a few days earlier. One evening we are at the Las Vegas Hilton, where our fight will take place, and who should come over but Sugar Ray. We sort of bump head-to-head into each other in the lobby. Leonard is doing a very nice thing: he has come over to see a young fighter named Michael Nunn. Nunn idolizes him, so Sugar is there to wish Nunn well—a nice gesture even if it is Leonard doing it. (I give credit where credit is due!)

Well, I know that the Leonard-Lalonde fight is hell-bent toward turning into a financial bomb. Leonard's camp has the mistaken impression that all they need to do is throw the doors open and people will flock in just because Sugar Ray is fighting. But I know different, and I can tell

by the way things are going that they are going to blow two million or more at Caesars Palace.

So Ray and I come face-to-face and I say, "Ray, I see there's a lot of horseshit work going on over there at Caesars with your fight. I got news for you; we're having a final press conference here. Why don't you come here tomorrow and see how the pros do it?"

Just like that, Leonard gives me a big smile. He is used to getting the zapperoo from me. "C'mon, Ray," I add, "come over and get some insight." He just smiles. He will win the fight, but the ticket sales aren't up to expectations.

In contrast to Sugar Ray Leonard we have one of my favorite people of the 1980s, Thomas Hearns. I put Hearns in the number-one slot, not only as a fighter but also as an all-time great athlete and, more importantly, a super mensch. I first meet Thomas in 1979 at the Superdome in New Orleans. He is a welterweight out of Detroit fighting a full-fledged middleweight named Mike Colbert. Hearns beats the shit out of him—breaks his jaw in three places.

Thomas has a mean, hit man look and a sinister stare, but behind it all he's a pussycat. One Thanksgiving Day I take Thomas to an old folks' home. He's just a kid then, but he has a great presence. The cameras are there and all that, but he would have been just the same if there hadn't been a single media person within miles. He walks up to an eighty-five-year-old white lady and says, "Can I have this dance with you?" Then the big black man and the tiny white senior citizen waltz around the floor.

Hearns is far and away the most cooperative person I have met in my life—a dreamboat. I once told his mother, "Lois, if you ever get tired of him, I'll adopt Thomas."

A press agent couldn't ask for a better subject than Hearns. We are training down in Florida in 1985 for the Hagler fight when four reporters who had been at the

Texas Rangers' training camp walk in unannounced and one of them says, "Can we see Thomas Hearns?" Imagine some reporters trying that on Sugar Ray Leonard. "When do you want to see him?" I ask.

At first they figure maybe tomorrow or, if they are lucky, later in the day. "How about now?" I say and march them right into Thomas's suite. They are dumbfounded, absolutely can't believe it, and of course, Hearns is a gem.

I get reporters from all the Florida cities—Orlando, Naples, Jacksonville—and bus them into Miami so they can see Thomas work out. Afterward he holds court for them. That's the way you promote a fight through the media these days. Every day Hearns holds court for some newsman or other. Some TV guy would call and say, "We want Thomas live tonight!" And live he gets him, right from Hearns's hotel room.

In the process, Hearns and I become good and close friends, not unlike my earlier relationship with Muhammad Ali. We are alone one day and Thomas says to me, "I'm gonna tell you something and if any word of this reaches outside of here, I'll kick your ass all over the USA. We call you 'Bro' as far as I'm concerned. Irvin'"— all the Blacks call me "Irvin'," but in Australia, I'm "Irvine" and in Paris "Monsieur Airving"—"you are a nigger like the rest of us!"

I laugh then, and even harder when the next day he walks over to me wearing a deadpan expression. "How long you married to your wife?" he says.

"Forty-four years," I reply.

"Does she know she married to a nigger for forty-four years?"

Not long after that we are together one afternoon at Caesars, where Thomas is working out for the Hagler fight. All of a sudden he says, "Will Irving Rudd please come up here." This in front of two thousand people.

So I get into the ring and he has a package in his hand.

Then he grabs the microphone and announces, "Ladies and Gentlemen, this guy here is our bro; not honorary, a full-fledged bro! And this is a token of our esteem."

I open up the package. It is a Kronk Gym warm-up suit with THE GREAT IRVING RUDD emblazoned across the pocket and KRONK BOXING TEAM on the back. It still is one of my fondest pieces of what I like to call "nos-tag-lia."

If Thomas has one shortcoming it is his frugality, which is matched, by the way, by Marvin Haglers. Some-one once says to me, "Would you like to see Hagler fight Hearns again?" I answer, "Shit, no. I'd rather see them do lunch. I'd want to see who picks that tab up because I have a feeling that cobwebs would grow around them be-fore either guy would move for the check."

One of my favorite Hearns stories involves the after-math of the Hagler fight, when he is knocked out with a devastating right. When I get to Thomas's dressing room, his mother is there, crying her eyes out. Hearns stands in the middle of the room, staring into space. At times like these, a publicity guy has to be very careful, sensitive to the fighter's feelings and needs. I don't have to be Albert Einstein to realize that Hearns is in no mood to meet the media.

"Thomas," I say, "I'll understand if you don't make it to the press conference. You just stay where you are."

He grabs my arm. "Irvin', there are good days and there are bad days. This was a bad day but there will be good days again. I *have* to go out there."

Hearns puts on a fresh pair of sweatpants and we head toward the ring, where the press waits. Suddenly he stops, wheels around, and walks directly toward Hagler's dressing room. When he opens the door, Hagler's face drops. The two guys who only minutes earlier had been trying to kill each other embrace warmly. "Boy," says Hearns, "you are some kind of fighter."

Hagler smiles. "Thomas, you're not so bad yourself.

And next time we fight—if we do—you and me will sit down and then go to Dub Arum together and we make more money!"

Hearns pumps his hand and then leaves for the interviews. Looking at Thomas, you'd never think he had just lost a fight. One by one, he handles each of the media characters till he is blue in the face. Finally he turns to me. "Now, Irvin', we've done NBC, ABC, CBS, CNN, ESPN. We have done the locals. Who's next?" To me, that sense of cooperation is what Thomas Hearns is all about and I'll never forget him as long as I live.

My relationship with Hearns is cemented so hard that I have no problem kidding around with him, even in print. Once, while at training camp, one of the reporters asks me how the two of us get along.

"Hearns and I have a very close relationship," I say. "There's nothing I wouldn't do for him and there's nothing he wouldn't do for me, and that's how it's been for ten years now—we've done nothing for each other!"

Granted, the line isn't about to bring back vaudeville, but what coverage we get from that one-liner. It runs right across the country, from the *Los Angeles Times* to *Newsday*. Best of all, it even gets picked up in the "Scorecard" section of *Sports Illustrated*.

It's a good thing Hearns has a sense of humor, otherwise I wouldn't get away with such tomfoolery. He can take those verbal jabs from me, and because of that, I have no compunctions about planting a good line about him wherever I can.

Somebody from *Newsday* wants to know a bit about Thomas. I remark, "People ask me if Thomas Hearns is cheap. I say, 'Not anymore.' When he was just starting out, he was cheap. Now that he's a great champion, he's frugal!" Sure enough, it runs in the next day's edition of *Newsday*, and Thomas laughs.

If nothing else, Hearns differs from Leonard in his sincerity. He proves to me he is a very good, kind guy, and he certainly makes my job easier with his sensitivity to my needs. Before the 1989 fight with Leonard in Las Vegas I am sitting in with Bob Arum at a staff skull session while Arum reviews the requests being made of Hearns's time. All of a sudden Arum says, "Nobody goes to Thomas Hearns that don't go to Irving Rudd first! Irving Rudd *is* Thomas Hearns. You got that? No favor, story, quote, angle, appearance, nothing. The guy that you have to go to is Irving."

Usually a press agent doesn't get into the business of predicting fights, but by June 1989 I have been around the game long enough to put my two cents in and get my forecast printed as well. Besides, the controversy regarding my prediction will surely generate more stories about the fight in the press. The bout I am talking about is the Hearns-Leonard fight in Las Vegas.

The oddsmakers have made Hearns no better than a three to one underdog, and if you polled the sportswriters Hearns would be a thirty-to-one underdog. But I am not swayed. My opinion has been formed while watching Hearns train in Kronk Gym in Detroit and when John Adams, sports editor of the *Knoxville News-Sentinel*, approaches me, I tell him I won't change my mind. "I believe Hearns is going to win, and I think he's going to win by a decision. I may be the only person who thinks that."

Adams asks me for evidence and I mention Lon Myers, a middleweight who is Hearns's sparring partner. He was supplied with a Leonard video by Emanuel Steward, Hearns's trainer. "Myers did a tremendous impersonation," I tell Adams. "He did everything Leonard does." I have seen Hearns picking off Myers's punches, bobbing and weaving. I also see the single-minded resolve in Hearns that was evident in Leonard before he beat Marvin Hagler in 1987. My controversial decision may be scoffed at by oddsmakers, but I believe in it and it gets us some great ink to boot!

On the Saturday before the fight, disaster strikes. A story comes over the wires that a young woman has been fatally shot at Hearns's home in Southfield, Michigan. Reports are that Hearns's younger brother Henry has been arrested and scheduled for arraignment on an open murder charge. Bob Arum goes to Thomas to commiserate with him, but Hearns stops him. "Bob, that won't affect me," he says. "I've been waiting for eight years to get Leonard in the ring."

It is fascinating to see how the writers respond to the two fighters and their chances of winning. When I tell certain newspapermen—including Phil Berger of *The New York Times*—that Hearns will win, they raise their eyebrows. One Detroit reporter says, "Gee, Irving, I wish you're right, but I can't see it."

I'm not concerned about my pick because either you're gifted with the knowledge of what a fighter is about or not. I am with Hearns, and I see what he is doing and I see what Manny Steward, Thomas's trainer, is doing. I have no doubt in my mind that Hearns will lick Leonard. Thomas has the stamina and Leonard's legs are shot. He doesn't have the movement anymore.

One of the best things Steward does is put a stationary bike right in the middle of Kronk's Gym. Seeing that stationary bike in that old gym is like finding a mink in a sewer. The bike does wonders for Hearns because it strengthens his legs, which have betrayed him in the past, and also it gets Leonard talking—and that means more ink. "You can't punch a man when you're on a bike," Sugar needles. "Nobody ever hit a man on a bike." There are times when more people are talking about the bike than the boxers!

However, in all seriousness, I am so glad that after the fight Thomas feels that he is vindicated. Unfortunately, the lousy decision of a draw comes down. I initially feared for Thomas's mental health if he were to be knocked out or defeated by Leonard. He said to me, and even to the press, "If I lose I am never coming back to Detroit again." He was dead serious, too. My fears are calmed when Hearns maturely acknowledges that "You can't argue with the officials." Personally, I think those officials are all a bunch of lunkheads.

This is the first time in my life, I must confess, that I've had a bias toward a fighter. Usually I am very neutral, for the mere fact that you work at one fighter's camp and who knows, the next day you might be working at his opponent's camp. I have always been very objective. I have never rooted at ringside in my life.

This being the case, still I box inwardly for Hearns on the night of the Leonard fight. I sit in the corner with Manny Steward, Prentiss Byrd, and Walter Smith, who are all working with Hearns.

During the fifth round of the fight, Hearns is showing stress. It all could end here. The whole time I keep asking the people next to me, "How much more time? How much more time?" I never root out loud for Thomas, but it is obvious who I favor. As one newspaperman says to me later on that evening, "I saw you bobbing and weaving. I saw you slipping punches."

To this day, after seeing the fight and watching the videotape, I still say Hearns won. Call me a Hearns man, but Hearns knocked Leonard down twice and clubbed him real good. Take the much-disputed twelfth round as an example. The lunkhead judge gave Leonard two points and the decision. However, the first minute of the twelfth round was absolutely dominated by Hearns. He won it all by himself and he scored some good punches. That in itself erases the two-point scoring. Sure, Leonard pasted him all over the ring for the last two minutes, sure it was a convincing winning round, but I still feel you have to look back to the first minute, where Hearns got some good licks in. Also, doesn't defense count for anything? Not to those incompetent judges. Hearns won in my mind, and that's the final count for this boxing fan!

*   *   *

No mention of my favorite fighters of the 1980s would be complete without Ray "Boom Boom" Mancini, who I like to refer to as "the all-American boy—with a touch of mozzarella." Ray and I have a special relationship, mostly because I knew his father Lenny—one hell of a fighter in the 1930s—very well. The Boomer and I hit it off right away. (In fact, to this day my phone will ring and the secretary will say, "Mister Rudd, somebody who says he's your grandson is on the phone." Of course, it's Ray.)

It's a lot easier to talk about the good times with Mancini than the bad, but in truth, the bad episode is the one that tested me most as a professional press agent so it's the one that's got to be chronicled. This goes back to a bout Boomer had with a Korean fighter named Deuk Koo Kim in Vegas. I am standing near ringside with Bill Cosby and the baseball star Willie Stargell. It is a savage, son of a bitch of a fight. The Korean is tenacious, banging away and giving Mancini more than he can handle.

Late in the fight Boomer begins to rally, and finally, with a barrage of punches, down goes the Korean. Now, if you've been around boxing as long as I have you get to know when a guy is *really* hurt, and I can tell immediately that Deuk Koo Kim is in deep, deep trouble. My suspicions are confirmed when Doctor Donald Romeo of the Nevada State Boxing Commission jumps into the ring to check him out.

I sense we might have a tragedy on our hands, and with this in mind I notice a couple of Korean newspapermen in the press row, guys whom I dealt with earlier and treated pretty good and who speak fluent English. I go over to them and say, "Do me a kind favor. Please go with Doctor Romeo and do whatever interpreting you have to do," and into the ring they climb.

Unfortunately, there is little that they could do. Their countryman has fallen into a coma and is taken to the hospital. I shuttle back and forth between the hospital and

265

the pressroom with bulletins on the kid's condition. The next day, Sunday, at six in the morning, I knock on the door of Dave Wolf, Mancini's manager. "Look," I say, "do you want me to be with you or Ray or what?"

Wolf is a wreck and asks me to see what Ray's needs are and come back to him with a report. When I arrive at Mancini's room he has a priest with him, one who always goes to the fights, a nice young padre. They are discussing a mass that the priest would conduct that day in the auditorium of the Tropicana to pray for the welfare of Kim. Mancini's mother and father are there, but I stay with Boom Boom throughout the service.

After the mass we all go over to the coffee shop at Caesars to get a bite, when who should walk in but Pete Alfano of *The New York Times*. He was covering some basketball game in Reno but was rerouted to Vegas by his paper to follow up on the fate of the Korean. Until this point nobody in the media has talked to Mancini since it became apparent that Kim's life is hanging by a thread. Alfano wants to talk to Mancini, and somebody told Pete that if anybody can get it done, it's Irving.

My first thought is to protect my fighter. Boom Boom's psyche is not in the best of shape ever since he learned how badly he hurt Kim. You can be damn sure I won't let *anybody* from the press talk to my guy unless he gives me a clear green light.

I walk over to Ray. "It's your call," I say. "I don't know how to tell you this, but there's a pretty decent guy from *The New York Times*—that's the newspaper of record. If you see fit, will you give him a few minutes?"

Mancini graciously says he will and sits down with Alfano, who comes away with one hell of a story. Meanwhile, Kim lingers on the brink and there are some important decisions to be made in terms of what, if anything, our fighter should do. Finally Boom Boom takes off to go home, and shortly thereafter, the Korean dies.

Wolf immediately phones and asks me whether I think

Mancini ought to double back for the funeral in Las Vegas. I think no, Boom Boom went to church and said a prayer. He offered his sincere regrets. He offered to help in any way he could. I reason that sending him back to the funeral will only subject Mancini to a whole series of interviews, questions, and generally getting his balls busted. "Let me handle it from here on, Dave," I insist and he agrees.

I get hold of a guy who promotes fights in the Philippines and is closely involved with the Koreans—Pol Tiglao is his name—and tell him what I want for the funeral: a huge wreath of flowers from Ray Mancini placed in front of the coffin. (It so happens that this bit of information and photos also get on the wire services, which doesn't exactly hurt Boom Boom's image.)

You might say that this was a callous way to operate, but I don't think so. Mancini could not have been more upset about the fighter's death and he expressed his deepest regret. In my estimation sending flowers was as meaningful, in this case, as it would have been had he gone to the funeral in Las Vegas and then been subject to all the hassling that would have come with such a move.

In any event, Mancini appreciated my action and we got to be very close. He confided in me about a lot of things and regards me as his surrogate father. Too bad he ain't Jewish!

= 18 =
To Rest Is
to Rust:
Press-agenting
Yesterday and
Today

S ugar Ray Leonard lived in a luxury suite at the
Hotel Inter-Continental at Hilton Head, South Carolina,
during one of my stints with him. The daily rate for Leonard's suite was $425. And if you figure in for inflation it
would come to about $500 today. Meals were extra.

Across the country at the Canyon Hotel in Palm
Springs, California, where Marvelous Marvin Hagler
worked out, he enjoyed the same type of palatial suite as
Leonard. From Marvin's digs you could see Bob Hope's
house high up on a hill.

Both fighters broke camp eventually and concluded
their conditioning at Caesars Palace in Las Vegas, where

they faced off for the middleweight championship in April 1987. As I gazed around the pressroom at Casears Palace, I couldn't help but realize that boxing press agentry has entered the age of Buck Rogers. I was now using a tele-copier, telex, and the telephone. It was nothing for me to make or receive calls to or from both fighters' camps, from coast to coast, from London, Rome, Paris, and the Orient as well as Central and South America. I put a guy calling from Paris on hold because I was talking to somebody from London. I find that a little awe-inspiring still, espe-cially when I recall that Al Weill, who managed Rocky Marciano, was the first guy to have a desk phone in his office—and he had a lock on it!

Not that *all* camp jobs in this ultramodern era of box-ing are in posh palaces like the Hotel Inter-Continental at Hilton Head. I had Earnie Shavers in—are you ready?—Calcutta, Ohio. Not even veteran Ohio newspapermen knew where the camp was situated. I always joke: "You heard of *Oh! Calcutta!*? Well, I spent seven weeks in Cal-cutta, OH!"

In 1985 I spent some time with Thomas Hearns in Laughlin, Nevada. Never heard of Laughlin? Well, you should. It's fifty miles east of Searchlight, Nevada, and right across the Colorado River from the noise and clamor of downtown Bullhead City, Arizona. There's a restaurant in Laughlin serving chicken and fish dinner combinations that invites you to "try our Cluck and Hook Special."

Mostly, though, the contemporary fight camps are in exotic, if not luxurious, settings. I handled Ray Mancini in picturesque St. Vincent, Italy, at the Italian-Swiss-French border, in 1983, and Mike Weaver at beautiful Lake Tahoe. The luxury of today's fight camps is a far cry from the primitive settings I remember when I was just breaking into the fight game.

The first training camp I ever visited was Dr. Bier's in Pompton Lakes, New Jersey. Joe Louis was training for a fight with Tommy Farr. Pompton Lakes, some two hours' drive from New York City, in those days was what we Brooklynites used to call "the country." It was remote, heavily wooded, and hardly in the same class with Hilton Head. The camp consisted of cottages or cabins and a main guest house. This held true for Madame Bey's in Summit, New Jersey—now a ritzy bedroom suburb but then considered far, far away—and Orangeburg, New York, site of Gus Wilson's place.

Press agentry in boxing has changed as dramatically during my five decades in the business. When I was breaking in, we would go to any lengths to drum up a story. And usually we'd get away with it—something that couldn't happen today.

There were two staples of gimmickry back in the old days. One was the maiden drowning in the lake, the other was a photo of the champion chopping down a tree. You see, our boxing hero was doing roadwork early in the morning when he heard this cry for help. A maiden, the reports from camp always read, was drowning in a lake and the heroic fighter stopped his running long enough to effect a rescue. Later I used to wonder what the maiden was doing in the lake at around six in the morning, especially when it was freezing cold in the winter.

Then there was the woodchopping. I once asked the great trainer Ray Arcel about the woodchopping and he looked at me as though I was punchy. The great danger and risk should have been apparent. Also, if one examined the photos carefully, the ax-wielding boxer was probably wearing fancy pressed slacks and polished Oxford Street shoes.

Speaking of old-time gimmicks reminds me of a fighter back then billed as King Solomon. He was supposed to be Jewish, and just to underline the point, he wore the Star of David on his trunks. Once, King Solomon was training to fight Jack Sharkey and a reporter happened to be in the gym on Yom Kippur, the Jewish Day of Atonement, the highest of the High Holy Days. Well, there on Yom Kippur was King Solomon working out like crazy. The newsman walked over to him and said, "Whadaya doin'?"

Solomon said, "Training for Jack Sharkey."

"But what about Yom Kippur?"

"I'll fight him next!"

The new champs, like Ali or Mike Tyson, travel with an entourage that would rival that of President George Bush. Back in the pre–World War II days the entourage as we know it today did not exist. Instead we had the odd hangers-on and characters such as Foulproof Taylor, who popped up in June 1941 when I was working Bummy Davis's camp at Madame Bey's, where Davis was training for a fight with Fritzi Zivic.

Foulproof Taylor lived in Brooklyn and worked for the Postal Telegraph Company. He fancied himself an inventor and in the late 1930s he fashioned a crude forerunner of the baseball safety helmet. He also invented a "foulproof cup." To market his armored jockstrap, Foulproof would visit Stillman's Gym or the Pioneer Gym in Manhattan and, wearing his cup, would stand, his feet apart, inviting anyone to punch or kick him in the groin area.

The offer was often accepted, and it was not unusual to see a giant heavyweight shoot a mean hook below the belt. Taylor would be knocked rear-over-teakettle but bounce up unhurt. Once at Madame Bey's he asked the Hearst newspapers' boxing writer, Hype Igoe, to test the Foulproof Taylor Cup. Igoe did, and Taylor crashed into a baseboard wall from which it took several men several minutes to extricate him.

A makeshift plaque was put over the hole in the wall that read:

> Hypus Igoe through this wall
> Knocked Foulproof Taylor—Cup
> and all!

Talk about changing times, when I worked the Davis camp I slept under the ring at Madame Bey's. Now I scuffle from a $275-a-day suite—but I still scuffle, and I'm still going strong at age seventy-two. Part of it is due to my philosophy, best put in a line from ninety-year-old trainer Ray Arcel, who once told me, "To rest is to rust." If there is one key to my success it is that I won't let rust gather under my feet, my typewriter, or my fax machine, and maybe that helps explain why the good lines keep growing in my head. Which reminds me of the time I handled the Hearns-Hagler fight in 1986 and a security cop who didn't know me wouldn't let I. Rudd into the dressing room.

"Listen, you bum," I snapped, "just because you make four bucks an hour don't make you no Sherlock Holmes!" *That* got me in.

Or, as I tell my boss Bob Arum, "I've been with you a dozen years and it's amazing what you've learned in that time!"

Right from the start my theory has been that nothing sells itself. Even the Bible had to have a PR man. But boxing always needs its special kind of shtick. There's the world of sports and there's boxing. I had Hagler and Hearns on a twelve-day tour of twenty-one cities to hype the fight. I had Hearns waltzing with grandmothers down in Miami. The toughest thing was keeping these guys from killing each other before they got into the ring.

The term PR always has fascinated me. In the 1930s and 1940s there was no such character as a "public relations man" in the sports world. You were a press agent or a publicity man. Period. These days PR people have meetings about meetings; they're posturing phonies. Take the Mets' Dwight Gooden situation with the cocaine. The reason that was badly handled—and believe me, it *was* badly handled—was because their PR guy had no street smarts; he didn't come from Brownsville. I'd have spotted the mugs around Dwight Gooden and I'd have gone up to management and said, "Hey, let me tell you, Gooden is hangin' out with guys that don't look right." Instead they put a cocoon around him. That's not the way to do it. You have to be out front.

I'm not naive enough—not after seven-plus decades on this earth—to believe that times don't change. You don't see trolley cars on the streets of New York anymore and you can't buy a good five-cent cigar, but that's no reason for me to forget how good things were when fighters had real names: Ruby Goldstein, the "Jewel of the Ghetto," Tin Can Romanelli, and the Whitechapel Whirlwind, *all the way from OVVV-erSEAS! The ppp-RIDE of the BRITTT-ish EMP-ahhhhhhh!*

You'll forgive me if I tell you that I wouldn't mind one more Saturday fight night in the 1930s when Duke Ellington and Cab Calloway and Ethel Waters came to the Rockland Palace. It was a time when you could walk Harlem, and I did, and I knew Sugar Ray—*Robinson*, that is—when he was an amateur in 1939. After you put Ray on Mt. Olympus, there's Ali and Louis and Tony Canzoneri, then you come to Hagler and Holmes and Willie Pep and Rocky Marciano. Then there's Jake LaMotta, whom I've known since 1945. When the movie about him, *Raging Bull*, came out, people asked, Was Jake that bad? "Hey," I say, "*that's* Sunnybrook Farm!" What a mean mother this was.

Nostalgia can be a problem if it's overdone, but I don't mind an occasional stroll down Memory Lane, and every so often I indulge myself in a walk on Manhattan's West Side. A periodic dip at the wellspring of boxing always elevates my soul. It still pains me that they tore down the Madison Square Garden at Eighth Avenue and Fiftieth Street. Now there's a big, sterile office building on the site. A block away, on the corner of Forty-ninth and Eighth, southwest corner, to be precise, sat Mickey Walker's saloon, run by Mickey, alias the Toy Bulldog, one of our great fighters.

Mickey was always bugged by the fact that people thought he couldn't have licked Stanley Ketchel. Ketchel was shot and killed in Conway, Missouri, in 1910, nine years *before* Walker began his career. Anyhow, this guy came into Walker's bar and said, "Hey, Mickey, what a fighter you were. I seen you fight a draw with Jack Sharkey. You were just a middleweight and you fought a draw with the great [heavyweight] Jack Sharkey. And you beat that King Levinsky [another heavyweight]. What a fight."

"Have another drink," said Mickey.

This fighter, that fighter. The guy's just warming up. At length, Mickey leans over and says, "Tell me, my friend, how do you think I'd have done with Stanley Ketchel?"

The guy rears up and says, "Ketchel would have murdered you!"

Occasionally I traipse up to Eighth and Fifty-fifth Street where the Neutral Corner was located. The noted author and columnist A. J. Leibling—also a big fight fan—used to visit there. It was there that Rocky Marciano's trainer, Charley Goldman, pinpointed the problem with modern boxers: "One of the troubles with fighters now is they don't start before they're interested in dames."

It was always that way. For every generation, boxing was better in bygone decades, but I don't buy that one bit. I like modern-day fighters. The problem today has nothing to do with the boxers and everything to do with a scarcity of trainers. Boxing has retrogressed technique-wise. Who are the teachers? Boxing is an art; it may be hurtful, but it's an art. So where are the cabinetmakers? Where are the guys making Stradivarius violins?

And where are the Eddie Bordens? Eddie who? you ask. Eddie Borden was, as they say in boxing, "around." He was a fight manager but he also was a writer, a general all-round guy—what the intellectuals today would call a Renaissance man. One time after a Garden fight, somehow the conversation got around to whether or not Eddie could go across Broadway—that is, Broadway at Times Square—on three hops, one, two, three.

Sound crazy? Not at two in the morning after some good Friday night fights. Everybody gets their money down. It seemed like a safe bet. The guys stop traffic and then, what do you know, Eddie negotiates Broadway in three hops—three hops!—and wins five hundred simoleons.

Bert Randolph Sugar, the cigar-chomping man-about-fights and publisher of *Boxing Illustrated* magazine, likes to say, "Irving Rudd is so old that when he goes to Atlantic City and hits the jackpot, the slot machine shows three prunes!"

Well, I *am* celebrating my fifty-third year as a press agent, but I still feel like a kid. Granted, the fight game has changed, but I. Rudd hasn't changed much since I hosted my first big press conference at Eastern Parkway Arena in Brownsville, Brooklyn, circa 1947. I learned a lesson that night.

On that night I had invited the cream of local society, including the popular baseball player Sid Gordon of the Giants, to mingle with the press before the fights. I spared no expense and ordered turkeys from a deli. This, of course, was supposed to be for the newspaper guys, but when the waiters marched in with the trays, a couple of dozen hungry Brownsvillians reached up and picked them clean. Blanched bones were all that remained.

My, how times have changed! In June 1941 I was hired by Mike Jacobs for the princely sum of $25 a week for three weeks to be with Bummy Davis. Now I make $60,000 plus. When I handled Rockland Palace, nobody even had a Baby Brown camera. Now when I handle a press conference we have a dozen magazine photographers at one throw, not to mention TV cameras and whatnot.

In terms of getting publicity, the biggest changes in the last forty years would center on persuasiveness. You have to be more convincing today. The young writers of the 1990s are more sophisticated; they are not like the old-fashioned boxing reporter, who worked strictly on his beat and welcomed almost anything. You can still scheme and dream up some things that would be called sensational, but you cannot ever lie. If you do, you're finished.

People ask me what is my claim to fame. Well, I could think of a lot of things. For one, I took two years off Marvelous Marvin Hagler's age, two inches off Sugar Ray Leonard's reach, and a half inch off Thomas Hearns's height. When Hagler went to court to have his name legally changed to Marvelous, I noticed his birth certificate said 1954. But, his publicized age was two years older, because when he started fighting at age fifteen, his managers tacked on the years so there wouldn't be any problems with his age. I always carry a tape measure, and because I had my doubts, I put it to Hearns and found he was just six-two and not six-two-and-a-half, and Leonard's reach was four inches shorter than publicized.

I can also claim that I have rubbed shoulders, shared drinks, and been friends with some of the titans of the writing game, guys like Jimmy Cannon, Frank Graham, Red Smith, W. C. Heinz, Dave Anderson, and Damon Runyon. Not only was Runyon a magnificent writer and chronicler of Broadway characters but Damon was quite a character himself.

One of my favorite Runyon stories took place near the end of his life. He had throat cancer and could not talk. He used to carry a pad with him and he would scribble comments and answers, then tear off the page and just drop it. Bystanders would scramble like mad for these bits of paper as souvenirs.

Eddie Walker, a fight manager at the time, took it on himself to be Damon's valet, bodyguard, self-appointed whatever. One night they were at ringside watching the young Ray Robinson box, move, and punch as only he could. Finally Walker said, "Damon, this is the greatest fighter of all time."

Runyon shook his head and wrote on his pad, "Benny Leonard."

"Good fighter, sure, but not as good as Robinson," Walker argued.

"Leonard," Runyon wrote more emphatically on his pad.

"Nope, Robinson," Walker insisted.

"*Leonard!*" Runyon scribbled furiously.

"Okay, okay," Walker surrendered in exasperation. "But do you have to write so damn *loud!*"

Damon Runyon isn't with us anymore, but there are some damn good writers around today who have the same kind of feel for the little guy that Runyon did. One of them is Bill Reel of the *New York Daily News*. I've watched Bill grow as a journalist over the past decade and we've become good friends. I'll never forget the time when I was working with Muhammad Ali, came back from a big promotion, and sent Reel some T-shirts for his kids. His son Joe wrote me a thank you letter and ended it by saying, "Have a Merry Christmas, Mr. Rudd."

A few days later, Reel is on the blower asking me if I had received Joe's letter. I told him that I had. "Well," he said, "disregard that Christmas greeting, Irving. Joe assumes that everybody celebrates Christmas. He didn't know you were Jewish."

I laughed. "The heck I'll disregard it!" I replied. "Don't forget, Jesus was one of *our* boys."

I've always believed that wit is the best retort to stupidity, particularly when the rednecks or tunnel-visioned religious fanatics get on their soapboxes. I'm reminded of the time a spokesman for a certain group of fundamentalist Christians once told my pal Reel that Jews are barred from Heaven. Bill kept a straight face and then went back to the office and wrote a piece saying that if Jews were unwelcome in Heaven, he wouldn't want to spend eternity there because Irving Rudd wouldn't be around to swap lies with and go over the hitters.

I phoned him after his column ran and said, "That guy who told you Jews can't get into Heaven is confused. He's got Heaven mixed up with the telephone company!"

It was Reel who had one of the most meaningful lines ever written about me. He noted, "You're only as old as you feel, and Irving feels like it's still 1937."

He's right in the sense that I'm hustling as hard as I did then and thinking as sharply as when I was a twenty-two-year-old instead of a seventy-two-year-old. If my mind wasn't as fertile as any youngster's, I doubt that I could have pulled off the press smash that I did for the Gerrie Coetzee–John Tate fight in South Africa. I had read that Coetzee had had several operations on his right hand. So I got Ace Miller, Tate's manager, to protest and demand a prefight examination on the grounds that Coetzee had a *bionic hand.* It was a biggie—great publicity for a fight outside the United States.

At a time when most guys my age were retired or looking forward to their pensions, I was just hitting my prime. Just before my seventieth birthday I pulled off one of the greatest stunts of my career. This surrounded the Hagler-Hearns title fight on April 15, 1985.

It suddenly dawned on me while directing the fight's road show that April 15 was deadline day for the filing of income tax returns. I also knew that the Internal Revenue people always have a devil of a time trying to get the public to send in their forms early, and a lot of money is spent on educating them accordingly.

The bulb flashed in my cranium. With the fight being April 15 we had to tie it in with it being the last day to file your income tax. So I called a guy at the IRS, and within two weeks we were in Sugar Ray Leonard's gym in Maryland doing the commercial.

The thirty-second spot begins with Hagler and Hearns and their handlers in the center of the ring listening as the referee is giving instructions. Suddenly Hagler interrupts:

"Thomas Hearns and I will be busy on April 15, so we're filing our income tax returns early."

"Yes," says Hearns, resting a hand on Hagler's shoulder, "you'll be less likely to overlook deductions or make last-minute mistakes. And, if you have a refund coming, you'll get it faster. So if you file now, you can relax on April 15."

"Not you, Hearns!" Hagler shouts. The ref then continues, an IRS logo appears, and the spot is over.

The shoot lasted eight hours and the fighters were thorough professionals. They weren't chummy—they kept their distance between takes—but they didn't get silly and start yelling.

The result was a press agent's dream. The commercial flashed on screens from coast to coast, morning, noon, and night. Best of all, the government footed every cent of the bill. (Bob Arum loved me for that!) And to top it all, Phil Mushnick, the *New York Post*'s sports columnist, wrote an entire story about it. It had a headline all the way across the top of the page: "Greatest Coup of Century."

Even *I* wouldn't go that far, but I do thank him for the compliment, and you might say without fear of contradiction that I. Rudd has come a long way since that Harlem afternoon when Al Douglas slipped me $18 for a week's worth of publicity at the Rockland Palace.

Now I'm looking ahead to the year 2000 and, perhaps, a few more "coups of the century." I can't help wondering with whom or where my next training camp will take me. It could be Reno, Nevada, where I spent August 1989, or Show Low, Arizona, where I spent part of 1976 with Muhammad Ali, or some unheard-of whistle stop next to nowhere.

Wouldn't miss it for a million!

Index